MOON SIGNS

MOON SIGNS

Discover the Hidden Power of Your Emotions

Sasha Fenton

Aquarian/Thorsons
An Imprint of HarperCollins*Publishers*

The Aquarian Press
An Imprint of HarperCollins*Publishers*
77–85 Fulham Palace Road,
Hammersmith, London W6 8JB

Published by The Aquarian Press 1987
7   9   10   8

© Sasha Fenton 1987

Sasha Fenton asserts the moral right to
be identified as the author of this work

A catalogue record for this book
is available from the British Library

ISBN 0 85030 552 7

Printed in Great Britain by
HarperCollinsManufacturing Glasgow

Contents

This book is dedicated to 'Merlin', otherwise known as Brian Mountford, who magic'd it into existence.

Acknowledgements

Thanks to Tony Fenton for practical help and support.

Helen Fenton for some illustrations.

Stuart Fenton whose spelling is better than mine.

Malcolm Wright for illustrations, especially the signs of the Zodiac.

Linda Tulley for word processing.

Jason Russell for some of the diagrams.

Douglas Ashby for contributing heavily to the magical section and for much astrological information and constant help and kindness.

Nina Ashby for astrological help and the free use of her bookshelf.

Sam and Frances Waxman, David Dunn and Joan Jackson for gardening, mythological and kabbalistic information.

Denise Russell for more astrological information, free use of her bookshelf and for keeping my head together.

Simon Franklin for just about everything.

Robert Curry for astrological information and free use of his computer.

David Baker for help and advice regarding the diagrams.

Robin Lown for criticizing, getting on my nerves and always making me go back and do it BETTER.

The Moon is riding high and clear,
O lovely one, draw near, draw near;
To lonely men on lonely ways
Come down in dream of silver haze.
Persephone, Persephone,
All in the end shall come to thee.

Aspects of Occultism
Dion Fortune

Introduction

What is a Birthchart?

The sign of the Zodiac which you are born under is called your Sun sign. Most people are aware of their own particular Sun sign and probably have some idea of the characteristics contained in that sign. When an astrologer makes up a birthchart he takes into account much more than the Sun sign on its own. For instance, he will look at the house* placement of the Sun, the placement of the Moon and also each of the ten planets of our solar system by house and by sign. He will look at the Ascendant, Mid-heaven, nodes of the Moon and the aspects (geometrical angles) which each of these factors make to each of the others. He may, depending upon his approach to astrology, look at the immum-coeli, Descendant, mid-points, arabic parts, fixed stars, harmonic vibrations, vertices and anything else he can think of.

All this will give him an insight into the native's character but not into the passage of time in the form of the daily, monthly and yearly events of his life. For this he will need to look at day-for-a-year progressions (also called secondary directions), transits and phases of the Moon. Please don't let all this put you off the subject, it is not necessary to look into *all* these effects, often there is enough information to be gleaned from the simpler forms of astrology. Anyway, do please consider that if *I* can master this subject, then so can you. In this book we are going to confine ourselves to an in-depth study of the Moon and its effects on all of our natures.

* For the astrological houses see chapter 8.

——Some background to astrological thinking——

The study of the Sun, Moon and visible planets figure strongly in man's earliest attempts to understand himself and his environment. This consideration of the heavens probably grew up out of the need to establish a calendar and to understand the passage of time. As man watched the crops and animals around him growing and prospering under varying heavenly circumstances, he began also to notice the differences of personality pertaining to those born with the planets in certain positions. The first horoscopes were made up by Chaldean priests solely for the use of kings, princes and potential military leaders, the first birthcharts for ordinary people were produced by the ancient Greeks.

Astrology has waxed and waned in popularity over the centuries, become mixed up with magic and mysticism, then derided and rejected completely during the age of reason. It has been revived during our own century as a useful aid to the study of psychology.

————The layers of your personality————

Most of us appear to have personalities which are constructed somewhat like an onion. We have an inviting outer skin which may be completely different in colour and texture to whatever is lying underneath. As we peel away the layers one by one we go on an inward journey until we hit the tender heart of the onion's personality, these are the layers which are ruled by the Moon and therefore associated with the innermost needs of the personality. The position of the Moon will reveal our inner feelings and underlying urges. It shows how we react to situations which are presented to us by others and how we behave when our passions are aroused. This underlying personality will reveal itself more readily when we are tired, ill or overwrought. The Moon position shows our ability to adapt, our bodily processes, moods, obsessions and deepest needs. One's Moon sign may be the same as the Sun or it may be in something completely different.

The first impression which we give to others is probably

shown by the Ascendant.† I say *probably* because nothing is black and white in astrology. Most people are outwardly like their Ascendant, some project a strong Sun sign, and yet others have birthcharts which are dominated by the fact that they have a number of planets placed in one particular sign. In the very simplest of terms, we can expect the face which is shown to the world to be the Ascendant, the basic day to day personality to be represented by the Sun, variations on a theme to be shown by the planets, worldly aims and aspirations to be shown by the Mid-heaven and the deepest, most hidden aspect to be shown by the Moon. Therefore a person with, for example, a Leo ascendant, a Sun in Taurus and the Moon in Gemini would be something like the following:

Leo rising: Dignified outer manner, apparently responsible and organized attitude, fondness for children.

Sun in Taurus: Practical kindly nature, stubborn, home-loving but businesslike attitude.

Moon in Gemini: Underlying personality needs freedom, changes of scene and new people in his life, cannot cope with other people's emotional problems, highly ambitious.

Here is another scenario:

Pisces rising: Outer manner is soft, gentle, caring and woolly-headed. He appears to need looking after.

Sun in Libra: Businesslike, sociable, friendly, attractive, sexy.

Moon in Capricorn: Inwardly very ambitious, good to one's parents, shy, real feelings very well hidden.

---

† Ascendant. The starting point on a birthchart; it represents the place on the Earth's surface where day-break occurred on the day of birth.

Some astrologers think that a man is influenced in his choice of a wife by the position of the Moon in his birthchart but, personally, I'm not so sure about that, it would depend upon what the man requires from his woman. A man who wants a woman to understand his career aspirations may choose someone whose Sun is in the same sign as his Mid-heaven, a man who wants a woman to have a particular kind of appearance may look for someone who compliments his planet Venus, but this is all complicated and rather off the point. Let's just stick with the Moon and its placement for now.

To find your own Moon position firstly look at the instructions and the tables in Appendix 1 on page 240.

CHAPTER 1

Moon Data

Astronomical Data

The Moon's mean distance from the Earth, surface to surface is 376,284 kilometres, or about a quarter of a million miles. It takes 27.32 days for the Moon to travel round the Earth and also 27.32 days for it to rotate on its axis, therefore it always has the same 'face' pointing towards the Earth. Its diameter is 3475.6 kilometres and its temperature varies between plus 101° centigrade and minus 153° centigrade. The interior of the Moon is still hot enough to be made of molten rock and there are about 3000 moonquakes per year. The surface of the Moon is fatter on the side which faces towards the Earth, it is also warmer on the Earth side.

The Moon and the Earth were both formed when the solar system came into being. The Moon became attracted to the Earth's gravitational field and formed a double or binary planet system. Double planets spin round each other rather like children swinging round each other on a rope; in this case, the relative sizes of the Earth and the Moon mean that the Moon does most (not all) of the swinging. The first Moon landing was at 2.56 GMT on the 20 July 1969 by Armstrong, Aldrin and Collins in Apollo 11.

The Moon is about a quarter of the size of the Earth and its surface area is about the size of Asia, nevertheless its mountains reach 8000 metres which is higher than any on earth. There is no atmosphere on the Moon, therefore meteorites fall on to it without being burned up by friction on their way down.

Eclipses

Eclipses of the Moon occur when the Earth is between it and the Sun and only when the Moon is full. There are roughly three to

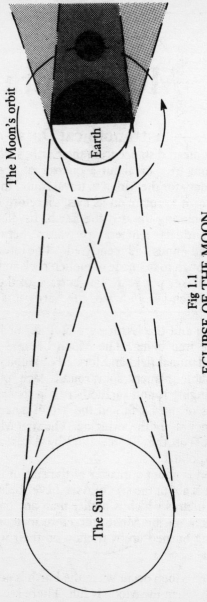

**Fig 1.1
ECLIPSE OF THE MOON**

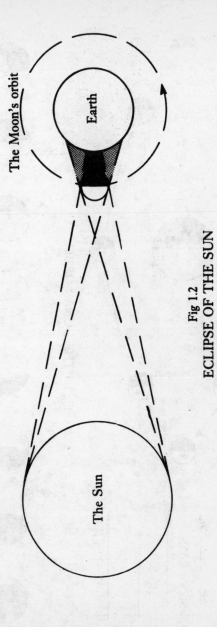

Fig 1.2
ECLIPSE OF THE SUN

20

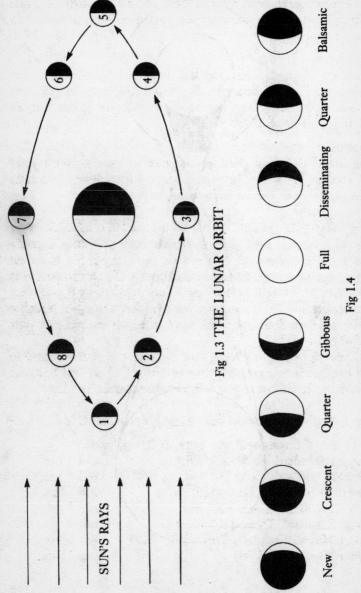

SUN'S RAYS

Fig 1.3 THE LUNAR ORBIT

New   Crescent   Quarter   Gibbous   Full   Disseminating   Quarter   Balsamic

Fig 1.4

THE PHASES OF THE MOON

four eclipses each year, most of these are partial eclipses. Total eclipses last for a few minutes but a partial eclipse can last for an hour or so.

Tides
There are two high tides a day and the areas of high tide revolve around the Earth in line with the Moon. At the time of the new Moon and the full Moon, when the Sun, Moon and Earth are in line the tides are higher.

Phases of the Moon
The Moon does not shed any light of its own, only the light reflected by the Sun. The phases of the Moon depend upon its position between the Earth and the Sun.

——Adjustments to the Moon Sign Tables——
The tables in this book show the times when the Moon enters a new sign *at Greenwich*. If you were born anywhere in Great Britain the times mentioned in this book will apply to you. It is unlikely that you will have to make any adjustment if you were born in Europe but if you were born further afield, for instance in the USA or India, you will have to adjust the time of your birth back to GMT.

If you were born in New York for instance you will have to add five hours to your birth time to bring it up to GMT; if you were born in Calcutta, you will have to subtract five hours.

The following list should help those born in the USA.

GMT (used throughout this book) 0° Longitude
Eastern Standard Time: 75° West   add 5 hrs.
Central Standard Time: 90° West   add 6 hrs.
Mountain Standard Time: 105° West   add 7 hrs.
Pacific Standard Time: 120° West   add 7 hrs.
Yukon Standard Time: 135° West   add 9 hrs.
Alaska/Hawaii Standard Time: 150° West   add 10 hrs.
Bering Time: 165° West   add 11 hrs.

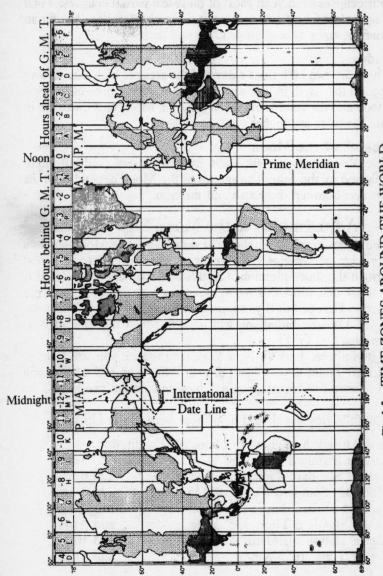

Fig 1.5   TIME ZONES AROUND THE WORLD

The time zone map on page 22 will help for most birthplaces but please do find out if there was daylight saving at the time of your birth, if there was, then subtract one hour.

CHAPTER 2

Lunar Lore

Lunar Gardening

If you with flowers stick the pregnant earth
Mark well the Moon propitious to their birth
For earth the silent midnight queen obeys
And waits her course, who clad in silver rays
The eternal round of time and seasons guides

from *The English Gardener*
(seventeenth century)

If you wish to make the best use of the position of the Moon in your garden, then you must take into account both the phases of the Moon and the signs that it travels through. When the Moon is growing from new to full it is called a waxing Moon, when it goes from the full to new it is called a waning Moon. It is considered best to plant crops which produce their crops above the ground by a waxing Moon and those plants which produce crops below the ground by a waning Moon. However, those plants which spend the winter in the ground (biennials and perennials) are better off planted when the Moon is waxing.

It is well known, of course, that rain usually follows the full or new Moon but there have been recent studies on the effect of the Moon on crops and animals.

Some studies on potatoes which, when grown in laboratory conditions at a constant rate of heat and light, still respond to lunar rhythms. A scientist called Frank A. Brown took some oysters from the Atlantic coast of America to artificial oyster beds in inland Illinois. By the time two weeks had passed, the oysters had adapted their opening and closing times from the

Atlantic tidal times to suit the times of the supposed 'tides' of Illinois.

Gardening by the phases of the Moon

First quarter: Leafy plants such as cabbage, celery, endive, spinach and lettuce, also cucumber.

Second quarter: Beans, peas, peppers, courgettes, tomatoes, melon, garlic, hay, cereals and grains in either the first or the second quarter.

Third quarter: Biennials and perennials, also root crops, onions, winter wheat, trees and shrubs.

Fourth quarter: Don't plant anything, do the weeding instead.

Gardening by the signs of the Zodiac

Aries: Seeds will be quick to germinate and quick to go to seed but could be used to get an early crop.

Taurus: Advantageous for most plants especially root growth, transplanting and many flowers.

Gemini: Not particularly good except for plants grown in wet conditions such as celery.

Cancer: A very productive time to plant, promotes the growth of foliage stalks. Vines will produce sturdy plants which can survive bad weather.

Leo: This is not a productive time to plant or to transplant.

Virgo: Planting now will result in tough, woody, useless plants.

Libra: A fruitful time to plant but there might be
                    too much bloom and not enough seed.

Scorpio: Good time for transplanting and pruning,
                    also for plants which have to survive the
                    winter.

Sagittarius: Plant fruit trees, hay and onions, otherwise
                    not a good time to plant.

Capricorn: Good time for grafting and pruning wood,
                    also for planting ornamental trees and
                    shrubs.

Aquarius: Only onions and pine trees should be
                    planted now.

Pisces: This is supposed to be a good time to plant
                    anything with the exception of potatoes
                    which will sprout at the eye.

Some more lunar gardening tips

Start a compost heap when the Moon is in the fourth quarter,
especially in Scorpio.

Cultivate and plough the ground when the Moon is in the fourth
quarter in Aries, Gemini, Leo, Virgo or Aquarius.

Dry crops in the third quarter of a fire sign.

Fertilize when the Moon is in Cancer, Scorpio or Pisces;
Taurus or Capricorn will do although less well. If using an
organic fertilizer, do so while the Moon is waning.

Graft during Capricorn, Cancer or Scorpio on a waxing Moon.

Harvest during the third and fourth quarters in Aries, Leo,
Sagittarius, Gemini or Aquarius. Harvest roots intended for
seed at the full Moon, grain which is to be stored just after the
full Moon in a fire or air sign. Harvest on a waning moon during
an air or fire sign.

Irrigate when the Moon is in Cancer, Scorpio or Pisces.

Mow the lawn in the first or second quarters to increase growth, during the third or fourth quarters to decrease growth.

Pick mushrooms at the full Moon.

Prune during a decreasing Moon.

Spray, weed and destroy pests during the fourth quarter in a fire sign.

Plant potatoes during the 'dark of the Moon' (i.e. new Moon) one suggestion that I have come across is to plant them on Good Friday when the holy powers are at their strongest! Peas should be planted in the 'light of the Moon' (full Moon).

(My husband tried mowing the lawn this year according to these ancient instructions in order to decrease its growth. The lawn grew like the clappers and my name was mud all summer long!)

CHAPTER 3

The Goddess of the Moon

The Myriad Faces
of the Goddess of the Moon

The Moon in mythology and in many religions represents the female force which reflects the male force of the Sun. In Hebrew she is known as Levanah, in Roman mythology Diana and in the Greek tradition as Persephone and also Aphrodite. In the Egyptian tradition she is Isis the female member of the powerful trinity of Osiris, Isis and Horus.

To the followers of the ancient traditions of witchcraft, she is Brid, Maiden-Goddess of the waxing Moon; Diana, Mother-Goddess of the full Moon and Morrigan, Crone-Goddess of the waning Moon. The following lines are an extract from a ritual associated with the Moon Goddess.

> Behold the Three-Formed Goddess;
> She who is ever Three — Maid, Mother and Crone.
> Yet she is ever One;
> She in all women, and they all in her.
> Behold her, remember her,
> Forget not one of her faces;

If you would like the goddess to grant you a wish, then take a piece of paper in the planetary colour of the person (or object) that your wish concerns; then light the candle and wait for it to burn down, as it does so, the spell will be working. Here is the invocation which will help the spell to work.

Upon this candle will I write
What I request of thee this night.
Grant what I wish you to do;
I dedicate this rite to you.
I trust that you will grant this boon
O lovely Goddess of the Moon.

Early man's initial concern was to survive. In some parts of the world even now where life is primitive, survival is still not guaranteed. For such people, the business of growing food and rearing animals went alongside the development of the calendar and also the development of religion and superstition. If an offering to a particular diety would help the crops grow; then obviously, that was the right thing to do. Even now, many good people like to say grace before or after a meal to thank God for feeding them. Even a total heathen such as I simply cannot eat the first fruits and vegetables of the season without offering up a Hebrew blessing.

Most religions take some account of the Moon's position in their festival calendar; for instance, in the Christian tradition, Easter and Whitsun still 'float' according to the Moon's orbit. It is interesting to note that Easter was a Greco-Roman festival associated with Aphrodite and Diana and, before that a festival associated with Ishtarte, the predecessor of Aphrodite/Diana. These goddesses, like the beginning of the spring season itself, speak of fertility and growth and the renewal of life. If you can take a trip to the re-discovered city of Ephesus in Turkey, just at the bottom of the hill on the left-hand side you will find the Temple of Diana which is close by the even more ancient site of the Temple of Aphrodite/Ishtarte. Ishtarte is the many-breasted Goddess of Fertility who was sometimes shown hung about with eggs — Easter eggs perhaps?

In the Jewish tradition, special prayers are said when festivals fall at the time of the New Moon (Boruha Levanah), prayers for each new Moon are said at the beginning of the lunar month (Rosh Hadesh). Astrologers watch the Moon carefully and there are some who will not even discuss a new project on a 'void of course Moon' which is when the Moon makes no major aspects to other planets. It is my guess that in all traditions and beliefs the Sun and Moon were, are and always will be the light which makes us turn our heads to the sky and our thoughts heavenwards.

The image of the Moon as the supreme female, the complete mother, is strongly represented in the Egyptian goddess, Isis, who presided over herbal remedies and Lunar magic. If you wish to invoke the goddess Isis, draw a circle late at night, concentrate your thoughts and visualize an image of the goddess while asking for what you want. Above all, ask for the love and strength to be able to cope with your troubles and live a kindly and decent life. Here is a tiny extract from The Worship of Isis rituals.

And over these tides the Great Goddess presides under her aspect of the Moon. As she passeth from her rising to her setting, so answer these tides unto her. She riseth from the sea as the evening Star, and the waters of the earth rise in flood. She sinketh as Luna in the western ocean, and the waters flow back into the inner Earth and are still in that great lake of darkness wherein are the Moon and Stars reflected. Whoso is still as the dark underworld lake of Persephone shall see the tides of the Unseen moving therein and shall know all things. Therefore is Luna also called giver of visions.

In the Kabbalistic tradition, the Moon, this time known as Levanah, is associated with the section of the Tree of Life which is called Yesod. Yesod, the Foundation, is situated towards the base of the Tree just above Malkuth. Yesod is the ninth path of pure intelligence and it purifies the emanations. Yesod contains two totally different images; the watery Moon of Levanah under the presidency of the water element archangel, Gabriel, and also the magical image of a beautiful naked young man who is known for his strength alongside the powerful God name of Shaddai el Chai, the Almighty living God. Nothing in the Kabbalah is easy to understand, but the idea behind Yesod is that the universe was a vaporous and watery chaos which was gathered into order by the strength and power of God. Genesis — Boraishis. Here is a Greco/Hebrew version of the Isis worship ritual.

> Our Lady is also the Moon, called of some Selene, of others Luna, but by the wise Levanah, for therein is contained the number of her name. She is the ruler of the tides of flux and reflux. The waters of the Great Sea answer unto her, likewise the tides of all earthly seas, and she ruleth the nature of women.

Whilst reading through the proofs of this section I decided to look a little more closely into the phrase 'for therein is contained the number of her name'. This led me into a fascinating line of research where I discovered that the 'alphabet number' Hebrew letters for the names Levanah and Luna were the same, e.g. lamed, vov, nun and hey. The numerology was, of course the same: 30, 6, 50, 5, making a total of 91*. I haven't had a chance yet to find an ancient Greek alphabet, but my guess is that when I do Selene will turn out to have the same numeric value. This led me further into Hebrew Kabbalistic numerology, which had been a speciality of my grandfather's during his lifetime. This type of esoteric thinking is obviously beyond the scope of this book. but it just goes to show how much knowledge is wrapped up in these old sayings.

In Kabbalistic divination, Yesod rules the instincts, habit patterns, food, home environment, sex and sexual organs. This is also the wife in a male reading, and the ninth month of pregnancy.

Before we leave the world of religion and magical belief I would like to advise you to perform all ritual and psychic work during daylight (except for the Isis invocation), even if you are only trying out ideas for size. This is because one's resistance is low after dark, and low-level entities may be drawn in due to the

---

* True Hebrew numerology is like Roman numerology with some letters representing hundreds and thousands etc.

unbalanced forces of the Moon and your tired mind. If you are
at all tuned in to your own lunar phases, then avoid doing any
psychic work at those times when you know you will be at a low
ebb. I know, for example, that I tend to feel tired, ratty and
off-colour just after the new Moon each month, probably
because I was born a couple of days after a full Moon.

   Good luck with your magic, may the Goddess of the Moon
guide your instincts towards greater understanding and the
ability to help others along their paths towards enlightenment.

CHAPTER 4
Elements and Triplicities

The Elements

You will notice as you read on through this book that I use the ancient ideas of earth, air, fire and water plus the astrological triplicities of cardinal, fixed and mutable signs, also the ideas of masculine, feminine, negative and positive signs. This ancient form of shorthand gives an invaluable clue to the basic character of each sign. The following should help you to understand the thinking behind these principles.

Earth

This is concerned with security, structure, slow growth, conventional behaviour, and concrete results. People whose charts contain a heavy concentration of planets and features in earth are sensible, possibly rather plodding and very practical in outlook. They do things thoroughly and carefully, they are unlikely to be extravagant and are very caring towards their family and close friends. They hold on to their possessions and may be a little too money-minded at times. They hate to give up anything and will always try to finish any job that they start. There is a sense of maturity with these people but perhaps a lack of spontaneity. Their virtue is their reliability, their vices are fussiness and an eye-on-the-main-chance attitude.

Air

This is concerned with communications, networks of all kinds, education, theoretical ideas, finding answers to questions and all-round enlightenment; also the network of one's nervous system. These subjects may be serious-minded, highly involved with the education system or the media or chirpy happy-go-lucky types who pick up their streetwise knowledge from the tabloid papers and the local pub. They will be found expounding on some pet idea or arguing a point over anything from a literary reference to a sporting event. They make good journalists and shopkeepers, teachers and travellers because they are always up to date. Although kind-hearted, they tend to forget their many friends when they are out of sight.

Fire
The key ideas here are of scintillating enthusiasm, initiative, intuition, optimism and faith in the future. People who have a strong fire stellium on their birthcharts never quite relinquish their childhood and, therefore, are very much in tune with young people and young ideas. These entertaining people display considerable egotism but also spontaneous generosity. They are concerned to get things started, to create action and pace but may leave the details to others to cope with later on. Fire sign people are quick to grasp an idea, and being on the ball, they approach life with a degree of sportsmanship as if it were a kind of game. These people find it impossible to save money but invariably earn their way out of disaster.

Water
This is concerned with the emotions and feelings, the beginnings, endings and major transformations of life also one's moods and inner urges. Watery people respond slowly when asked a question and may appear to be slow when grasping a new concept. They are slow to change, preferring to stay on tried and tested paths. Their chief need is to be near the family, also to have financial security. Faithful, loyal and often quite tense, these people have an intuitive feeling for what is going to be right for themselves and their families. They are sensible and reliable but can fall into depression and illness if life doesn't go their way. There is a corresponding understanding of the needs of others but sometimes an unwillingness to make the effort to

do something about these needs. Most watery people have an artistic streak in them, they are particularly fond of music.

────────── The Triplicities ──────────

Cardinal

This implies action, initiative. People with a strong cardinal element in their charts cannot be held down under anyone's thumb, they initiate ideas, especially those connected with business. There is an inner sense of determination and an irrepressible desire to succeed. Another way of looking at cardinality is to see it as a beginning because it provides the energy and initiative to get things off the ground.

Fixed

These people like to stay put; in the same house and the same job for as long as possible. They have the strength and endurance to see things through and to uphold the status quo. There is always a measure of stability here, even if it is just the following through of mental exercises and ideas. This can be viewed as a form of continuation as it implies the steady effort of working things through.

Mutable

These people can also hang on to outworn lifestyles, either because they fear change or because they want to keep the peace. They will try to adapt to the behaviour of others and to supply the needs of others. They have the ability to adapt their style of work to whatever situation is prevailing at the time and can steer projects through all their necessary modifications without too much difficulty. Their thinking is wider and more lateral than the other two types but they may prefer to sit in a stew and moan about it than to grit their teeth and either bear it (fixed) or make a new start (cardinal). A further way of viewing mutability is to see it as a transforming element which can either change a situation or bring it to a conclusion.

Masculine and Positive

Outgoing, social, assertive, *apparently* confident, *apparently* courageous.

Feminine and Negative
Introspective, shy, moody, unassertive, *apparently* weak, *apparently* fearful, receptive.

NB: Remember, all that is apparent, ain't necessarily so!

CHAPTER 5
Your Natal Moon Sign

——MOON IN ARIES——
♈ (Ruled by Mars) ♂

The sun shall not smite thee by day, nor the moon by night.
Psalm 121

The sign of Aries is masculine, positive, fiery and cardinal whilst the Moon, through its association with the sign of Cancer, is feminine, negative, watery and cardinal. This Moon position gives its owner an underlying need for power and a desire for leadership. This may lead you to reach for the top in your career or to become the leader of whichever group you find yourself in. Women with this Moon placement face emotional conflict within their personality due to their highly assertive inner nature and they frequently resolve this by choosing weak partners so that they can reverse the traditional man/woman roles. One such woman is Bernadette.

Bernadette is a hard working and successful businesswoman

who travels far and wide to earn the money which her family needs. Her sensitive and artistic husband has a rather humdrum job in a local garage and is super-supportive and caring towards the children. 'I didn't choose this way of life,' says Bernadette, 'it just seems to work out better this way. David cannot take too much hassle and he is really much better with the children than I am.'

Some choose single life and a demanding career in preference to housework and motherhood. Carol is now in her late thirties and is running a successful public relations business of her own. She has had long-term lovers but has never married. 'Some years ago I debated whether to have a child and bring it up on my own because I knew by then that marriage was not for me. In the end, I decided to stay as I am but I'm not always sure that I took the right decision even now.'

Both sexes have an inner power pack of energy, forcefulness and courage, the cardinality of this sign means that you rarely allow the grass to grow beneath your feet. If faced with a problem you would rather sort it out immediately. You may actually get others to do this for you but help is appreciated when it is given. Your mind is highly original and, given other encouraging factors on your birthchart, you may be able to turn your ideas into money-making projects which could give you the means to get yourself up the ladder of success, however you may be so idealistic and enthusiastic as to be unrealistic. You have a tendency to do things on too large a scale sometimes, over-optimism can cloud your brain and make you unrealistic in your expectations. You need to have an element of risk in your life which may be reflected in the job you do or in your personal life.

Being quickly responsive to any situation, you can be relied on in a crisis; you're not embarrassed by the sight of people who are in trouble, indeed you will do what you can to help them. Your emotional reactions are fast and instinctive, your behaviour can be over-impulsive but time and experience of life may soften some of the rough edges. Care should be taken not to be critical and impatient with those who see and do things differently from you, as this can lead you into a narrow-minded and bigoted stance. You quickly become irritated and may have difficulty in keeping your temper due to the combined blanketing effect of the watery moon and the fiery impulsiveness of the sign of Aries. This tension may be released in sudden outbursts of temper and biting sarcastic remarks. Your energy, if there are some Aquarian traits on your chart, could make you an energetic social reformer. You prefer other people to be forthright and honest in their dealings with you and unless there is a very good reason for secrecy, you prefer to be direct and honest yourself. Your excellent sense of humour gets you out of a lot of trouble and you have the ability to take a joke against yourself.

Your ability to put ideas into action can be an inspiration to others, also you can motivate people by your optimistic outlook and your faith in the future. You know instinctively how to raise the spirits of others. However, you can go 'over the top' on occasion and plunge into action without weighing the consequences and therefore, you need to cultivate a sense of proportion. When being carried away on a cloud of enthusiasm be careful not to override the feelings of others, however, it is never your intention to hurt anyone. You have little patience with people who withdraw into their shell, sulk and won't tell you what's the matter with them, your own hot temper can make you insensitive at times but you don't hold a grudge. The lunar Arian heart is warm and you are the first to help and comfort those who are in trouble. You respect the beliefs of others and are happy to preserve their independence; your broad mind makes you able to relate to people of all classes and colours. You really cannot stand neurotic people who whine for nothing. You will help anyone who has practical problems but have little patience with emotional doubts and worries and you tend to avoid having them yourself.

You are more of a city person than a country type but you like to get away into the fresh air and love being in the sun. It is a fact that many lunar Arians are excellent sportsmen and sports-women. The fiery quality of Aries indicates a need for excitement and change, a monotonous job may pay the bills but won't satisfy you for long. This need for excitement can also make steady relationships appear unappealing and this may even lead you to choose unreliable partners. Some of you, on the other hand, seek to steady your own inner nature by marrying a much more placid and reliable personality than yourself; a few of you may possibly destroy a relationship simply because it has become boring. I have a theory that Moon in Aries subjects of both sexes prefer a younger partner, this suggests that you would enjoy moulding them to your own design. Many of you choose a partner who is careful with money because you don't seem to be able to trust yourself not to overspend. You enjoy the pursuit of love and fall in love fairly easily but the flame can burn out quickly. A relationship based on friendship is more likely to be enduring that a swift passion but there must be excitement, sex and warmth or it will not work at all. Women with the Moon in Aries have a touch of masculinity at their core, that is *not* to say that they are all budding lesbians, just that there is dissatisfaction with the traditional feminine role. Whatever your gender, if you have this Moon placement, you may be hard to live with at times, because you can fall into the habit of being picky and fault-finding due to unreasonable fears based on imagined threats to your independence.

You can be quite a good homemaker as long as you have time and money to spare, but if you are short of both, you will ignore your surroundings. You enjoy buying gadgets for the home and you can put up with noisy or messy major alterations better than most people can.

You are a caring parent but unfortunately you could belittle any child whom you considered weak and silly. You do your best to see that your children have all that they require and will move heaven and earth to get them a good education. You may not actually wish to spend too much time with your children, the relationship works better if you have a fulfilling job and can, therefore, direct most of your energies away from the home situation. You will never hesitate to spend money on your family's appearance as you consider that good clothes give a good impression.

Sexually your attitude should be straightforward but you may wish to dominate your partner and control him or her. Talk of sex excites you but background music during love-making may put you off! You enjoy fun and laughter while making love but, above all, you need friendship with your partner as much as you need sex.

Many of you love the arts, especially music and dancing, some of you will find your way into an artistic career, certainly you need a measure of creativity in your work. Many subjects with the Sun, Moon or Ascendant in Aries have a lifelong *desire* to study music or art but somehow never quite get around to it, perhaps the fear of failure is too great.

Attitude to Career

The position of the Moon on a birthchart rarely determines one's actual career but can show inner motivations. You are happiest in a job where you can make your own decisions and may prefer to be self-employed. If not too impatient, you can rise to an executive position in a large and well structured organization. You enjoy wielding power and should make a sensible and benevolent manager or employer, you have the ability to delegate tasks to others and then leave them to get on with the job. Taking orders from someone you don't respect is impossible for you and you would respond very angrily to anyone who tried to bully you; however you, in turn, must try not to bully or to laugh at others.

You need to be able to use your initiative, you would find it impossible to work for a wet blanket type. Work in the military or paramilitary field might appeal to you as might engineering, electronics or work which influences the public. You may enjoy working in the media and being in the public eye so that you can receive open adulation. Marketing, promoting and thinking up new ideas comes easily to you. Your Achilles' heel may be that you are susceptible to flattery. If there are other indications on your birthchart, you could make quite a good teacher. Your love of mechanics and vehicles makes you a good driver, and even a good pilot. The modern technologies of computers and telecommunications would come fairly easily to you. You could make a living from sport or dancing, possibly as a teacher.

Parents and Background

This Moon position shows a difficult relationship with the father, you may have loved him and hated him at the same time and also tried to emulate him. Whilst growing up, you probably found yourself in a number of nose-to-nose shouting matches with him. There is a fight for emotional supremacy in this relationship with the father seeing the child as being unrealistic and the child seeing the parent as being overly restrictive or unhelpful. Sometimes the father actually shows contempt towards the child. Your mother may have been cold towards you or just too busy to take much notice of you. The family itself may be attached to a large and very structured organization such as the armed forces or the civil service. The Aries Moon child may follow his parents into the same organization but would only be happy in that environment if he quickly gained a position of rank and decision-making.

Your parents encouraged you to stand on your own feet at an early age. They would have applauded and encouraged any physical activity (sports, swimming, dancing) and wanted you to do well at school. You don't have much attachment to the past or even to your own family, this is especially true if you feel that they don't appreciate you.

Your mother might have had to face some kind of circumstances where she was forced to leave you to cope alone. This was probably due to problems at that time; however it is possible that she was vain, selfish and all too easily bored by the tasks of motherhood. The Moon sign sometimes jumps back a generation, therefore, some of the circumstances given here for *your* childhood could actually apply to *your mother's experience* when young. There may even have been jealousy and bitterness between you and your brothers and sisters.

Health

In so far as the Moon sometimes reflects continuous or chronic health conditions, any trouble in this case would be in the area of the head, eyes, nose, ears (upper) teeth and throat. Your impetuosity may lead you to have silly accidents such as cuts, burns and possibly bruises as a result of dropping things on your feet.

──MOON IN TAURUS──
♉ (Ruled by Venus) ♀

Ah, Moon of my Delight who know'st no wane,
The Moon of Heaven is rising once again:
How oft hereafter rising shall she look
Through this same Garden after me — in vain!

from *The Rubaiyat* of Omar Khayyam.

The sign of Taurus is feminine, negative, earth and fixed, while the Moon, through its connections with the sign of Cancer is feminine, negative, water and cardinal. The Moon, therefore is fairly comfortable in Taurus adding a measure of stability to the personality and bestowing an uncomplicated response to sensual pleasures. You enjoy eating, drinking, making love and listening to music. The feminine aspect of this placement prevents you from being much of an initiator, indeed you prefer to spend your life sailing along on a steady course than for it to be full of storms and disruption. The fixity of Taurus stabilizes the natural restlessness of the Moon makes you very purposeful and determined, particularly when it comes to getting what you want or hanging on to what you have. You try at all times to maintain the status quo, you may find that the circumstances of your life force you into this position. You might even find yourself putting up with a long-term lifestyle which is not of your choosing. The Moon is said to be 'exalted' in the sign of Taurus which gives an inner sense of strength and resilience. Lunar Taureans, therefore, are noted for their generally robust health and their ability to obtain practical results in all that they undertake.

People who have the Moon in an earth sign love the natural world which means that you make a hobby out of botany or animal biology. You could become involved with some scheme that seeks to preserve the countryside (this is even more likely if there is any Aquarius on your birthchart). Even if you are not actively involved with these pursuits, you will love getting out into the fresh air and into your garden. Many lunar Taureans choose to work as representatives or even milkmen, so that they can be out and about and keep in tune with the seasons. You have a strong need to build for the future and create things which will be useful and long-lasting, this could be reflected in your choice of a career. You like the sea but not with the same intensity as the solar or lunar Cancerian, you wouldn't have any great urge to run off and join the navy. Your affinity with nature could lead you to take an interest in the old religions of earth magic and the 'craft'.

You don't enter into relationships lightly, the fixity of Taurus plus your inner urge to build and preserve leads you to take any form of emotional commitment very seriously. Most astrology books tell us that this Moon position leads to possessiveness and jealousy and, to some extent, this is true. Possessiveness is more of a problem than envy or jealousy but this is a rather subtle concept to grasp. You don't envy the things that other people have or the relationships that they enjoy but if *your* partner were to leave you for another, you would be very jealous indeed. If the object of your love promised to leave his or her partner for you, you would believe him, if you then find him (or her) dragging his feet, you would become very upset indeed and would remain that way for years. It is not easy for you to give in gracefully and accept defeat, especially in the face of what you see as a form of betrayal. This tenacity and endurance are both the strengths and the weaknesses of this particular Moon Sign placement.

Your senses are strong, especially touch and smell; you love the scent of flowers and the feel of velvet. Your musical taste is well developed; one Moon in Taurus lady told me that she hates the sound of a 'murdered song' but loves the sound of laughter. Obviously this sensuality leads to a love of sex with all its scents, textures and passions, however, relating is more important to you than sex for its own sake. You love to be cuddled and stroked in both a sexual and an affectionate manner and ideally for you all this snuggling should take place within marriage.

You are, under normal circumstances, reliable and steady in relationships. You prefer to be faithful to your partner, but if for some reason you find this impossible, then you would try hard to wait for your children to grow up before actually leaving the family home; you try to do your duty for however long it takes. Oddly enough you are quite a flirt but this is 'social' flirting which is not intended to be taken seriously. You don't flirt in order to make your partner jealous, you do it just for the fun of it. You can appear to be intrusive or possessive to those who are close to you ('Where are you going and when do you intend to be back?'), this is not intended to irritate them or to show any lack of trust on your part, you just need to make sure that your family is safe. My Moon in Taurus husband, Tony, likes me to be around. He isn't afraid that I will run off with someone else, he just worries about me. When a friend commented to him about this he told them, 'If Sasha is not home at the time she says that she will be, I start to think that she has had an accident. I have to get up early for my work and if I am kept awake worrying about her, then I get annoyed.' There is no way of changing this person's nature, one just has to be grateful that they care — there are plenty who don't.

You take naturally to parenthood, you love your own children and have patience with those of others. If you marry someone who already has a family, you cope with this very well. You take a responsible attitude towards those who depend upon you, both older and younger members of the family, even pets, without making heavy weather of this. You are very loving and caring and really enjoy looking after, even waiting upon, those you love but you become understandably resentful if this care is taken for granted and not appreciated. You are good with sick people as long as there is not too much mess to clear up, the one thing you really hate is the sight of blood (especially your own). Sometimes this practical type of caring is not enough and you may miss some essential element in your partner's make-up and fail to give him or her the understanding that he needs. Bethany, a really sensitive and intelligent friend of mine summed this up by telling me that 'I just couldn't figure out what it was that my ex-husband really wanted from me half the time. I obviously missed something but, even now, I'm not sure that I can see what it was.'

You yourself strongly need the closeness of a family around you, your sense of loyalty makes you jump to the defence of any member of your family who is criticized by an outsider. However, you yourself are convinced that you have every right to criticize them! Your own deep attachment to your family, occasional misplaced pride in them and desire for them to have the best, be the best, can make you over-critical and even tyrannical at times (especially when you are in a bad mood). A strange fault of yours is that you seem unable to cope with people who lack confidence in themselves. You could even squash the little that they have, you need a certain amount of standing up to, you could actually belittle a partner, even belittle your own children if you suspected too much weakness. You respect strength, possibly because you need to 'tap into' the strength of the other person. You are not necessarily competitive though, and would help a partner or workmate to get ahead. Above all you need a stimulating partner who has similar interests to yourself. You are emotionally habit-forming, not keen on too much change or excitement, you must beware that monotony does not seep into your sexual behaviour.

You are attracted to beauty and people who have cheerful, pleasant natures. Your pet hates are fatness, ugliness and people who wear dirty, tatty clothing. Both the people around you and your own surroundings must be clean and attractive.

You have the quality of basic common sense (rare sense perhaps?). You like your bills to be paid on time, are careful with money and like to have some savings to fall back on but despite this, you are not unduly lucky with money and *can* be taken in by a confidence trickster. There are times when your judgement deserts you. Occasionally your patience deserts you and this can be an interesting experience for those around you as your temper is really fearful when it is unleashed; it can overwhelm you and cause you to cut your nose off to spite your face.

You control your feelings very well and are adept at hiding them from others, probably due to childhood training; being a feminine and emotional sign this repression can lead to moodiness. You may break out in a sudden angry response; if someone were to push in front of you in a queue for instance, you may react differently from one day to another. Being naturally rather cautious, you prefer to allow new acquaintances to do the talking, it is only when you know people better that you can relax and open up. You are not above a bit of manipulation in social circumstances but will generally use it in the form of humour to defuse a tense situation. You usually guard your tongue well and rarely run off at the mouth. Once you have formed an opinion it is hard for you to alter it. You can have the rather unfortunate habit of laying the law down to others.

Attitude to Career

I use the word 'attitude' because the Moon position alone would not suggest any specific career, however one spends so much time at work that it helps to understand one's inner motivations.

You are undoubtedly ambitious, both for yourself and your family. Women with this placement seem to be given the message by their parents that they should stick to the old-fashioned idea of the feminine role and, therefore, often start out as secretaries, nurses or children's nannies. All the lunar Taurean women whom I have spoken to tell me that they resented this bitterly, and also resented the associated implication that they were not as bright or as important as their brothers. They have all subsequently drifted towards less overtly feminine forms of work.

In common with the other earth signs of Capricorn and Virgo, lunar Taureans of both sexes have to put aside their dreams and ambitions for the sake of practicalities, later on in life they may not bother to revive those dreams which I think is rather a shame. One lady told me that she always dreamed of carrying the Olympic torch. Many of you dream about being a musician, dancer or singer but with a bit of luck from elsewhere on your birthchart, you may just be able to make it into showbusiness. Your practical side leads you to supply people with the things that they need, therefore you may deal in food, furniture, household objects or even the things which help people make themselves and their homes attractive. Other typical Taurean trades are building, architecture, farming, market gardening, make-up artist, musician, artist and dancer. Because it is the Moon that we are dealing with here, you will not necessarily follow a Taurean trade at all, however the need to be useful, get out and about and help to create something which is both durable and pleasing to the eye is a strong motivating force. You are not drawn to speculative ventures which is just as well as you are neither a lucky gambler nor particularly good at handling business crises. You are not keen on sending memo's or making up office reports — for one thing, you hate anything to be too cut and dried; however, if you have to produce these, you will do so thoroughly.

A couple of final comments on attitude to work. You prefer to find a steady job and stick to it. You finish practically everything that you start and although not terrifically analytical, you can deal with details without becoming bored. Your persistence makes you good in the field of sales, your flair for beauty could lead to a career in marketing (especially luxury products). A lot of this depends upon the rest of the chart as a touch of Pisces, Aquarius or Sagittarius for instance would add the ingredient of imagination. You hate to be rushed, you can cope with anything when left to work at your own pace.

Parents and Background

According to most astrology books you should have good
parents and have enjoyed a happy and peaceful childhood. My
experience as an astrologer tells me that this is just not so.
Whenever the Moon is in a fixed sign there is at least one parent
who has a bullying or intransigent attitude towards the subject.
This may be due to the fact that the parent has had a hard life
him or herself and has subsequently developed a hard and
unsympathetic outlook. A high proportion of lunar Taureans
have at least one parent born under the sign of Aquarius which
leads to total lack of understanding and communication. All this
leads to an almost Scorpionic ability to keep your thoughts and
feelings away from your parents. This is fair enough as a survival
mechanism but the danger is that this behaviour will be carried
over into other relationships or later dealings with 'authority'
figures.

It seems that one of your parents grew up in some kind of
deprived circumstances, this is more likely to have been poverty,
a lack of opportunity and a lack of material security than lack of
love (although that could apply too). This parent, therefore, is
left with the feeling that *things* are safer than people and that one
must obtain goods and money in order to survive, there seems to
be little space in the parent's head for love, understanding and
sensitivity to the child. You may have come from a comfortable
home where your practical needs were taken care of but there
will have been some lack of understanding. One of your parents
may have been ill, a hypochondriac or just weak-willed, you
probably harbour feelings of contempt for this parent, these are
very well hidden — even from yourself. You may feel that the
weaker parent could have done more for you, and more for
themselves as well.

Most women with this Moon placement marry quite young
and have children early. Lunar Taurean judgement being what
it is, the first marriage might well turn out to be a mistake. It
appears that you are attracted to exciting types who in your eyes
complement your own stodginess. These types are *too* exciting to
be good family men, therefore the disappointments are a kind of

double blow. The result of this can push female Taureans into exciting careers as a result of the need for financial survival.

Health

In so far as the Moon influences health on a birthchart, an afflicted Moon in Taurus would bring problems in the area of the lower jaw, ears, throat, voice and tonsils. There may be thyroid problems and even, just possibly diabetes. You may have that famous Taurean tendency to gain weight, but this will be mitigated if there is a lot of air on your chart.

——MOON IN GEMINI——
♊ (Ruled by Mercury) ☿

When they got there, the West Wind asked him if he could tell her the way to the castle that lay *East of the Sun and West of the Moon*, for it was she who ought to have had the *Prince* who lived there.

(from a book of old Norse legends which I read and re-read, scribbled on and nearly wore out when I was very young.)

The sign of Gemini is masculine, positive, airy and mutable; the Moon, through its association with Cancer, is feminine, negative, watery and cardinal. The Moon, therefore, is not really comfortable in this sign and this may lead to some conflict within the personality. The instability of Gemini plus the fluctuating nature of the Moon could make your emotions a little too changeable and your nerves jumpy. If you have something steady such as Leo or Taurus on your Sun or Ascendant, then the Gemini nervousness would just be confined to bouts of irritability. You are impatient with demanding people and cannot cope with those who are chronically ill. Your own health is not all that good but you try to ignore bouts of illness and hardly ever take time off work to recover or recuperate.

The mutability of this sign gives you a fascination for new and interesting people and places and this leads you into the kind of job where you continually come across new people and get around from place to place. You like to be in the swing of things and hate to miss anything that is going on. Your private life is probably less changeable but you certainly have many friends and can usually be found on the end of a phone somewhere.

Women with the Moon in Gemini need to be out at work. This is even stronger with the lunar type than in women who have the Sun in Gemini because the underlying nature is highly ambitious and rather calculating. Both sexes like the home to be clean and orderly but are not interested in doing much housework themselves. Both sexes like to look nice and tend to feel confident if they go out knowing that they are well dressed. Your mind is very active and you may be intellectual; even with very little formal education; you would be a deep reader and a self-educator. Your mind (unless Mercury is badly placed) is very quick and acute and you have a fine, fast sense of humour and a gift for making amusing and witty comments. The reverse of this coin is that you may become sarcastic if irritated. Lunar Geminians think fairly deeply and are less likely to be content with surface knowledge than are Sun in Gemini subjects, however, in addition to this depth of thought, you also have a dustbin-like mind full of rag-tag bits of knowledge. Although chatty and friendly to every new face on your scene, you do have strong relationships with your family and you will keep your most personal friends for years. Your moods change quickly but you don't sulk and you have no patience with those who do. Your attention span is strange; people who moan about their problems or go on at length about their pet subject bore you, but an interesting book or TV programme will hold you riveted for ages. Your thought processes are logical and you learn in an orderly fashion but you can blend this logical aproach with instinctive or even psychic awareness if there is help from other areas of your birthchart.

There is a kind of Peter Pan aspect to this Moon position

which I think may also apply to the other air signs of Libra and Aquarius. Somehow you never see yourself as quite grown up and can continue to display quite babyish behaviour when away from the outside world. The reverse side of this coin is that you do seem to keep your youthful looks and a young outlook on life far longer than most. You have creative and artistic ability and may paint, make ornaments or interesting clothes, you may be interested in model-making or computer techniques. You have strong dress sense and a good eye for matching up an outfit.

If given the opportunity, you learn to drive a car while you are in your teens, explore your own neighbourhood and then travel the world as soon as you are able to. Cities appeal to you more than the countryside and you particularly enjoy visiting foreign cities. You are resourceful and can usually find a way to solve practical problems, you are probably quite good with your hands.

Although not a social reformer, you hate racialism and ill treatment towards those who can't stand up for themselves such as children or animals. As a parent you would make quite sure that your own children were being well treated but would not want to spend all your time looking after them. Your worst fault is a certain inner coldness, you really cannot take to people who wish to lean upon you, and may give the appearance of having very little depth of concern for others. You can give practical help when it is needed but you may find people's emotional problems hard to cope with. Being logical by nature, you cannot see how or why they fell into their particular emotional mess in the first place. Care must be taken to watch that your witty tongue does not spill over into sarcasm.

Oddly enough you can suffer from depression at times and can become so down-hearted that you feel life to be a total waste of time. One case of these feelings might be exhaustion because you have few reserves of energy to call on and you have the habit of going beyond your limit if there is work to be done.

Some of you may delay marriage or parenthood until you feel that you are sufficiently grown up to cope with it, but when you do take the plunge, you are quite serious in your attitude. You make a delightful parent because you never quite grow up yourself, therefore you relate easily to children. You will break the bank to provide them with a good education and your children will never be short of books, materials or any other kind of mental stimulation. You will try to remain close to your grandchildren as you value family life.

You can have a real problem in the realm of relationships, leading a very busy life which leaves you too tired and over-stretched for much relating. To some extent this is a mechanism which helps you to avoid the reality of responsible relating. This 'busy-busy' business could hide a deep well of unspoken unhappiness. You may avoid emotional commitment, preferring to keep your contacts with the opposite sex on a somewhat shallow level. You could attract (or choose) a rather weak dependent type of partner who would be drawn to your inner strength — remember Gemini is a *positive* sign, but you are better off with one who can stand on his or her own feet. Helen, a young Moon in Gemini travel agent tells me 'I'm not so much afraid of commitment as bored by it. I still feel at my age (early twenties) that I want to play the field. I have to admit that to some extent I dread the thought of being tied down.' Perhaps you need to get in touch with your own feelings before being able to handle those of others. You could be a theorizer and, as far as emotions are concerned, you may prefer to read about emotional matters and to rationalize them than to feel the reality of them. To some extent this derives from a mistrust of the opposite sex and possibly a lack of sexual self-confidence. You don't like to be emotionally fenced in. Malcolm, a highly successful Sales Manager for a vehicle hire firm, told me recently that he had just fallen in love for the first time at the age of forty-eight. 'Why?' I asked him, 'why now?' 'Well', he replied, 'I suppose I was always nervous of being vulnerable or of committing myself totally. I did go through some really stupid escapades with a number of totally mindless women at one time — escaping reality, I suppose.'

You don't suffer from jealousy if you see other people making a success of themselves and, like most of the lunar masculine signs, you measure your own successes against *your own* achievements. Not being jealous or possessive yourself you strongly resent being on the receiving end of this behaviour by others. You are proud of your achievements however, and also proud of your family, you could push your children educationally, and will make sacrifices in order to help your family.

Sex has to start in your mind and, if you are not careful, it can stay there too; like lunar Pisceans you may be happier fantasizing about sex than actually indulging in it. If you find a compatible partner who encourages you to relax you can bring all that sexuality down from your mind to reach the parts that the other beers cannot reach, then you could become the lover you always wanted to be. You are easily put off by coarseness. Your nerves are sensitive, therefore a quiet atmosphere, an amusing lover and a couple of drinks will work wonders. You may possibly experiment with bisexuality and may privately enjoy rude books and even blue films! Oddly enough both solar and lunar Geminians are tactile. They enjoy hugging, touching and being touched as long as they are not smothered or held too close. Before leaving the fascinating subject of sex, it is worth noting that anyone with Gemini strongly marked on his chart can do two things at once!

Attitude to Career

The position of the Moon will not indicate any specific career but will show your inner motivations. People, mental activity, words and travel are essential ingredients for your working life. You may work in sales, telephone or telex communications or marketing. Writing, especially journalism may appeal, also all forms of teaching. Your own education may have been of almost any quality but many of you do teach yourself, then others, possibly in the realms of sports or dancing. You are generally respected by others both for what you know and for your pleasant way of handling people.

Your mind should be orderly (unless there are other indications on your birthchart) and you can organize both yourself and others. Travel appeals to you, especially air travel, and many lunar Geminians work in the airforce or the travel industry. You all seem to love driving and may be able to pilot a plane as well. You have a quick grasp of new ideas and can communicate them well to others, you are very good at handling people and make a wonderful manager. You can be canny and crafty in business; you love wheeling and dealing and you may not always be a hundred per cent honest. You are at your best when teamed up with a practical partner. As this sign rules the hands and arms, you could be a super craftsman, printer, manicurist or even a palmist.

Oddly enough, religion and mysticism may interest you but only on a surface level. You may enjoy the social side of a religious group rather more than the deeper elements of its philosophy.

Parents and Background

The chances are that you had one parent, probably your father, who tended to lay down the law to you, this gave you an awareness of the need to be obedient and to conform with the parent's ideas of behaviour. Your childhood home was probably filled with books and educational aids and your parents will have been quite happy for you to have tuition in practically anything. There would have been good conversation and interesting visitors in your home. You should have been born fairly easily and may have been the youngest child in a small family or the only one of one sex among a family of the opposite one. There is some evidence of deep unhappiness in childhood and a sense of not fitting in somewhere, this may have been within the family or at school. You may have been on the receiving end of racial or religious prejudice! You may have been compared to other brothers and sisters, a dead child or even one of your parents and found wanting. It is possible that you fancied working in the services or in a hospital but somehow this either doesn't happen or just doesn't work for you when you try it.

An unusual mother is indicated for you, she may be a career woman, highly intellectual or just plain eccentric! Your mother would have shown you, either by direct reference or by example, that women must be able to stand on their own two feet in life.

This will influence you, if you are female, to become a career woman; if male, to choose a career woman for your partner.

The problems associated with this placement could jump back one generation and apply more closely to one of your parent's experiences of childhood.

Health

This is not a healthy placement for the Moon especially if it is also badly aspected by other planets. Your lungs may be weak also there could be problems with your hands and arms. Some lunar Geminians suffer really horrendous accidents which affect their arms, hands, teeth and faces. This lunar position can lead to bones and features having to be rebuilt! You can suffer allergies and may have one or two ailments from among the range of nervous or auto-immune diseases. This could be asthma, eczema, rheumatism, migraine, psoriasis, ulcers, colitis, etc. Your nerves may be your worst enemy. You need to find an outlet for your nervous energy; sports, fresh air pursuits or even sex could help!

─────MOON IN CANCER─────
♋ (Ruled by the Moon) ☽

'It was the lovely moon — she lifted
Slowly her white brow among
Bronze cloud-waves that ebbed and drifted
Faintly, faintlier afar.'

It was the lovely Moon,
by John Freeman (1880–1929)

The sign of Cancer is feminine, negative, watery and cardinal. The Moon is the planet which rules this sign, therefore it is quite at home here. The Moon rules the inner person, therefore like those who have the Sun in Cancer, your reactions to people and places are very strong and this will be automatically taken into account in any decisions which you make. Your feelings are very sensitive, which means that you link in very quickly to other people's feelings to the point where you can feel whether they are unhappy or in pain. You can sense a 'funny' atmosphere as soon as you walk into a room. Unless there are very conflicting forces on your chart, you should have the usual Cancerian ability to listen sympathetically. In business, you would have an instinctive feel about a deal which was about to go wrong — or go right!

The negative side of this coin is over-sensitivity. Like the other feminine water signs of Pisces and Scorpio you can take things too personally, brood, sulk and shut yourself off from others. They say that Cancerians' moods change with each tide but this is an exaggeration. Women with the Moon in any of the water signs will be very susceptible to period problems and hormone-related mood swings. The very worst aspect of this placement is that you may indulge in emotional blackmail by shutting off from others and sending out disapproving vibes. On a very bad day, you might be beset by feelings of paranoia or the kind of envy which would make you behave in a thoroughly resentful manner. You can also be over-critical and fault-finding on occasions. This kind of behaviour is rare because you are much too kind and thoughtful a person, far too receptive to the needs of others to be this unpleasant for long.

You have the ability to adjust yourself to your surroundings and fit in fairly well with other people (water signs find their own level). You may complain about the situation you find yourself in but you will make the best of it and will often find a way of changing and manipulating the circumstances to suit yourself. Remember Cancer is a *cardinal* sign and the Moon represents one's instincts. *Your* instinctive reaction is to put things right and create a better atmosphere. Some people are starters and others are runners, the ability to initiate projects and/or to see them through would depend upon a variety of factors in your birthchart, but your instinctive reaction is to set things in motion and then encourage others (or find someone else) to see them through. If you are really stuck for an answer to your problems you can always look a bit pathetic in the hope that someone will take pity on you and help you solve them.

You are considerate towards others, especially your family, it would be almost impossible for you to desert them; you would only do so under extreme duress. I think that you would try several times to put things right before giving up on them. You have patience with children and young people and are probably very fond of animals. You are not entirely selfless, it is only when *you* are settled and satisfied that you can relax and give sustenance to others. Your greatest requirements are for *emotional* security, e.g. a partner you can rely upon, harmony in the home and friends who help build up your confidence. Lack of confidence in your own abilities and feelings of relative worthlessness are your worst enemy and it's these that can make you feel jealous and resentful towards others, often quite without justification.

You like children and enjoy having them around you, not only being good to your own children but kind to other people's as well. However, you greatly resent having other people's children being dumped on you. Your gentle inner nature responds to the vulnerability and honesty of children. You may remain a bit too close to your own children after they have grown up or you may want them to be independent but find that you can't get rid of them! Alternatively, your own mother may continue to smother *you* long after *you* have grown up! It may be quite difficult for you to forget your own childhood as you have a slight tendency to live in the past.

You react to any difficult situation by worrying. You genuinely worry about your family; also money, health, the state of the nation and the imminence of nuclear war. There is a tendency for you to attract parasitical people who hang themselves on to you and make demands upon you. This is most evident among those of you who have your Sun or ascendant in a steady earth sign or an enthusiastic fire sign. Fortunately for you, you are astute enough to be able to spot these types coming and to off-load them far more easily than, for instance, a soft-hearted Moon in Pisces person could. When you care for someone you are very good to them if they are ill; being kind and sympathetic, you can become worked up on their behalf if you think that they are being hurt by someone else. Unfortunately, unless there is a lot of strength elsewhere on the chart, you won't actually *do* anything practical to help.

You might be sensual but you are not greedy. You don't have a large appetite for food, you prefer small amounts that are very well cooked and presented. Your sensitive stomach may reject spicy foods. (One Moon in Cancer friend tells me that he cannot eat raw onions.) You probably enjoy good wines but there is no evidence of this Moon placement leading to overindulgence. You could be a good cook yourself but this will depend upon other factors in your birthchart, also your lifestyle. You hate scenes and rows and are easily upset by harsh discordant noises. You can put up with any amount of chaos around you at work but you need peace and harmony in the home. You may have the Cancerian trait of collecting things, ranging from valuable antiques to junk. You don't like losing anything — or anyone.

Your senses are all strong, especially that of hearing, you really hate discordant noises. The senses of smell, touch and taste are well developed and you could be long-sighted. Sexually, you absolutely come into your own. The whole concept of an experience which involves all the senses plus love and affection is just too much for you to miss. Being basically kind and thoughtful, you should be a considerate — even a practised lover. The fact that you are the faithful type possibly mitigates against much variety in sexual experiences. Two of my friends who happen to be married to Moon in Cancer subjects tell me that their partners are good lovers.

You enjoy the company of new people and visiting new places but also you have an attachment to old ones. You enjoy gossiping almost as much as your Gemini cousins do. You have a habit of observing the behaviour of others as a form of self-protection. Being emotionally cautious, you are slow to fall in love and open yourself to the prospect of hurt and rejection. Others may fall in love with you because you have an immediate understanding of their problems. You seem to *know* others psychically. If the one who falls for your sympathetic attitude expects you to go on and solve their problems they may be disappointed. This rather depends on your Sun and rising signs.

Being cautious, you may react in a slightly hostile manner towards new people. If you have something very outgoing, such as Sagittarius, on your Ascendant, there will be an open, confident attitude, however the caution will still be there hidden away underneath. You are basically honest both with money and in most other senses; you can be trusted in any kind of confidential situation and with any information. However, one less pleasant attribute is that you can occasionally display a touch of smarminess, flattering those whom you wish to get round or make capital out of. This is a successful ploy in most cases, but it won't wash when dealing with people who are particularly perceptive.

You can be slightly mean in small matters. This peculiarity also applies to the Moon in Pisces and Scorpio. My friend Linda tells me that she gets annoyed when her children waste toothpaste and she saves the last bits of used bars of soap, jams them together so that they can be completely finished off! I have the Moon in Pisces and have to admit to the same small economy measures. Both solar and lunar Cancerians find it hard to get rid of anything. Once in a while you decide to turn out the cupboards only to put almost everything back again. There is too much sentiment attached to your junk for you to be able to throw it out. You need a base to operate from, therefore, not only your home but also your office are important to you and you don't want these to be disturbed or 'cleaned-up' too much. Unless there is a strong dose of Libra or Virgo on your birthchart, you are not over-fussy about the appearance of your home; you could make a home anywhere.

Your likes and dislikes are strong; remember Cancer is a cardinal sign, you also have courage in odd places where others lack it. For instance, you are adept at asking questions, probing, finding out what makes people tick and keeping up to date with the local gossip. You are not above giving a gentle form of 'third degree'.

Lunar Cancerians have a long memory, therefore, you can hold a grudge if you are hurt, but you also remember those who have helped you. Being rather sentimental, you like to remember birthdays and anniversaries and you feel peeved if yours are forgotten. Your intuition is very strong and this may just be a helpful tool in everyday life or you can actually be drawn towards psychic work of some kind. Quite a few lunar Cancerians have paranormal or psychic hobbies. Because you can be trusted with secrets, you could work as a psychic consultant of some kind where you have to listen to people's confidences. You like the countryside and really love the sea. If a Cancerian Moon is *very* prominent in your birthchart, you could choose a job on or near the sea. Another of your interests is the past. You may study history or collect things which have been around for a long time such as antiquities.

In relationships you play the part of parent and may take an over-responsible attitude to others and try to organize them too much or dictate to them too much or play the child hoping to be forgiven for bad behaviour just one more time. This too may jump back one generation and you may be on the receiving end of this behaviour rather than dishing it out yourself. It is natural for you to worry about those whom you care about. If backed up by other planetary factors, you could be a blamer and complainer in a relationship — this would be especially true if there was a strong Pisces factor somewhere on your chart.

Attitude to Career

The Moon will show how you approach the *idea* of work rather than give specific career guidance. Unless there are other factors on the chart, such as an emphasis on the sign of Libra, you will be a hard and conscientious worker. Your inner nature leads you towards the kind of job where you can be helpful. Many lunar Cancerians work in hospitals, schools and with the elderly; others are attracted to the world of business. Some of you are drawn towards the field of antiques, rare coins, stately homes or genealogy. Insurance may attract you because of its 'protective' image. Many of you retrain later in life if your original career ceases to be viable or if you find that you lack certain qualifications which would help you to get up the career ladder. Many solar and lunar Cancerians run small businesses, shops and small agencies. Being good with your hands, you could work as a plumber, carpenter etc. Lunar Cancerians make excellent teachers too.

You will not stand in the way of a partner who wants a career, in most cases you are only too willing to see them get on and you will help if you can. Your sensitivity means that you could make a good salesman or business executive, personnel manager or counsellor. Politics may appeal, as could accountancy. Most of you have a theatrical side to your nature and might be drawn to the world of entertainment or sports. The drawback to this is the irregularity of work and the general uncertainty of this field, being a worrier, you would probably be happier in a secure job while singing and dancing during your time off. You would be a good partner for a very go-ahead person but you haven't really got the stomach for high risk or slightly criminal ventures.

Parents and Background

The Moon in this position suggests that your mother gave birth to you easily. Your parents' home will have been comfortable and the relationships there will have been pleasant. The chances are that you are the eldest in your family (although this is much more likely if the Ascendant were in Cancer). The background and history of your family is important to you and you may try to trace your family tree. The family may travel a bit, taking you with them, but there is no evidence that you moved home a lot. Mother may have been traditional and ordinary but possibly over-protective towards you.

Health

This Moon position suggests strong health with good recovery from illness and operations. The weak areas associated with the Moon in Cancer would be chest, breasts and stomach, but the Moon is not the most obvious indicator of health in a chart.

You are very much in tune with your body, therefore, you would feel pain almost before something began to go wrong! Unless the Moon is very afflicted and there are other very important factors on the birthchart, there is no reason to suppose that you are any more susceptible to the dreaded disease of cancer itself than any other sign.

──MOON IN LEO──
♌ (Ruled by the Sun) ☉

Or when the moon was overhead,
Came two young lovers lately wed;
'I am half sick of shadows,' said
The lady of Shalott.

by Alfred Tennyson

The sign of Leo is masculine, positive, fiery and fixed, while the Moon, through its associations with the sign of Cancer, is feminine, negative, watery and cardinal. At first sight it doesn't look as if the Moon would be very comfortable in Leo but in many ways it is. For the sake of convenience, astrologers call *all* the bodies in the Solar system 'planets'. The Sun is, of course, a small star whilst the Moon is a satellite of the Earth. These two objects dominate man's view of the sky and their movements dominate the lives of every being on the face of the Earth.

The main differences between the Sun and the Moon from an astrologer's point of view are in the attitudes which they lend to relationships, especially inter-generation relationships. The power of the Sun seems to dominate the Moon, permeating the deepest layers of the personality with Leonine characteristics which then bubble their way up to the surface. If you have this Moon placement you are basically kind, generous and honourable with an instinctive need to encourage others. There is a real touch of Leo nobility deep down inside of you. It is worth remembering that many members of the royal family have the Moon in Leo. Being naturally dignified, honest and trustworthy, you would find it hard to behave in a callous or a crafty manner and you are far too proud to scrounge off others. Your need to *appear* honest and honourable may not reflect reality; but if you are caught out in a cowardly or underhanded act or if it becomes obvious that you harbour jealous feelings, you can react in an angry and aggressive manner. You can get on your high horse if your dignity is pricked.

The fixity of the sign gives you the determination to see things through and to finish everything that you start. It is possible that you may dig your heels in too much and try to lay the law down to others. You could be stubborn and unbending at times.

You sometimes appear to behave in a distant and superior manner, this is your shield for those times when you are in unfamiliar situations. When hurt, you retreat into something which you see as dignified silence and others see as the sulks; however, under normal circumstances you are cheerful, friendly and open. You occasionally have doubts about your own self-worth, also occasional feelings of intense superiority. The emotions are always held under control when the Moon is in a fixed sign and therefore they may break out strongly from time to time. You could become quite aggressive if pushed, or are on the receiving end of aggression from others. If hurt enough you would become jealous, full of hate, revengeful.

Lunar Leo's can be surprisingly self-sacrificing towards loved ones but heaven help them if the loved one doesn't appreciate the sacrifices. You place the objects of your love on a pedestal and feel hurt when you discover that they are only human. Your intense feelings give you a longing for excitement, drama, romance and passion; with a bit of luck you will find this within a steady relationship; if not, then you will look for romance, passion etc. outside of marriage. You may even create tension within a relationship to keep it alive. For the same reason you must have an exciting career, you can put up with an insecure one but not a boring one. Too much contentment bores you.

Your mind is broad and you are unlikely to follow any of the more fanatical religious or political beliefs. You may have a religious and philosophical outlook which is different from that of your parents but this should not be a big problem in your life. Although not in any way bigoted, you may find it hard to change your mind once it is made up and you can have rather entrenched views.

The Moon is associated with the home, therefore, yours will be attractive with an interesting sort of decor. You are very fussy about your own appearance and may even be vain (men with this Moon placement are actually worse than women). The one thing which is the bane of your life is your hair. You may consider this to be too thick, thin, wiry, curly or even if male, too bald! You may be vain about your body and even your sexual performance. One lady who is married to a very nice Moon in Leo guy tells me that he doles out sex as if it were a treat! As a lover you could, like Sun in Leo, be bossy and demanding but also comfortable, relaxed and kind. It would be most unusual to find an out and out pervert with this Moon placement. Being romantic, you enjoy dining out, giving and receiving presents and remembering birthdays. You are fussy about your choice of partner, nothing less than the best will do for you. You have a strong sex drive but couldn't cope for long with a relationship based on sex alone. You need romance, passion and you need above all to be loved. Even so you would find it difficult to live without the comfort and release of sex; life without love, in all its applications would be too cold to contemplate. You don't mind taking the lead sexually and can encourage a partner who is less experienced than you. Your senses are strong, therefore everything about sex appeals to you as long as you can perform with a certain amount of decorum. The back seat of a car in a rainy car park is just not for you (except maybe a Rolls Royce!).

You may feel a need to attach yourself to some source of

power. You may work with powerful and successful people, with large and powerful animals; alternatively, you might be fascinated by the power of magic and the spiritual world. This would enable you to enjoy risk-taking at second hand which is a lunar trait. Your courage, fire and enthusiasm could lead you to learn from the powerful people around you and put their lessons into action for yourself which is, of course, a solar trait.

You will do anything for those whom you love but you need your generosity of spirit to be appreciated. Being a fixed sign, you resist change and would find it hard to admit defeat in any situation, therefore, you would find it difficult to cut your losses and start again. You can put up with the wrong job for far too long and also hang on to a rotten relationship long after the time has come to end it. You are possibly a little too good at maintaining the status quo, especially in emotional situations. You may be self-centred emotionally and possibly inclined to hang on to those you love — this applies to your children as well. Laura, a gentle and skilled palmist now in her mid-forties, recently left her paranoid and violent husband after many years of abuse; but still feels that she is unable to make the final break and divorce him. 'It's too final,' she says.

Unless there are very different characteristics in your Sun and Ascendant you are sociable and enjoy being entertained but, being much shyer than the solar Leo type of personality, you can only entertain others in a quiet way. Sports and the company of young people appeal to you. You might become involved in some organization like the Boy Scouts, Girl Guides, the Territorial Army or the Red Cross. There is no need for you to be the centre of attraction in the world outside, but you do like to be in the centre of things within your own home. If you did find yourself in the spotlight, you could cope with it but you don't seek it consciously in the way that Sun in Leo would. You like to know where the various members of your family are and to make sure that they are all right, you have an inner need to organize them and keep them on the right lines.

Your inner nature, unless you are feeling hurt, is playful, sunny and friendly which makes you popular in a quiet kind of way. You appreciate beauty, creativity and art and have an instinctive sense of style. You are proud of your loved ones and even of your friends, you prefer not to be surrounded by dirty down-at-heel types. You never forget a hurt but your strong loyalty means that you remember those who have helped you too. You need to belong somewhere and may be attached to a particular set of bricks and mortar or to an area of the country with which you feel a particular affinity. Needing space, you hate cramped surroundings, you love to get away into the countryside and to take your holidays in a warm and pleasant place. You need holidays and breaks because you tend to put a lot of effort into your job and into life itself. Your vitality is never drained for long as you have inner reserves of strength.

You make an excellent parent, often treating your children as young adults and always preserving their dignity. You don't seek to hang on to them when they grow up. You are able to teach and encourage them through play, but you may not be too patient with them at times, you can be relied on to give them a cuddle whenever they are down-hearted or ill.

Attitude to Career
The position of the Moon does not indicate any specific career but will show your inner leanings and drives. Both solar and lunar Leo subjects learn more easily after leaving school than before. You may take a quite demanding course when already busy with a career, home and family; this may be in order to get yourself a better job or just to fulfil yourself. You lack confidence in your abilities, therefore any achievement that you make will help you to go on to further successes. Even if you do not have much formal education, you understand people and learn well from life. You have an inner need to be in an executive position, and if your circumstances mitigate against this you could be self-employed, the king of your own field, although you might need someone else around to help you cope with the details.

You make a good employer, with an understanding of the need to preserve the dignity of others.

You are career-minded and with your good concentration and good organizational skills, can climb the career ladder in a steady manner. You need to gain a reputation in some kind of creative field and may strive hard to perfect something which will bring you a quiet kind of renown. Your ability to make the right impression could lead you to the fields of marketing, personnel work, the display of works of art or antiques. The biggest problem is that you could have big dreams but may be too lazy to make them come true. You want to come out on top of your field but are strangely uncompetitive, being too self-centred to worry about others, your own high standards would give you enough to compete against. You are good at calming people down and dealing with touchy situations, therefore some kind of social work with troubled people, especially troubled youngsters might appeal. Your attraction to glamour might interest you in some form of show business. There is a creative side to you which means that you would take to dancing, singing or artistic work of some kind. Being drawn towards children and young people, you could be a teacher, (especially if there is Gemini, Aquarius or Sagittarius on your chart). You might prefer to be a nursery nurse or probation officer. Your love of the good things in life could make you a good restaurateur or hotelier but you might be best employed out in the front. You would be all right behind the scenes organizing others, but under no circumstances would you want to be the one to do the cleaning and cooking.

You are competent and capable as long as you are allowed to work at your own pace but you detest being hussled and put under pressure.

Parents and Background

There is probably something wrong here. The chances are that your father was autocratic, authoritarian or just unable to relate to children. You probably got on much better with your mother. You yourself might be too ready to push your own children but this may reflect back one generation, meaning that *you* were pushed by your parents and that they expected more from you than you were able to produce at that time. The background may have been traditional, even religious in some way involving rituals and certain kinds of behaviour. At the worst end of this spectrum you may have been afraid of your father or made to feel that you couldn't live up to some impossible image of perfection. He may have been a very successful man himself or he may have achieved a great deal while he was still young. Lunar Leos are far more likely to succeed later in life. You need parental love, encouragement and appreciation and if you get this from at least one parent plus brothers and sisters, fine, if not you could become something of an emotional cripple. The last thing you need is a cool intellectual air sign for a parent.

Health
The Moon is not the only indicator of health problems on a chart but it might point out any underlying chronic condition. You need to keep your intake of food and drink down and to take exercise and lead a moderate life because your heart may be weak. There could be spinal trouble; this is particularly prone to occur when you are unhappy or worried.

MOON IN VIRGO
♍ (Ruled by Mercury) ☿

Pale moon doth rain, red moon doth blow,
White moon doth neither rain nor snow.

(Proverb)

The sign of Virgo is feminine, negative, earthy and mutable; the Moon, through its association with Cancer, is feminine, negative, watery and cardinal. This means that there is an uneasy alliance between the sign of Virgo and the energy of the Moon. You may find it very difficult to shape your world the way that you would like, it seems that the cardinality of the Moon (cardinality implies action) is halted in mutable, negative Virgo. If you cannot make your job work for you, create the right kind of environment or find the right partner, you could retreat into fiddling about and fidgeting. You may never quite finish decorating your home, you may try out one partner after another or you could become your own worst enemy at work. If thwarted, you will develop a tendency to meddle, criticize, ruin, lose or destroy the very things which you most need. You could over-analyse yourself and everything around you then hide your fears and phobias under a layer of fussiness. Be careful not to fall prey to a psychological need to organize every detail, prepare for every eventuality so that you program out not only life's unexpected problems and but also its pleasant surprises.

Virgo is a difficult sign to understand and the Moon in this placement adds to the complications. I shall now borrow a bit of logic from my own planet of Mercury, which is placed in its own sign of Virgo, in order to analyse the problems. Virgo being an earth sign suggests an inner need to serve people in a practical way, therefore you will prefer to work in a field where you can be useful to others. You feel more comfortable in the workplace than in a social setting, especially if your talents are being used to the limit. Being dutiful and caring towards your family, you show your love for them by helping them in a practical way or by giving them material things, rather than by open displays of affection or of verbal love. You are especially helpful and understanding if they are ill. You are reliable, businesslike, tidy and efficient in all that you do, being loyal and trustworthy, you would never betray a confidence. Most lunar Virgoans are early risers and seem to be more alert in the morning than in the evening. Your mind is very clear and logical, your thinking is usually along realistic lines and you prefer to think before acting. You could be quite imaginative if there were something like Pisces or Leo on your birthchart, but the imagination would be harnessed to some kind of structure — writing poetry, making a garden or computer programming for example. You enjoy debating when you are among people with whom you can relax, you never swallow what you are told without verification. Be careful not to spend too much energy on details and miss the main point, also try not to let problems revolve round in your head growing out of all proportion. Some lunar Virgoans are vigorous social reformers, especially if there is any Aquarius on the birthchart or if the Sun or the Ascendant are in fairly confident outgoing signs. You can take practical decisions almost instantly and will go anywhere at the drop of a hat; when decisions have an emotional content, this is not so easy. Oddly enough, although the mind is quick, your bodily movements may be slow. Female lunar Virgoans are good homemakers, often loving their homes, but they need an intellectual outlet and the chance to work and earn money of their own. Although your thought processes are particularly logical, you can be very psychic. There is an acceptable logic to psychic matters which you seem to grasp more easily than many other people. Religion may not interest you overmuch, and blind faith is never acceptable to you.

Virgo being a mutable sign suggests that you can fit yourself in to almost any type of company. You are unlikely to be prejudiced about race, religion etc. because all people interest you. Lunar Virgoans rarely manipulate others for their own ends. You are shy at first but very sociable when you feel that you can relax. Although hardly likely to be the life and soul of the party, and even less likely to get drunk and make a fool of yourself, you do enjoy socializing, especially in the company of witty and interesting people. Despite being shy, you like to welcome new people but will sit back and analyse them later on.

I very much doubt whether you see money in terms of the power it may give you, and you have little desire to waste your hard-earned pennies on flashy things, you prefer to pay your bills on time and then have a bit left over for treats. A favourite treat for you would be a trip out into the country and a nice meal out. You like the fresh air and the seaside, you enjoy physical exercise of a fairly gentle nature, e.g. walking, dancing, badminton. Being an earth sign, gardening appeals to you, especially growing your own fruit and vegetables plus filling the house and garden with sweet-smelling flowers. Your senses of taste and smell (and your stomach) are easily upset, therefore good home-grown produce is a favourite with you. Reading and listening to music provide you with a passive form of escapism. One active form of escapism which is very popular among both solar and lunar Virgoans is acting, here you can forget yourself for a while and take on a completely different personality. This gives you the opportunity of behaving foolishly or even outrageously without having to risk being taken seriously.

Relationships can be a minefield for you; you tend to make yourself useful to your partner and then wonder why you are being used. In a way the most successful relationship for you would be with a partner who has an important and interesting career of his or her own where you could help to smooth their path for them. There must be a mental rapport between you and your partner, shared interests or work in common will help. You are prepared to make an effort in a relationship. Some of you attach yourselves to a glamorous glittering personality and enjoy being a part of their life. Any relationship based solely on sex alone wouldn't hold you for long. Many astrology books suggest that solar and lunar Virgoans are sexless *this is just not true*, however there can be some really vicious problems associated with sex and sexual relationships. I think that the trouble stems from two sources; the first being that you are easily embarrassed by the apparent ludicrousness of the sex act, you find it hard to relinquish your dignity and make the necessary adjustment which would enable you to surrender to your feelings. The second problem is that you may be ashamed of your own capacity for passion, possibly due to early childhood influences and incidents. Anyone who has *any* of the personal planets (Sun, Moon, Mercury, Venus and Mars) placed in Virgo will immediately freeze up if criticized for their performance.

You may fill up your time with work in order to avoid dealing with the whole relating and sexual scene. Shyness doesn't help here, but most of this can be overcome if you find yourself a kind encouraging partner. One thing which does help is your ability to adapt; all mutable signs will try to fit in with other people's requirements, therefore, given a chance and much tender loving care, you could realize your sexual potential, especially with the 'right' lover. Coarseness puts you off immediately. Criticism will squash you, not only sexually but in every other way. You have intensely critical feelings towards others but being the lunar, inner, side of your nature, you probably keep your remarks to yourself — unless you become very angry when it all bursts out.

If a relationship goes wrong you can become desperate, even suicidally depressed. You have to beware of self-fulfilling prophecies where you tell yourself that you are going to be let down and then you allow yourself to become so; lack of confidence and too little faith in the future can actually bring this about. You may go too far the other way, keeping your emotions on such a tight rein that you never allow yourself the luxury of love and romance, this is a shame because you do need a partner and also a family.

You may find it hard to relate to your own children and may pay too much attention to their practical and educational needs and not enough to their need for love and affection. On the other hand, children may be the ideal outlet for your bottled up love, giving you the opportunity to give and receive affection unreservedly. You may be able to romp, roll around and act out parts for their amusement in a way which you could never do with adults. Teaching comes naturally to you, therefore you enjoy opening your children's minds to the world of books, museums, nature. Given a secure and loving partnership you will gain confidence and really begin to blossom.

You have an acute sense of humour which so often is able to save you from much of the unhappiness associated with this sign, if you can find an intelligent partner to laugh with, then you are really made. Being loyal yourself and having very high standards of behaviour, you may expect others to be the same with regard to you. If your partner makes a habit of wandering off and leaving you alone whenever you go to a party, you would be most put out. You need to be hugged and comforted especially if things are not going well for you and, most of all, you require a feeling of solidarity in your relationships, a feeling that your family circle will stick together and stick up for each other against the world.

Attitude to Career

As a rule the position of the Moon does not indicate any specific career, only one's internal motivations. However, in this case, the sign of Virgo will dominate the personality in such a way that you identify yourself far more by what you *do* than what you *are*. There are enough wasters and losers in this world already, perhaps we could do with a few more lunar Virgoans to prevent us from losing and wasting what is left of our planet. You learn quickly and like to keep your mind and body occupied, even your leisure pursuits are healthy or useful ones such as gentle sports or working for a charity or political organization. You have a creative side which can be expressed in sewing, carpentry, cooking or writing because you like problem-solving and the bringing together of separate parts in order to make a whole.

Skills such as typing, driving and accounting come easily to you. You make an exemplary office worker, being neat, efficient, quiet, clean, practical and helpful. Given that your Sun and Ascendant are placed in an outgoing sign, you may enjoy a life in a skilled branch of the armed forces. Learning and coming to grips with highly technical matters would hold no terrors for you.

The whole field of health comes naturally to you, lunar Virgoans make good nurses, doctors and dieticians. Although unlikely to make much display of your own feelings, you are able to understand the pain of others. Your interest in health is not just in the field of caring and healing but of preventing disease from taking root in the first place, therefore, you advocate diet, exercise and moderate living. You yourself could be a hypochondriac or could genuinely suffer from a series of minor but irritating ailments and nervous disorders. Having a clear, logical and analytical mind you would be a natural for computing, accounting, systems analysing and electronic weighing and measuring. Research, especially in the medical field would please you. Teaching might appeal, either teaching infants or older students who are highly intelligent, quiet and ready to learn. Maths and scientific subjects would suit you, but languages may be a problem. You could learn the grammar all right, it is the speaking that would get you down unless you had something fairly uninhibited like Sagittarius on your Ascendant.

It may be difficult for you to manage others because delegating requires confidence both in one's own leadership qualities plus confidence in the ability of others to do a good job on your behalf. You tend to become angry when faced with an attitude of uncaring inefficiency. You may not be overly

ambitious, but you like to do things well and to be appreciated
for it. The success of others doesn't upset you.

Parents and Background

At best your childhood would have been a fairly cool affair, at
worst it may have had nightmarish qualities. 'Nightmarish is just
about right,' said Anne, an elegant, divorced systems analyst. 'I
used to study my father to judge which rules I should be playing
by and just when I got the hang of the game, he changed the
rules. I could never win, my place was always in the wrong.'

To start with, being born wasn't all that easy, therefore the
relationship between you and your mother probably started
badly. There was a great deal of discipline in your childhood, an
emphasis on being on time for meals, washing behind your ears
and doing your homework. You may have been compared to
other children and told that you were not as good, clever, pretty,
tall, etc. as them. If you were a diligent child, naturally tidy,
quiet, organized and clever at school, you would have pleased
your parents and would therefore have had an easier time of it.
You may have only been able to win their approval by success in
exams or winning medals at sports, dancing, etc. Some of your
self-esteem and lack of confidence results from having been
nervous or even afraid of your parents; you found them hard to
please. It is even possible that you were a naturally timid child
with rather boisterous parents, or one of your parents might
have been particularly hard to get on with.

If your parents were born under the signs of Aries, Scorpio or
Sagittarius, they would have been far too impatient, lacking in
understanding and quick to criticize. This lack of praise and
encouragement caused you to feel resentful, worthless, lonely
and repressed. You may have been shoved aside for other
reasons, e.g. family problems, a handicapped sibling or lack of
money. You may have learned how to hate early in life. Your
hatred of being accused of laziness is a hangover from
childhood. Your shyness and repression may have been the
result of severe and prolonged illness in childhood rather than
awful parents.

There is always the possibility that the Moon's position reflects the mother's experience of life, so the interpretation could be an indication that your mother had a hard time while young.

Health

Both solar and lunar Virgoans are strong and healthy but the nervous system is delicate. Ailments include migraine and asthma, allergies, skin conditions and stomach ulcers. Tension and overwork is your enemy and you must take exercise in order to relax. Severe Virgoan health problems which sometimes arise are appendicitis, typhoid, peritonitis and anaemia. Tall subjects may have back problems.

──MOON IN LIBRA──
♎ (Ruled by Venus) ♀

'Fly me to the Moon
Let me play among the stars
Let me see what Spring is like on Jupiter and Mars
In other words, hold my hand
In other words, darling kiss me.'

Sung by Frank Sinatra

The sign of Libra is masculine, positive, airy and cardinal. The Moon, through its association with the sign of Cancer is feminine, negative, watery and also cardinal. The cardinality is the most important factor here because, even if the Moon is not really at home in such a strong sign as Libra, its cardinality will give you the inner dynamism to put things into action, albeit *slowly*. Being an air sign, your thought processes are logical and, provided you have a fairly active Sun sign, you could achieve a high position in life. You are both ambitious and lazy at the same time but you should be able to motivate yourself enough to get things done. You never lose sight of your objectives, you never give up on a goal. Your mind is fair and balanced and you hate any form of injustice, some of you will take up a cause which champions the underdog. You object strongly to any form of racialism. When others argue, you seek to be the peacemaker but you can argue like a Jesuit when the mood takes you. You're always open to new ideas but will not swallow what others tell you without proof. A surprisingly large number of people who have the Moon in Libra also have Aquarius strongly represented on their charts thereby emphasizing the need to be independent.

You seem to need a touch of glamour in your life and could be drawn to work in some kind of glamorous or luxurious trade. You make sure that both your home and your working environment are comfortable and attractive with a pleasant peaceful atmosphere. You have no patience with ugliness in any form, especially ugly or dirty people. Being fussy about your personal appearance you are also rather inclined to be vain about your own good looks. Indeed, while you are young, your partners may be chosen for their looks rather than their personality.

Whenever the Moon is in a masculine sign, the native is naturally competitive and a high climber but is only really impressed by *his own* measurements of success. With the Moon in Libra, you could have a similar 'what right do they think they have to tell me what to do!' attitude as you would expect from Moon in Aries. Although charming most of the time, you can be extremely sarcastic and hurtful when provoked, showing a grasp of vocabulary worthy of any solar Gemini!

Your nerves can sometimes let you down, therefore you need peace in the home environment. Both sexes of this Moon placement are good homemakers and are attached to their own plots of land and their property. You enjoy do-it-yourself jobs, cooking, mending and gardening, however, a life made up purely of housework would stifle you. Your good taste will ensure that your surroundings are always comfortable and elegant. Some subjects may have artistic talent, especially in the field of music. You could have a nice deepish speaking and singing voice too. You certainly enjoy listening to music and hate discordant noises. All your senses are strong but sight could probably be the strongest; if something doesn't *look* right, you couldn't live with it.

Being an air sign, you need the stimulation of meeting new people and are usually welcoming towards newcomers. Travel is liked, as long as you can do it in comfort, you feel perfectly at home in the world's nicest hotels and watering places. Although you enjoy your own company from time to time, you really cannot live or work alone for long. There is a need to keep in touch with the world and to keep your mind stimulated with new people and up-to-date experiences. You enjoy being part of a group and seem to need the approval of your peers but you wouldn't necessarily wish to lead the group. Given the chance, you prefer to be fairly near the top so that you could delegate the more distasteful chores to others!

You are excellent in a crisis but unable to give sustained help because you quickly become bored with problems. You have no patience with fools although you can hide your irritation under a layer of urbanity. Your mental responses are surprisingly fast and you can be quite calculating when necessary.

Your pet hates are loud discordant noises and, according to my lunar Libra friends, being travel sick! Perhaps this has something to do with your need to control your own environment or maybe it is because you have delicate eyesight and hearing (through the reflected association with Aries). You like the sea and the countryside but are really a city person at heart, in amongst it all, where it's all going on.

Relationships are really where you come into your own; not that you are easy to live with. You can be critical, fussy, demanding and occasionally downright childish. However, you need to love and be loved, you also need friendship with people of both sexes. You can be capable of using, even of manipulating others but you need to be needed, therefore you also allow yourself to be used by those whom you love. As a young person you can be inconsistent in emotional relationships wanting the challenge and excitement of new faces practically each week. You enjoy the opening phase of a romance more than the later stage of commitment, because you don't like to be emotionally fenced in. Later on, your need for the security of a family and the love of children will encourage you to settle down into domesticity. Even then you will always be a flirt! Apart from the need for an attractive partner, you need one you can take anywhere. A classy type who can be relied upon to be the genial host or gracious hostess who will help out with the social side of your career. You need someone with a gentle and witty sense of humour as you hate coarseness or hurtful remarks. I have actually seen Moon in Libra subjects become ill because they were unhappy at work or home. Men with the Moon in Libra have a curious split in their personality which, on the one hand, gives them a somewhat 'macho' image, while at the same time endowing them with an almost feminine gentleness.

Lunar Librans are very clever with intricate machinery, and like the other air signs, they all seem to have a love affair with vehicles and speed. Another facet of this complex placement is that you are careful and gentle when around small children and weak people. There is no evidence to my mind of you being an animal lover, but you couldn't hurt an animal or see one hurt by others. Your gentle manner with those who are weaker than you adds to the attractiveness of your personality. You respect the dignity of others and treat them with tact and charm. Those of you who have a strong Sun sign may hide strong feelings and opinions under this charming exterior, but those who have an unassertive Sun sign may need to develop your own point of view and learn how to make a stand.

Sexually speaking you could turn out to be one of the best lovers in the Zodiac! This, of course, depends upon other factors in your birthchart. However, given a fair crack of the whip, leather underwear, luminous suspenders and an exuberant and co-operative partner, you could live out your fantasies to the full. Your sensual nature cannot be denied, and with a bit of luck you will find fulfilment within marriage. If this is not so, you will still seek fulfilment even if it is at the expense of your marriage. You could actually relate well to a difficult partner who keeps you on your toes. Someone unpredictable enough to give you a few lively arguments and passionate enough to satisfy your strong sexual needs.

Knowing instinctively when your partner is ill or unhappy, you rise to the occasion and do all that you can to make them feel better, you don't really like to see anyone down-hearted. You are good at providing little treats but cannot always be relied on to remember anniversaries etc. this is because your giving is spontaneous rather than organized. Lunar Librans need to give and to receive affection, tenderness and sympathy, also to alternate at being the 'parent' or the 'child' in a relationship. If you have the Sun or ascendant in fire signs, you could be a little too dependent on the approval of others. Some lunar Librans can be easily influenced and swayed by others but most of you have a mature outlook and can make up your own mind about life, most of you try to keep your emotions under the control of your mind.

Attitude to Career
The position of the Moon alone is unlikely to suggest any specific type of career but it can show one's inner motivations. Firstly you will want a job which gives you scope to express your creativity this may be in an artistic or semi-artistic world such as architecture or fashion. You are persuasive enough to make a good salesman but unless there are strong factors elsewhere on the birthchart, you would not have the kind of sustained energy which selling requires. Public relations and marketing would be better.

The world of catering might appeal, certainly glamorous hotels and restaurants are your natural habitat. Being good at calming others and even better in a crisis, you could make a good negotiator. You have a talent for arbitration and your quick mind and sense of humour can be used to defuse potentially dangerous situations therefore you might succeed as a union negotiator or as a particularly urbane politician. Personnel and recruitment are also possible career ideas. You can appear to be lackadaisical while working furiously behind the scenes. I call this the 'duck' syndrome because a duck looks as if it is gliding along the surface of the water while it is actually paddling like fury underneath. You are a good listener, so long as the person who is doing the talking doesn't go on too long.

You enjoy money for what it brings but can have something of a 'convenient' memory when owing money to others, this memory is far less 'convenient' when money is owed to you. You don't need to have power but you do need a largish income to really enjoy life, therefore you will aim for the top anyway. The only thing you really cannot do is rough and dirty work among coarse people.

You get on well with workmates and colleagues. With your logical mind, you would make a good engineer. Driving and even flying come easily to you. Finally, you could earn a few pennies as a spare-time musician.

Parents and Background

There is some evidence from this Moon position that you were born easily. You may have had a father who pushed you educationally and possibly a rather peculiar mother! This does not mean to say that you were unhappy as a child, you seem to have been loved and understood by your parents and even overindulged a little. Your charm, even as a baby, will have got you everywhere. Your mother was probably ambitious, clever or even eccentric, she may have forgotten to feed you or wash you on occasion but she never forgot to love you. The home was a stimulating place full of books, conversation and interesting visitors. This means you grew up without having to develop a suspicious attitude or a strong shell to hide behind. Nevertheless you are happier to be an adult, this could be because your schooldays were not a very happy time for you. It is possible that you found exams troublesome because *they* test what you *know* rather than the power of your personality!

Health

You are generally strong but may develop diabetes, cystitis or skin problems. You need to take exercise and keep your weight down (and not smoke) or you could develop both chest problems and arterial or arthritic problems. Hay fever and farmer's lung are other possibilities.

—————MOON IN SCORPIO—————
♏ **(Ruled by Pluto and Mars)** ♇ ♂

She's got some cruelty,
See it in the dark of the Moon,
Brother take her cruelty, face it
with her beauty and show it.

Pagan Easter
by Seldiy Bate
by kind permission of Temple Music

The sign of Scorpio is feminine, negative, watery and fixed whilst the Moon, through its association with the sign of Cancer, is feminine, negative, watery and cardinal. This would suggest that the Moon is comfortable in Scorpio but it must be remembered that this is the sign of the Moon's 'fall' and therefore, projects some of the most difficult aspects of both the sign and the planet. Scorpio's influence on the Moon adds intensity to the nature, also tenacity, capability and strong resistance to disease. It endows its natives with a strong instinct for survival plus an attraction to the more dangerous aspects of life. If this is your Moon placement, you have a tremendous ability to bounce back from illness, disappointment and even the door of death itself.

There are two quite separate needs within your personality
and, bearing in mind that these needs are lying underneath the
more outward and obvious aspects of your nature (as depicted
by your Sun and Ascendant signs), this can make you very hard
for others to understand. You seem to require challenge and
excitement on one hand plus constancy and security on the
other. Like all fixed signs, Scorpio Moon people want to
maintain the status quo. You prefer to stay in a job with which
you are familiar, occupy the same house for years and remain
with the same partner even when the partnership is no longer
viable. The other side of you cries out for the brink, the edge,
the place where you can test your strength. Some lunar
Scorpions become involved with risky or even illegal business
interests while others involve themselves in risky romances or
strange sexual encounters. You seem to have the feeling that you
are invincible, 'bomb-proof': and you are probably right! A
constructive way of dealing with this might be to build into your
life an interesting and risky hobby or some kind of part-time
attachment to a paramedical or paramilitary organization. You
may find yourself up against difficult situations without actually
going out and looking for trouble. One lunar Scorpio friend of
mine has a daughter who, after twice becoming involved with
the shady side of the law, turned up at her house eight and half
months pregnant!

Emotionally speaking, you are even more peculiar because
you have the ability to go at two speeds at once. When you meet
a new attraction, you are cautious, watchful and apt to sit back
and see what transpires; despite the fact that you are perfectly
able to psychically sum up anyone who is likely to become
important to you within minutes of meeting them. You can be
manipulative towards others but often only for their own benefit.
You are as caring towards your family and friends as any solar
Cancerian. Like all Moon in water people, you can occasionally
be emotionally wearing but you hate others being emotionally
demanding towards you. You are perfectly willing to come to the
aid of someone who is in a state of crisis, but if they continue to
demand help and support after the immediate problem is solved,

you become bored with the whole thing. You have a built-in detector for monitoring out lonely people and those types who seek to lean on you and draw from your inner strength. Moon in Scorpio subjects all have a built-in bullshit detector and therefore are quicker than most at spotting a phony. Sometimes the emotional sufferings of others make you feel helpless and powerless. Your worst fault emotionally is a tendency to become jealous and possessive towards others; however, secure people who have the Moon in Scorpio are able to go through life without most of these unpleasant feelings.

Your home must be peaceful, clean and attractive. Your taste runs towards the antique rather than the modern and you will spend a considerable amount of time and money on furniture and fitments. You probably spend even more time and money on your garden because your love of beauty and strong sensuality draws you towards the beauty and scent of flowers. You enjoy the countryside and outdoor pursuits. The sea is attractive to you and you love to feel both its power and its peace. You are probably a very good swimmer.

You keep a tight grip on your own emotions and tend to bottle up anger and allow your feelings to seep inwards. This can result in angry outburts which may affect your health. On those occasions when you do become ill or suffer from some set-back in life, your first reaction is anger, then if you cannot do something immediate and practical about the problem, you become silent, withdrawn and depressed. An athletic hobby would make a good outlet for your considerable energies, and some of you will turn to the occasional highly-charged sexual encounter. You can usually spot the feelings and motives of others quickly; you are able to find their weak spots and then, depending on circumstances, use this information to help and encourage them or in order to wind them up and throw them off balance. You are able to get at the truth and to face up to it but you tend to conceal your feelings from others so that *they* don't get a chance to make use of you.

Neither solar nor lunar Scorpios like officialdom but you seem to have an uncanny knack of 'working the system' when

you need to. You are persistent in pursuit of a goal and faced
with opposition you will either find a way around it or, as a last
resort will force your way through assertively. You rarely
consider asking others for help, seeing that as an admission of
weakness.

You enjoy family life and make a reliable parent as long as you
can step back a little from your children and let them be
themselves. Many of you seem to have difficult or sickly children
but you cope with these problems better than most. You must be
careful neither to smother your children nor try to mould them
too forcefully, you should make an effort to allow them to
develop their own individual personalities. Some of you may be
fussy about food; this may be due to a weight problem or just
faddiness. Many lunar Scorpios are vegetarians partly through
personal preference and partly due to a love of animals.

You are a hard tenacious worker and you try to finish
everything which you start, disliking being interrupted.
Preferring to work slowly and thoroughly you hate being rushed
or placed under a lot of pressure. If there is a little help from the
rest of the birthchart, you can be surprisingly artistic. Both solar
and lunar Scorpions have a strong sense of structure, an eye for
detail and a well developed sense of touch. This leads to a
natural ability to handle materials in a creative manner. You
could make an excellent sculptor, potter, design engineer or
design dressmaker. Other structured interests such as dancing
and sport appeal to you and being competitive, you would always
strive to be better than the next person.

Your sexual feelings are intense and, if not fully gratified, you
can become extremely irritable; you might even engineer
arguments in order to 'rev-up' the sexual excitement. Your
deepest need is for a stable relationship with a reliable person
who has a high and interesting sexual drive! If you do not find
satisfaction within your marriage, you will look for it on the
outside. You may fancy the occasional perversion! In this aspect
of your life, as in all others, you cannot seem to compromise.
You must not try to reform your partners but should try to learn
to accept them as they are. It would be better if you could pour

your energies and reforming drive into the outside world in order to bring about beneficial changes. The ability to do this would depend upon other political or reforming factors on your birthchart. Your compelling nature makes you a pretty exciting lover but you are also sensitive enough to 'tune in' to the needs of your partner and give as much pleasure as you yourself would like to receive. Depending upon your mood at the time, you can be extremely receptive to the needs of those around you or surprisingly (maybe conveniently) dense. This depends upon your mood and the state of your health at any one time.

There is some evidence of homosexuality and bisexuality being associated with this Moon sign. You may even marry someone who is attracted to their own sex.

You have strong intuitive and even psychic gifts and may be drawn to discover more about these aspects of life. Being mediumistic and clairvoyant, you may take a further interest by studying the occult in all its forms. You seek deeper meanings in everyday events and may consider them to be omens of some kind. Many of you feel that other people block your progress or even cause you to have bad luck instead of accepting that things do go wrong from time to time. You may be superstitious and inwardly fearful when faced with new circumstances and unknown factors in your life. Many of you are drawn to the arts of witchcraft and magic which give you the opportunity of linking into group energies and earth energies. The Kabbala is another potential interest. The healing and caring aspect of psychic work would immediately attract you and, particularly later in life, you could pour your considerable mental, physical and psychic energies into the philosophy of healing and the positive use of psychic powers. You have the potential to change the world, by politics, science or even by means of war but this would depend upon a strange combination of planets in your chart. Could you be the next and last person to use Mr Oppenheimer's little toy?

Attitude to Career

The position of the Moon in a birthchart does not show one's actual career but the inner motivations which may affect one's choice of job. You are a slow, methodical worker preferring to stick to a job that you are accustomed to. You have an exceptionally pleasant voice and manner which makes you a natural for dealing with people, your enjoyment of new and interesting people both at work and in a social setting, gives you the potential to be a good salesman or woman. You can inspire others to get things moving, are competitive and ambitious but may give up on your ambitions for the sake of safety and practicality later on in life. You *should* make a point of striving for success as you could be jealous and resentful of others if you don't. You can learn from others and can, in your turn, encourage them and guide them but you don't have enough patience with *people* to make a good teacher.

Medical matters appeal to you and you are not easily upset by the sight of blood, your patience with things (as opposed to people) would make you a fine surgeon; psychiatry would also come naturally to you. Any work which brings you to the heart of matters will appeal to you and, therefore, you could find yourself involved in the legal, forensic or political field. In business you can make spectacular gains and even more spectacular losses on occasion.

Many lunar Scorpios love the sea and can make their living on it as sailors, fishermen or swimming and diving experts and also, of course, in the navy. A life in the armed services appeals to many of you as it requires the kind of skills and dedication which come so easily to you.

Parents and Background

There is evidence that your birth brought a problem to your parents. Many lunar Scorpios are born into some kind of 'inconvenient' situation and are adopted soon after birth. On the other hand, some of you are born to families who already have a number of children and don't really want any more. There is no doubt that you are on a different wavelength (possibly even a different planet) to that of your parents and you will have been constantly misunderstood as a child. Your experience may have been poor because you were not really the type of child that they were hoping for or that you were compared unfavourably to another child in the family. 'My parents always seemed to have much more time for my brother than they did for me', says Lorna, an attractive and active lady whom I meet regularly at the swimming baths. 'Being male gave him a head start, of course, but then he was also considered to be the "clever one". You know, looking back over our lives now, I think that I have done just as well in the long run even without academic qualifications or the unqualified love of my parents. No, I don't feel bitter; not now.'

You could, at the worst end of the spectrum, have been bullied by your parents, subjected to violence, sexual abuse or just made to feel thoroughly inadequate. You may have been told, or have been given the silent implication that you could never live up to their exalted standards. Negative attitudes die hard in fixed signs and you could, if not careful, go through life never shaking off the hatred and anger of your childhood. You may still feel yourself to be a nuisance to others and wonder why they put up with you. Nevertheless many lunar Scorpios do love their somewhat inadequate parents very much and take a really caring if rather dutiful attitude to them later in their lives.

One peculiarity associated with either the Sun or the Moon in Scorpio is there could be a death in the family at the time of your birth or soon after.

You may have been either very good or very bad at school. Sports and artistic subjects come easily to you but you could have had difficulty coping with the pace and imposed discipline of normal school lessons. Some of you will have worked hard when reaching your teens in order to overcome childhood shortages of one kind or another. Some of you will marry in order to improve your position in life.

Health
Although usually very fit you can be a worrier over your health. Your weak spots are your arteries and veins and you could suffer from high blood-pressure later in life. You may suffer from

headaches and migraine also other forms of allergies such as hay fever. The main problem seems to be in the reproductive organs, many women with this placement have terrible periods and may have to have a hysterectomy in the end just to stop the endless outpouring of blood.

———MOON IN SAGITTARIUS———
♐ (Ruled by Jupiter) ♃

Underneath your dreamlit eyes
Shades of sleep have driven you away
The moon is pale outside
And you are far from home.

from *When Tomorrow Comes*
sung by the Eurythmics

The sign of Sagittarius is masculine, positive, fiery and mutable, whilst the Moon, through its association with the sign of Cancer, is feminine, negative, watery and cardinal. Neither the planet nor the sign have anything in common with one another, therefore each will work against the other in some way. Problems which result from this will be felt in the area of your emotions and in your relationships with others. If this is your Moon sign, you probably didn't receive much physical affection from your parents. Maybe they weren't the kind who went in for touching and cuddling, or you yourself may have pushed them away. There are some children who hate being kissed and smothered by adults, although most children *do* enjoy receiving comfort and affection from their own family. It's possible that your parents had to work hard and didn't have much time to spare for you; all this could lead you, later in life, to separate the feelings of love from those of sex. I have found this to be a greater problem for male lunar Sagittarians than for females. You may shrink back from being touched by others in normal daily life, or you might find it difficult to caress and stroke your partner when making love! If this seems to be all too true, then don't despair, because you, above all the signs of the Zodiac, have the brains and the courage to face up to your problems, seek help and eventually sort yourself out. Those of you who don't have this problem are so cuddlesome that they actually prefer to choose a chubby partner for themselves!

Any physical problems which you may experience are more than made up for by the excellence of your mind. Everything interests you but you accept nothing at face value. You enjoy reading and, on the rare occasions when you watch the TV, you enjoy programmes which have something to say. Some of you are deeply philosophic in your manner of thinking. You may have been brought up in a religious family, rejected their ideas and later on found others which suited you better. There are many solar and lunar Sagittarians in the spiritualist movement and also in the psychic world, all trying to make life that bit more meaningful for others. You are intuitive, exceptionally clairvoyant and probably a good healer as well although you may not yet have discovered that you have these gifts.

You need personal freedom and independence, needing especially to be in charge of your own life rather than being under someone else's thumb. You must be able to come and go as you please, you cannot be cooped up anywhere, indeed, you may even suffer from claustrophobia when travelling in a lift or in the back seat of a two-door car. New faces fascinate you and you need plenty of friends because you become bored if you have to spend every day in the same company. Sagittarius being a mutable sign, you can adapt to most situations and enjoy all kinds of people, you are broad-minded and never racist or bigoted. Like most mutable sign subjects, you do need to get away on your own from time to time in order to think and to recharge your emotional batteries. You have exceptionally clear vision and can see to the heart of a problem when others can only see muddle, you are resourceful enough to solve most problems both for yourself and for others although you do appreciate a helping hand when it is offered. You will help anybody who is in trouble and in a crisis. Being sure of your own abilities at times of trouble, you may push others out of the way so that you can get on with sorting the problems out by yourself. This behaviour is not always appreciated by those whom you are pushing!

Solar Sagittarians are sociable and outgoing but lunar ones are shyer. This depends upon the kind of Sun and Ascendant you have on your birthchart but nevertheless, you will have some of the typically Sagittarian characteristics. You may be a good actor, certainly you have the ability to interest others, fill them with enthusiasm and motivate them. The traditional Sagittarian careers of the church, the law and teaching may not apply directly to you but you often find yourself teaching others in some way or another and your own codes of honour and ethics will be high. You may have the traditional Sagittarian tactlessness as well, but the Moon being sensitive to the feelings of others makes this less likely. You are sensitive to atmospheres, for instance, you are aware as soon as you go into a room if there has been an argument going on in there. You may over-react to people who show hostility towards you. Your temper is explosive and your tongue sharp and articulate, therefore you could make an unpleasant, if not actually dangerous adversary. However, like most fire signs, you don't hold a grudge and prefer to forget bad feelings and look towards the future with optimism.

The Moon is associated with the home and Sagittarius is a dextrous sign, therefore you should be good at do-it-yourself jobs, also cooking. This might at first seem a peculiar thing to say as the vast majority of you will spend as much time away from the home as you can and would *hate* to spend your life decorating or cooking. However, I have noticed that all lunar Sagittarians are absolutely inspired when it comes to cooking for guests and, even if you don't actually do the decorating yourself, your taste and choices in materials and decor would be perfect. If there is some Cancer on your chart, you would definitely go in for home carpentry work. Whatever you do, you will always clear up afterwards; you don't like mess and dirt and cannot stand living in chaotic surroundings. You need peace and calm in the home as you expend a lot of energy in your career and need to refresh yourself in a peaceful loving atmosphere at home in order to rest your delicate nervous system.

You enjoy sports and may be a good swimmer, you are too active to spend your spare time sitting about so any form of sports or dancing would appeal to you, this also brings out your competitive spirit. Although you may be a little on the shy side, you enjoy singing, music or artistic hobbies but probably would prefer to be among a group rather than out on your own as the solar Sagittarian would. Your active nature would make you choose a job where you have the chance to move around and meet people and also where you are up on your feet rather than sitting about. Your pattern of working may alternate between manic activity and apparent laziness. This is because you are not good at keeping to a steady routine but will go at something hammer and tongs while you are inspired and then recoup your energies, probably whilst planning for the next burst of activity.

If you have to leave your home for any reason, you would set about making another attractive place for yourself as soon as possible. Being attractive and rather vain about your appearance, you enjoy buying nice clothes and may tend to spoil yourself while conveniently forgetting that there are bills to be paid. Your appearance and your body are very important to you as activity is so much a part of your nature.

There is, like most of the mutable signs, a strange duality about you. You want something passionately and then go off it once you have got it. You need security at the same time as you need freedom, this can make you appear irresponsible to others but somehow you always find an answer and seem to be able to pull the irons out of the fire when things go wrong. You are no stranger to debts but hate to be in debt. You can soon put other people's problems in perspective for them but you may be hopeless at sorting out your own muddles. A friend of mine who is just about typical of this lunation, is responding to the fact that her husband has left her by giving up her job and spending money on clothes and nice things when it is the last thing she ought to be doing. This is an almost Piscean reaction in refusing to face reality — because reality right now is too much to face! The last split is in your attitude to personal relationships, you need and want to love and be loved but you may find it hard to be faithful because there are so many interesting people out there who will be equally fascinated by your looks and your charisma. You need a really understanding partner. Another oddity is that you *really* prefer friendship to affairs anyway, so you could appear to promise much and not really deliver anything at all! Very strange. You couldn't cope with someone who lays the law down to you, under those circumstances, you would assert your independence.

You can be a bit dual in the world of work too. You are highly ambitious but not necessarily money-minded. You need money to pay the bills and to make life fun but not for power or to impress others. Women of this lunation like to control their own finances. You need to work at something which you enjoy and which keeps you in touch with people. You can appear lazy to others because you have a habit of preparing your work at home either before or after your normal working hours, thus hiding the actual amount of effort which you put into your work. Metaphorically speaking, this gives you the appearance of a duck which as we all know, glides effortlessly over the surface of the water, but is actually paddling away like mad under the surface! However much you love your job, you also need to relax and socialize and are not as a rule a workaholic. You are, in all but shape, a well rounded person. Women of this particular sign can become wrapped up in causes and will be found saving the whale and banning the bomb. This could cause problems on the domestic front as there will sometimes be too little time left for the family. Being slightly bossy, a woman with the Moon in Sagittarius would need a very understanding husband, but she is wise enough to find the right one for herself, and if she doesn't do so the first time, she will have another go. Both sexes love children, but spending your days looking after small children wouldn't stimulate you enough mentally. Many of you are brilliant with older children and may involve yourself with the scout or guide movement or something similar. Lunar Sagittarians make excellent teachers.

Your sense of adventure means that you could take up anything from hang-gliding to mountain climbing, you enjoy every experience that comes along. This is the sign of the traveller, and the Moon being associated with travel, especially travel over water means that you take every opportunity to travel anywhere at the drop of a hat. You are fascinated by desert and mountainous areas where you can stand tall and see for miles.

Anyone choosing to live with you would find you a happy and optimistic partner as long as you have the freedom to do your own thing. You cannot stand people who try to dominate you or control your actions, neither could you live with a partner who whines and nags. The worst type for you to have to cope with, either at work or in your personal life, is someone who is critical of you whilst considering him or herself to be perfect. Your intense need for freedom and independence means that you spend time away from the home possibly travelling around in connection with your work. You would be happy to be married to someone rather like yourself as you wouldn't seek to tie *them* down either. If you have an ambitious partner, you help them to get ahead in their career. If you are allowed freedom and trust, you will probably choose to remain faithful but if restricted, you will show your resentment by straying from the straight and narrow. Your unpredictability can make you hard to live with.

You don't give up on a relationship at the first hurdle, you try to do all that you can to make it work. You will adapt your own nature and your own needs to that of the partner as far as you can in order to make the relationship work. There is a possibility that you could find yourself stuck with a partner who suffers from some kind of mental illness. I discovered while researching this book that lunar Sagittarians have many connections with mental illness, either through senile parents, a schizophrenic child or a depressive spouse. There are times when you are so busy trying to adapt to *their* unrealistic behaviour that you begin to wonder just *who* is the dotty one!

You may choose a partner who is out of the traditional mould, for instance someone older or younger than yourself or of a different racial or religious background. You may strongly attract people of a type which you really cannot stand or you may find yourself attracted to someone who pleases you in one way and repels you in another. It is hard to find someone who is right for you in every way, that is mentally, physically and spiritually.

As a parent you are proud of your offspring and will do all you can to help them get on in life. You respect their need for space and a separate identity and also their need for dignity. There is a possibility that you could live apart from them for some part of their childhood, either due to work which takes you away from home or as a result of a divorce.

Many of you will have parents who were born in a different country from the one in which you live. This is actually more often the case when the Ascendant is in Sagittarius but also applies to the Moon quite often. There may be Irish connections or Jewish ones — emigration or just living away from home are all possible. This may, to some extent explain some of the splits in your personality if, for example, you were educated in a different manner from those around you, brought up in a religion which is anachronistic in your present country or even speaking a different language when with your parents. I asked my friend Susan about her childhood which was spent in a variety of different countries and she told me that it was hard always to be the child who spoke the wrong language or who had the wrong accent.

Attitude to Career

The position of the Moon on a birthchart does not show which career you choose but it can show your inner motivation. In the case of Sagittarius, your greatest need is for freedom of action and the ability to communicate with others, possibly on a rather large scale. You are a natural teacher and if you don't work directly in education you would still enjoy helping and guiding others and passing on the knowledge which you have accumulated over the years. Most of you are surprisingly modest about your work and your achievements and tend not to promote yourselves very well, therefore, it is only when one gets to know you better that we learn just how knowledgeable you actually are.

You would enjoy a job in broadcasting or publishing or even as an entertainer. Many of you are good actors and singers but, unless you have a fair dose of Leo or Aries on your chart, you may be too shy to push yourself forward in this way. You are adaptable enough to get on with anyone and to work anywhere but you have high standards and a strong sense of your surroundings, therefore you couldn't do anything which was really down-market, under-handed or which involved working in dirty messy surroundings. You are stubborn enough to finish what you start but you may start too many projects and then become worn out from trying to do them all at once.

The travel trade would attract you as you love to expand your horizons in a practical sense as well as in a mental one. Some of you can work on dicey projects which involve intuition and the ability to guess right. This could be something like the futures market on the stock exchange or any other business connected with gambling. Being over-optimistic at times, this could occasionally run you into trouble. Whatever you do, and even if your own confidence deserts you at the wrong moment in your career, your pixilated sense of humour will always see you through. Lunar Sagittarians are excellent salespeople as long as they believe in the product they are handling.

Parents and Background

Your relationship with your parents was good but distant in some way, possibly because they were busy or because they didn't encourage closeness. 'I just couldn't keep my parents' attention', says Joe, a salesman for an electronics company, 'my father led a busy life which took him travelling, rather like I do I suppose. My mother was always preoccupied with her church cronies.' Joe's story is typical even down to the fact that the Lunar Sagittarian's experience of parenthood could turn out to be similar to his own parents' experiences.

Your parents may have come from a different country with a different culture from the one which you are now living in; possibly just a different part of the country and with a different outlook on life or a different religion.

You did well at school, if not in academic studies, then in something else such as art, dancing, music or sports. The greatest and most important part of your education will come later in life. Your pleasant appearance and friendly, open attitude make you popular at school.

Health
You could suffer from some of the Sagittarian ailments of leg and hip problems, varicose veins, phlebitis, rheumatism and blood disorders. Women of this lunation may have period problems followed by a hysterectomy.

MOON IN CAPRICORN
♑ (Ruled by Saturn) ♄

The first time ever I saw your face,
The Sun rose in your eyes,
The Moon and Stars were the gifts you gave.
Sung by Roberta Flack

The sign of Capricorn is feminine, negative, earthy and cardinal while the Moon, through its association with the sign of Cancer, is feminine, negative, watery and cardinal. Therefore the planet and the sign are quite compatible, however, the Moon is said to be in its detriment in Capricorn because the sign is opposite the sign of Cancer, the Moon's natural home. This means that the emotional side of your life could be a little suppressed.

Whatever you appear to be on the outside, inwardly you are sensitive, vulnerable and shy, especially where your personal feelings are concerned. The earthiness of Capricorn makes you practical and sensible, therefore if you find that an idea works for you you will use it, otherwise you will reject it. Even if you have an extroverted sign on your Ascendant, you will be shy when you are young but later in life you will cover this up with a layer of polish. Nevertheless, inwardly you are rather deep and unfathomable. You resist serious illness and have, in addition to bodily strength, considerable strength of character, these strengths enable you to survive almost anything plus giving you the kind of tenacity and determination which allows you to finish whatever you start. You rarely take time off from work, even when you *are* ill.

Many of you go into business for yourselves thereby giving yourself the opportunity to create something of your own which will stand the test of time. You learn self-discipline early in life and feel inwardly that life is a serious business. You have the feeling that you should work to build up your finances while you are young so that you can relax and enjoy the result later on. As you will probably live to a ripe old age, you are right to think like this. Another reason for self-employment is the fact that you enjoy being in a position of responsibility and you carry authority well without throwing your weight around.

You need security, your idea of hell would be to be dependent upon others because you hate to be a burden or to suffer the embarrassment of having to ask for help. You are resourceful and hard working but could be a little scheming and just a dash dishonest when chasing a goal (remember, tricky Dicky Nixon had the Moon in Capricorn). Your serious nature is relieved by a delightfully dry and witty sense of humour. You don't make hurtful jokes about others but just see the world in an off-beat way which those who share your sense of humour, will find very funny. You enjoy the company of humorous people too.

You learn well and may be academic, but practical subjects really suit you best. You can think and plan on a large scale and in a structured manner, rules and methods come easily to you, whether they be mathematical, engineering, or the pattern made by a series of dance steps. You prefer not to gamble on life but to plan your course, moving forward and then consolidating your position for a while.

Although your values are material rather than spiritual, the most important aspect of your life is probably your relationship with your family. You are very caring and you take your responsibilities towards them very seriously. You are dependable and faithful in marriage and will try to make almost any kind of situation work. Your work may occasionally come between you and your family but if they are ill, they get all of your attention immediately. Oddly enough you really enjoy hearing all the local gossip, not just family gossip either. You can really get your teeth into a nice juicy piece of scandal but you yourself would hate to be in the middle of any scandal.

Lunar Capricorns can find it difficult to form relationships due to shyness, but the intensity of this problem would depend on the type of Ascendant and Sun sign which you have; nevertheless, you are easily hurt and embarrassed. Being cautious, you take care to find yourself the right type of partner. As a parent you are gentle and caring, and although you would be unlikely to join in rough games with your children, you will do your best to teach them about the world we live in and to open their eyes to the possibilities which life has to offer. You may be a little old-fashioned in your aproach when they reach their teens but you will try to see things from their point of view. At least you would always be aware of your children's need to be treated with dignity.

You exert considerable control over your own inner nature, sometimes too much so, in order to prevent your feelings from getting the better of you. Your somewhat formal manner protects your vulnerability, it would be impossible to imagine you getting drunk and making an ass of yourself. Like the other earth signs, it takes a lot to make you lose your temper, but when you do so, it is over-poweringly destructive. Making friends is a slow process with you and the few friends whom you do have, you keep for years. You adapt better to *new places* than to new people and can fit in almost anywhere. Your pet hate is to be embarrassed and humiliated, a spell in a hospital which is staffed by insensitive people would be dreadful for you. Another pet hate is coarseness or vulgarity of any kind. You are kindly and helpful towards other people, especially in a work situation and you would make a good financial adviser or a good teacher on a small group basis. You need a strong and independent partner who can, to some extent, protect you. Your hidden sensitivity can give you nervous ailments such as skin problems, asthma, rheumatism or a tendency to have colds. You listen to any advice which is offered to you but in the end you prefer to make up your own mind.

You have a love of beauty and grace in all things and a hatred of any kind of ugliness, from an ugly appearance to ugly behaviour. Being reserved, you don't readily reach out to touch people but you love to be held and touched by your partner and your children. Earth signs are sensuous and this could show up in your case as a love of flowers, music or the seasons of the year. If you are insulted or pushed aside in a queue you would, as one lunar Capricorn friend told me, 'fume inwardly' but you are too polite to say much.

Where sex is concerned you improve with age, and also with the overcoming of your shyness and inhibitions. You are fastidious and very particular both in your choice of partner and in your behaviour. One night stands are *definitely* not for you! The feeling of closeness while making love is as important to you as the act itself. You may choose to marry someone who is older than yourself but whoever you choose, whatever their age or appearance, you will feel protective and caring to them. You even like to work together so that you can share the same problems.

Most lunar Capricornians are great holiday-makers, you need to get away from work from time to time and you really enjoy a break. You are not too experimental with foods as you are a sparing eater but you enjoy good surroundings with well cooked and presented foods. Comfort is a necessity for you when travelling, you are not likely to be found on a camping site.

Parents and Background

There is something strange here. You begin by being very close to your mother and then losing your idealized picture of her. There may even be tragic circumstances involving death of a family member or a spell in a home due to illness or divorce in the family. As you grow up you may realize that your mother is a loving woman who did her best under the circumstances. Peter explained the situation to me 'My parents were very caring towards me but there was just too much for them to cope with. My father never got over being shot up in the war and mother had to work hard during those years. The love was there but they were elderly and up against it. I felt it would be wrong to make too much noise or to bring other noisier youngsters into the house. I doubt whether they would have stopped me but I would have felt bad about it, that's all.'

There could have been some conflict and aggression between you and your father which accounts for your slight air of watchfulness when around new people. This Moon position suggests difficulties during childhood through poverty, too many other children in the family or a loss of some kind. Oddly enough this may jump back one generation and be, not your experience of childhood, but your *mother's* experience. Your parents loved you and were kind-hearted but they could have been slightly insensitive and critical of your school work. A conflict could have arisen if they wanted you to work in the same line as themselves and were disappointed when you chose not to. They, possibly due to their upbringing, taught you to be careful with money and highly realistic in your dreams, you would have learned to value (possibly over-value) material security and possessions.

Being a quiet and obedient child you did well at school and gave the teachers no problems, but you would have found sports difficult, possibly due to poor health and short-sightedness. Many of you go on to further education, especially of a practical nature.

Attitude to Career
The position of the Moon on a birthchart does not necessarily indicate your choice of career but it can show your inner motivations. Lunar Capricorns prefer to do something useful, this could be anything from structural engineering to making medical supplies. You could be drawn to accountancy, the law, also politics, especially if there are other political indications, such as the sign of Cancer or Libra somewhere on your

birthchart. Being interested in business, the world of insurance might appeal to you, or some kind of work in a government department. You prefer being in a position of management.

Travel and transport or a chain of shops are possibilities too. Being slow, thorough and efficient in all that you do, you become annoyed by petty inefficiencies in others; for instance buses being late or paperwork which has not been properly done. I have noticed that most people with the Sun, Moon or Ascendant in an earth sign are early risers. You are highly ambitious and will climb slowly towards the top of your career.

Health
Your weak spots are supposed to be the bones, especially the knees, therefore you could have rheumatism later in life. Hearing problems are a possibility, especially tinnitus. You may have skin problems, even alopecia and could be short-sighted. Generally speaking you should live a long and healthy, if rather hard-working life.

MOON IN AQUARIUS
♒ (Ruled by Uranus and Saturn) ⛢ ♄

When the moon is in the seventh house
And Jupiter aligns with Mars,
Then peace will be around us
And love is in the stars.
    This is the dawning of the age of Aquarius.

from the musical *Hair*.

The sign of Aquarius is masculine, positive, airy and fixed, while the Moon, through its association with the sign of Cancer is feminine, negative, watery and cardinal. The power of the Moon is rather muted in this sign, the greatest effect being to reduce the *feeling* element from the emotions. Inwardly you are detached, independent and rather cool. Although controlled and possibly a little bottled up at times you like others around you to show that *they* need and want you. When meeting people for the first time socially, you are pleasant and affable if a little shy; meanwhile you are weighing them up in a slightly watchful manner. You have a strong inner sense of self which would lead you to take a calculated risk in a career or even in a relationship. Although sensible, you are not over-cautious, therefore you would accept most of life's challenges whether they put your finances at risk or your feelings. This ability to inwardly weigh and measure could be confusing to those who fall in love with you because, although you can discuss feelings in an articulate manner, one wonders just how much you are actually able to feel yourself!

Your inner nature is off-beat, you could find yourself travelling in a different direction to everyone else. Like your solar Aquarian cousins, you are educationally minded and will choose a career where you can stretch your mind and also broaden the minds of others. You are kind, helpful and humanitarian but this may be directed more towards the world in general than to those who are closest to you. Although helpful in practical ways, there could be an element of embarrassment and helplessness when faced by the sight of other people's emotional pain. You are afraid that if you allow weak people to latch themselves on to you that they will drain your energies or, worse still, bore the daylights out of you! Your general outlook is balanced optimistic and cheerful, to all except the most neurotic you would be a good friend.

Your mind is excellent and it doesn't matter whether you are educated and academic or shrewd and streetwise, either way your thinking processes are fast and your intuition is strong. You possess a dry and intelligent sense of humour. Your ideas are often excellent and you have the ability to put them into practice.

Being strongly independent, you prefer to cope alone with your own problems, however harrowing they may be. One Moon in Aquarius friend of mind wouldn't allow anyone to go with him when he went into hospital for a major heart operation. You could reject outside help in case accepting it makes you appear weak and incapable, you may even view help as a form of interference. You're not at all keen on people who try to own you or to manipulate you although you can be adept at manipulating others. Another pet dislike is of being falsely accused — you are willing to admit to your own errors but will not carry the can for others. Your attitudes can sometimes cause others to stay at a distance to you, which can consequently cause misunderstandings both at work and at home.

Your friendliness is universal and you would not reject anyone due to colour, age, race or religion. Many lunar Aquarians belong to clubs and societies of one kind or another, you enjoy committing yourself to group activities. Most of your hobbies involve people and ideas which are sociable and charitable such as Masonry, or something directly helpful, such as youth work. There is one hobby which many of you enjoy entirely alone, although the results of this involve other people, and that is cooking. I have met some truly inspired solar and lunar Aquarian amateur chefs.

You can take any amount of chaos going on around you at work but you need peace in your home, where you can be in control of your own environment (creating a little bit of chaos for others maybe). You enjoy visitors but don't appreciate people who dump themselves upon you. Many of you are clever handymen (and women), enjoying the challenge of working on your home and garden and often finding imaginative and original ways of solving practical do it yourself problems.

Your memory is also rather original and may be strangely selective, easily recalling things you find interesting but 'tuning out' irrelevant details. However, you don't duck really important issues as you have high standards of honesty and integrity. You don't as a rule go in for petty jealousies, neither do you make mountains out of molehills. If your pride is hurt, you can be quite spiteful and very sarcastic. You really do need a creative or useful outlet or you can become bored, gossipy or aloof.

Some of you are lazy and too easygoing, especially if there are planets in the sign of Libra on your birthchart; yet others can be truly very eccentric, especially if there are other planets in the sign of Aquarius. For the most part, criticism brushes off you, you have a strong ego and feel that everyone is entitled to their own opinion, even their opinion of you. You are not likely to change your ways in the face of criticism anyway.

In close personal relationships you are kind, pleasant, thoughtful and passionate; you could even be rather romantic. Aquarius being a fixed sign suggests that you don't easily walk away from situations. You may stay in the same house, the same job or the same relationship long after the time when you should move on. However, if the day comes when you *do* move on, you seem to be able to do so in a decisive manner, looking mentally forward rather than backward. If necessary, you can wait years for the right person to come along, if this paragon does not appear, you spend years of your life alone. If you become bored with your permanent partner, you may look outside the relationship for change and excitement. If you fall in love with someone while you are still married, and especially if you have children, then you will be terribly torn between the need to be loyal and the need to be with the one you want. However, your famous Aquarian detachment may come to your aid here and allow you to work out logically what would be for the best. There is no doubt that you need an interesting and stimulating partner, another very important ingredient would be shared interests and mutual respect. Without shared interests, you would gravitate towards interests of your own and this would begin the process of allowing the marriage to drift into failure and loss. There is just a suspicion that lunar Aquarian males might find a very successful career-girl type of wife too much of a good thing, there could be just a tinge of jealousy creeping in here. You can be strangely blind to both the needs and feelings of those you love. You may never really get to know them on a deep level.

Women of this lunation must have some kind of interesting work outside the home. Neither sex seems keen to have a large family but the relationship between lunar Aquarian parents and their children is usually very good. There is a natural sensitivity to the needs of children and young people and you would offer help without making undue demands upon your children or smothering them. It is just possible that you could expect too much of a very timid child but for the most part you make a successful parent. You are always ready to stump up cash for education or hobbies but you might be a little absent-minded about some of the practical details, such as making sure that they have a clean shirt for school.

Both sexes with this Moon sign are attractive rather than

beautiful, in fact your features are more likely to be rugged and bony than soft and sweet. None of this matters much because your friendliness, charm, sex-appeal and humour are far more effective with the opposite sex than any amount of sterile beauty would be. Being rather shy, you might have a little difficulty in breaking the ice but your interest in people soon helps you to overcome this. Anyway, you always have the option of meeting people through mutual interests such as your work or social activities rather than, for instance, at a disco. People with fixed Moon signs can cope with a lot, it would take a great deal for you to break up a relationship, but when you do, there isn't a backward glance. In relationships, as in all things, you need freedom and independence and may demonstrate this by being deliberately forgetful, erratic and hard to pin down with regard to mutual arrangements. You seek an intelligent and independent partner and often are happiest with one who is much younger than yourself, so that to some extent you can advise or mould them. Be careful that when your good advice is taken and your pupil begins to blossom that *you* don't then become resentful. If your partner started laying the law down to you and restricting your movements, your first impulse would be to get out of the relationship.

Sex for you is a by-product of love, you *can* indulge in sex for its own sake but are much happier when love is the main motivating force. This may surprise many readers but this lunation produces amazingly sexy people! Your special combination of action, imagination and stamina seems to bring something special to the act of love. Friends who are married to lunar Aquarians have told me . . . . well, let's draw a veil over that! It's strange how the supposedly non-tactile air sign people seem to become so good at touching and cuddling when there's the chance of a bit of sexual activity.

Your temper can be a problem when you are young but later you learn to sit back and control it, however if hurt, you retain the ability to wound verbally. There may be a lack of adaptability in your attitude to others, you will only go so far in order to fit in with their wishes, you are inclined to consider that other people ought to take or leave you just as you are. Your partners are chosen to some extent because they have the right appearance. Fatness turns you right off, as does dirt and mess. A lively person who has many outside interests would attract you; if they have a sense of humour and also look nice, better still. Lunar Aquarians of both sexes prefer an equal partnership and will do all they can to promote the interests and job of the other, even trying to help the partner to enjoy his or her hobbies. There is evidence that you wouldn't be so happy if the hobby was a particularly noisy one because you hate loud discordant noises.

Needing a pleasant home and a nice garden, you have no special preference for the town or the country. I think you would make the best of it wherever you were, as long as you are not isolated from people or fenced into a very small space.

Attitude to Career

The position of the Moon on a birthchart rarely determines one's actual career but can show one's inner motivations. You take work seriously and don't like chopping and changing jobs preferring to find a career which you can settle into. You are interested in ideas and willing to learn, therefore you do well at school and continue to learn later on. Certainly your parents encouraged you to progress, but like all lunar masculine signs you are inwardly quite goal-orientated. You enjoy work which is useful to the community and you also like making things which are needed. You can pursue a goal persistently, therefore, you can *close* a deal if someone else will open the door for you.

Working with children might appeal to you, either directly in education or in something tough such as the probation service, because you have patience even for the awkward ones. You take well to challenges and can ride out most problems without falling apart, therefore the armed services or police may appeal. Your incisive mind may lead you into the legal sphere, medicine, psychiatry or even astrology. Being impatient with fools, you could find delegating difficult. You usually learn from your *own* mistakes and are fairly forgiving towards others for theirs, as long as the mistakes do not occur too frequently or are not too obviously stupid. You solve problems in an original way, but must learn to keep lists and use your memory rather than your forgettery.

You seem to be happiest when working in large enterprises; you may wind up in the civil service, a large commercial firm, the teaching profession or government. You have, in common with the other fixed signs of Scorpio, Leo and Taurus, the determination to finish what you start. You don't like being pressurized by others, preferring to work things out in your own way and to do things slowly and thoroughly. Some of you enjoy being attached to some kind of glamorous or powerful enterprise where your own dynamism can come to the fore. There is a reverse side to this coin in that you can run a *small* enterprise of your own as long as you have total control. Although ambitious while young, you are prepared to settle for something comfortable later in life.

You are clever with electronics. computers, radar and other modernistic ideas and may even dream of being a spaceman. You are capable and inventive and will give the whole of your attention to the task in hand, therefore you can create some highly original and very workable methods of production.

Most solar and lunar Aquarians have a need to do something worthwhile, to put something back into life. One lunar Aquarian friend of mine raises money for handicapped children, he does this very quietly despite being one of the most prominent members of this country's civil service, another is in the scouting movement. There is an inner desire to bring a sense of love to all people.

One occasionally runs across the type of Moon in Aquarius subject who is languid and arty, unambitious and lacking in self-discipline. There are a few others who may be theorizers, never quite able to put their theories into action. and too eccentric to fulfil any ordinary kind of role. Most of you, however, enjoy a challenge and will get a kick of making something succeed. Some of you are drawn to the arts or the world of drama and, if there are other encouraging factors on your birthchart, writing may come naturally to you.

Parents and Background

On the face of it you had a good childhood, certainly your practical needs were attended to. If you came from a background where there was little money to spare, your parents would have made sure that you had enough to eat and were dressed and equipped in a clean and decent manner.

Your mother may have been a busy career woman or may have poured her energies into some personal interest. One lunar Aquarian friend of mine had parents who were actively involved in the Salvation Army. Some of you will have had the kind of mother who did very little outside the home the results of which had the reverse effect of making you feel that families are definitely better off when the mother *has* outside interests. Another Moon in Aquarius peculiarity is that you may have had religion rammed down your throat in childhood which put you completely off the idea of formal religion later in life.

It is possible that you loved your father but inwardly considered him to be weak. He may have had poor health, oddly enough, many Moon in Aquarius subjects seem to have fathers who suffered from stomach ulcers. Mother would have been the more organized and capable parent, especially as far as money is concerned. You probably come from an average family of two or three children and would have been the older and/or more capable one of the group or of a different sex to the other children. You were taught not to make scenes or allow your emotions to become a nuisance to others. It is possible that you were never really able to feel very close to your parents, it is even possible that this is a circumstance of your own making. People who have the Moon in air signs do tend to be rather emotionally self-contained and you may just have been born that way.

Your parents took a reasonable view of your educational needs, they encouraged you to learn but didn't push you unduly. They may not have been so accommodating in respect of any hobbies you wished to pursue, which may have been due to shortage of money or conflict with their moral or religious views, for instance if the activity involved participation on the sabbath.

Health

You are basically very strong. Blood-pressure could be a problem especially for women during pregnancy. Allergies such as hay fever, asthma, eczema, psoriasis and hives can occur, also migraine, menstrual problems in women, rheumatism and diabetes are possibilities. The weakest part of the body is the lower legs and ankles, which could involve problems with veins, phlebitis and thrombosis, also leg ulcers later in life.

———MOON IN PISCES———
♓ (Ruled by Neptune and Jupiter) ♆ ♃

I am the star that rises from the sea-
  The twilight sea.
I bring men dreams that rule their destiny.
I bring the dream-tides to the souls of men

from *The Worship of Isis*.

The sign of Pisces is feminine, negative, watery and mutable
while the Moon, through its association with the sign of Cancer,
is feminine, negative, watery and cardinal. This would make the
Moon appear comfortable in Pisces but to some extent, the
mutability of Pisces weakens the active, cardinal nature of the
Moon. The Moon is associated with one's innermost feelings
and underlying emotions and the sign of Pisces, being devoted
to emotion, suggests that even if the subject's outer manner is
confident and capable, there will be a terribly soft heart hiding
deep inside.

If this is your Moon position, you will spend some part of your
life searching for answers to deep and indefinable questions.
You will contemplate the meaning of life and the possibility of
an after-life and could even be drawn to a religious or

quasi-religious way of living. Your energies to some extent will always be directed towards trying to improve the quality of life for others and to introducing people around you to a gentle and healthy understanding of their minds, bodies and spirits. Life may disappoint you as it may never match up to your idealistic dreams and indefinable yearnings. Yet, somehow, life must go on and you will probably wish to live it to the very full, therefore a particularly Piscean form of practicality often seems to combine with your desire for perfection, and the requirements of the hereafter.

You can be surprisingly ambitious. This ambition may take the normal route of upward mobility in the working and the suburban community or it may take a totally private form. You could push yourself to improve your performance in a creative capacity. Either way, you have the long-term patience to achieve your goals. You also have the gift of creative visualization. The only real drawback to you reaching your goals is your lack of confidence and your fear of making other people angry with you for competing with them. A sarcastic remark can wound deeply and is never forgotten.

On a more mundane level, you are extremely sensitive to the needs of others. Nobody is kinder, more thoughtful and considerate; you seem to feel other people's wants even before you are aware of your own and you can soak up other people's moods and desires psychically. There is a definite need for you to assess your own feelings from time to time to make sure that they *are* yours and not those of the people around you. You should also note that it doesn't always do to rush in and smooth the path of others, it might do them more good if you were to allow them to solve their own problems from time to time. Not everybody will want your intervention — although, human nature being what it is, most people will take advantage of free help when given the chance. If you become a permanent listening ear for neurotic friends and relatives, you will become worn out, depressed and even physically ill. There are people who *don't* want their problems solved because this would stop them from attracting the attention and sympathy of others. You must make a special effort to avoid the truly mad, bad and sad for your own mental health's sake, even if it means abandoning some of those who call themselves friends.

Like all those who have the Sun or Moon in mutable signs, you have an inner streak of resilience and can usually find a way round your own problems. If absolutely pressed, you can stand up for yourself very well and dish out a surprisingly devastating dose of criticism. People tend to forget that just because you are so ready to sympathize and to understand their needs, that you also see their faults and inner motivations. If you are wounded you withdraw into your shell, but if the problem is too great, you can be very spiteful and destructive. Destructive behaviour does not come naturally, you prefer to take the role of counsellor, teacher and guide.

Like Moon in Cancer subjects, you can be a really monumental worrier, beginning with worries on behalf of your family and friends, your health, money, the state of the nation and the imminence of nuclear war. You could be mean in small ways, smoothing out paper bags for reuse or moaning about small expenses. In a way, you can be penny-wise and pound-foolish because you are never mean about large issues. You are always broke but usually manage to do the things you want. You will spend money on musical and recording equipment, books, dining out and trips. Most astrologers will tell you that you like to be on or near the sea, but where travelling is concerned, you don't actually mind where you go as long as you don't get too worn out in the process.

You will not tolerate injustice in any form and, if you see a child, an animal or a person of a different race or religion being badly treated you truly go bananas. You value loyalty above all things and hate to let anyone down. Friendship is terribly important to you, especially as some of you have difficult or demanding family members thus making friendship outside the family essential.

All solar and lunar Pisceans are creative, many are artistic and you need to express this creativity somewhere in your daily life. You work at your own rather strange pace, often like a dervish for a month at a time and then switching off for a week in order to recharge your batteries. Most of you enjoy some kind of sport; swimming is probably high on your list, also dancing, tennis or just walking the dog. Every lunar Piscean that I have come across is a naturally good dancer, especially ballroom dancing. Some of you can be serious athletes or dancers, but this will require strongly competitive elements elsewhere on the chart. Those of you who have a very ordinary job will probably have a creative interest on the side. Some of you will privately work in the psychic or even the magical field, often without the people at your place of work having any idea of this other interest. You see omens in everyday events and may be superstitious and fearful of unexplainable dark forces which sometimes seem to gather around you. Even the most practical among you can feel patterns in events which seem to occur.

You are not as changeable in your moods as most astrology books would suppose, oddly enough people who have the Moon in fixed signs are by far the moodiest. However, when you do become emotional or upset, the feelings go deep. You are able to hold a grudge for ever but you are equally apt to remember those who stand by you in times of trouble. If someone hurts you gratuitously even in a minor way, you will never quite be able to trust or really like them again. Women who have the Moon in water signs can often attribute some of their mood swings to pre-menstrual tension — I'm not quite sure what *men* can blame their moods upon. In some ways your apparent moodiness stems from your inability to get the whole of your life together at any one time. It seems that if your work is going well, your love life will be in a state of collapse and vice versa. Even if *everything* is going well, you can be discontented due to boredom!

Your home is your haven, it is also a haven for a good many other people. Many of you work wholly or partially from home which often involves people coming in and out. The place is also permanently full of friends and neighbourhood children. Lunar and solar Pisceans are supposed to be loners, but I have yet to see any evidence of that, your phone and your doorbell are always ringing. Many of you literally don't bother to shut your door as there are so many people pounding in and out. Your home is attractive and comfortable but not over-decorated or cleaned to the point of sterility. You love warm colours, interesting textures, pictures and music, you fill your home with these plus, of course, books, books, books. You read almost anything but probably novels, books about the occult, history, psychology, health and magic will be lying about somewhere on your shelves.

You can be so adept at hiding your inner nature that your kind heart might be buried under a shield of efficiency, toughness or even sarcasm, this is mainly a self-protective shield. You are slow to reveal your own inner feelings and it takes some time for you to get to know and trust someone. Some lunar Pisceans even go through many years of marriage without their partner ever really being let into their innermost hearts. You can be a little manipulative at times, either to prevent yourself from hurt or in order to benefit those around you. When you are entirely comfortable with someone you can be surprisingly bossy in a rather mother-hen way but you do it for their own good.

Both solar and lunar Pisceans have an all or nothing relationship with vehicles, either being fabulous drivers or hating the whole business of learning to drive and not bothering with it. Some actually do learn and then avoid driving whenever possible. Very strange.

In marriage you are so supportive that you can spend more energy on your partner's behalf than on your own and you really have to beware of becoming a martyr or a doormat. You tend to moan a bit about your partner, especially when you are feeling tired or depressed but this is almost an expression of affection and often doesn't mean much. You certainly need love and approval and although you *can* live alone, you far prefer to have someone to love and be loved by. Not receiving the love and understanding which you need in childhood, you actively chase after it in adulthood. Some of you are so shy and repressed that you *never* get the love you want and then you may retreat into a life of daydreams and illusions which would make a Walter Mitty appear down to earth. Your powerful imagination is both your most valuable asset and the point of your greatest weakness. If you can channel this into creative pursuits, spiritual development or work in the counselling field, you could overcome most of this.

You make an excellent parent because you understand the needs of children and are happy to spend time playing with them. I'm not sure about this but I think it's probable that you don't relate to babies as much as slightly older children who can talk and play. Certainly you find no difficulty in playing 'let's pretend', you are probably way ahead of them on that one anyway. Your children are encouraged to respect adults but not to be afraid of them, you respect the dignity of children. You could be so busy teaching them about the universe, the world around them and giving them all the love that they need that you overlook their need for clean shirts and breakfast cereal. Don't worry, they will survive and will love you all the more for it.

Your greatest fault is of over-sensitivity to criticism. Nobody likes to be criticized but you really do seem to suffer. Your self-esteem is low enough to begin with, you don't need to have someone else giving it a further battering.

Although you are friendly and non-hostile in your approach to new people, if you really fancy someone, your first reaction may be to run in the opposite direction. You fear rejection, ridicule and loss. You are afraid to become close to someone, in case you learn to rely on them and then lose them again for some reason or other. Love relationships make you nervous because you are aware of your great need for emotional sustenance and of your vulnerability. Adolescent relating can be very painful; later on you learn some protective techniques but these may be ultimately manipulative in that you may not allow yourself to take a chance on expressing your genuine feelings, this again is due to your fear of rejection. Do try, if you can, to be *yourself* in a love relationship and not the pseudo person whom you think your lover wants you to be. In most cases, it is better for you to connect with someone whom you know on a friendly basis rather than to jump deeply into a new relationship. Being incredibly romantic, you appreciate little presents, birthday cards, candle-lit dinners and shared memories. You have a stock of romantic melodies and catch-phrases which you link to your lover.

An important ingredient in the lunar Piscean's nature is curiosity of all kinds. Sexual and emotional curiosity strike early. I can't really find any way of putting this delicately but the fact is that you love making love. The act of sex is a great outlet for you because it combines all your favourite feelings and sensations. Your senses are terrifically strong, especially your psychic sense; love-making gives expression to every one of them, including your powerful imagination. It may be a cold-blooded thought, but your nerves are delicate and often over-stretched, and therefore sex gives you a tremendous release of tension. A pal of mine tells me that he is 'horribly romantic' and couldn't enjoy sex without love. I think that goes for all the other lunar Pisceans too, there must be affection and fondness, if not outright adoration, for you to be able to really relax and enjoy yourself. My friend Nina says that she likes to have poetry read to her while she is in bed — I like poetry anywhere!

You might try too hard to please your partner both sexually and in other ways, remember the relationship stands more of a chance of lasting if *both* of your needs are being satisfied. Another difficulty for you is that you don't like being possessed. You yourself can be possessive, especially when in the early stages of a romance; possessive, hungry for love and desperate to be reassured. There may not be enough touch, comfort or words of love in the world for you, but you can in your turn fill your partner with love and reassurance until the cows come home. You need affection even more than you need sex, you need to be cuddled. You need to play a little and to have fun with your partner. (Welcome to the pleasure dome!) Oddly enough, you don't much like to be touched by strangers. You need to keep a little distance between you and 'touchers' this may be an instinctive need to protect your rather sensitive aura!

Some men are better avoided by Moon in Pisces women. The first is the self-destructive type, such as the confirmed alcoholic. You may wish to reform this person, to teach him by loving him endlessly to mend his ways. This will get you nowhere and will only deplete your small reserves of psychic energy. Another is the paternal type who appears over-protective but who is in fact threatened by the possibility of your becoming independent or taking control of your own life. The two Piscean fish can make you stupidly romantic and earthily practical both at the same time.

Here are a few more oddities from the Piscean wash-bag. You like fresh air and the countryside but not when the weather is cold, *then* you prefer sitting by an open fire. You can be too serious at times and you should let your friends encourage you to let your hair down and have some fun. You need to have good clothes and may be fussy about the type of shoes you wear.

Attitude to Career
The position of the Moon does not suggest any specific career but can show one's underlying motivations. You are creative, inventive and easily bored, therefore a routine job will not satisfy. Not having endless reserves of strength, you tend to work in fits and starts, therefore, you need a job where you can work at your own pace. Many of you have an urge to do something useful and find work in hospitals or even in prisons. Many solar and lunar Pisceans can be found in the world of music, acting, dancing and art. Creative work obviously appeals, floristry and cookery are typical interests. Glamorous work such as fashion interests you as does the more up-market kind of public relations work.

Many of you are skilled engineers, electricians, telephone engineers and precision sheet-metal workers. This is because the work is detailed, creative, requires problem-solving techniques and involves drawings. Obviously drawing office work appeals and many of you can be found working in aircraft factories!

I belong to an organization called the British Astrological and Psychic Society which has nine people on the committee. We all have different Sun signs and Ascendant signs but *all* nine of us have the Moon in water signs. Two of the group have the Moon in Cancer the other seven have the Moon in Pisces. This must be significant mustn't it? Some of us work full-time in the psychic field, others work on a part-time basis. One can find among our collective skills, astrologers, palmists, tarot readers, numerologists, clairvoyants, healers, aroma-therapists, trance mediums, aura-readers, graphologists, sand-readers etc. All lunar Pisceans are natural psychics but it is surprising how many are drawn specifically to work in the field. If you have Sagittarius, Aquarius or Gemini on your birthchart, you will probably want to teach. It seems that the Pisces connection gives one the urge to give gratuitious information to the world. Healing is also a naturally Piscean gift which many of you have.

Parents and Background

You may have been born with difficulty and could have been the youngest child in the family or perhaps an only child. The general feeling is that you were not an especially wanted child and were viewed right from the start as being a nuisance. Your parents would have been up against difficulties when you were very young, these could range from severe financial problems, deaths and tragedies in the family or the kind of situation where one half of the family doesn't talk to the other. There is, actually, strong evidence that you had early experience of the shortness and fragility of life due to the death of a parent or of someone close to you. Some of you would have been born at around the time of a death in the family; wartime births probably occurred during bombing raids!

One way or another your childhood was rather lonely. Some of you felt yourself to be 'different' in some way, possibly being the only artistic and sensitive child in a household full of very rugged and practical people. Even with nothing tragic or 'out of gear' in the childhood, there was a need to withdraw into your imagination, to get away and spend time on your own. Most of you are avid readers, often attracted to stories about magic or science fiction. Finding it hard to make friends, you could have been badly bullied at school or, worse still, badly bullied in the home. You may have felt embarrassed by your appearance, i.e. too tall, short, fat, thin, etc. Somehow, you found it hard to relate to your parents and may have been afraid of them or of other people around you. There may have been an over-emphasis on a particular kind of moral or religious observance, or there is the possibility that you were or you may have been pushed at school further and faster than was comfortable. This would be a difficult situation as your natural inclination was to please your parents and teachers. A few of you were rebels at school and hated authority.

You developed a watchful approach to adults and learned how to gauge their moods and how best to please them. This could be carried into adult life making you adept at finding out just how to please people and to manipulate them to suit your own ends. More likely, you would manipulate *yourself* to suit the other person and, therefore, *never* really learn to develop honesty and a sense of reality in personal relationships.

Adolescence is likely to have been a minefield as you learned to adapt to one person after another, not learning to appraise yourself of your own realistic needs and make them plain to others. All this can be sorted out later in life with an increase of awareness and self-awareness and, to give you your due, you do go to considerable lengths to discover what's wrong and to put things right. Pisces is a sign which is associated with illusion — as you grow and learn you should learn to channel your illusions into artistic or creative work and *out* of your dealings with others, especially in the personal sense.

Health

If you have this Moon placement, you may not enjoy the best of health. You could have been weak as a child and have spent a good deal of time alone because of this, later in life the legacies of your childhood have a habit of lingering on. Your energies are quickly depleted and your nerves are delicate. You can suffer from nervous ailments. The traditional problem area for Pisces is the feet, also the lungs. Heart trouble is a possibility, also skin allergies, migraine or asthmatic problems. You may retain water or have blood disorders. I have not yet come across a lunar

Piscean with a drink problem, but smoking seems to have a bad effect. An old-fashioned astrology book of mine tells me that you are susceptible to social diseases! Anybody who works with people in a counselling capacity will be able to tell you that social diseases are pretty common and don't apply to any one sign of the Zodiac or any one planet.

CHAPTER 6
Quick Clues to Your Moon Sign

—Quick Clues to the Natal Signs and Houses—

This is a very brief outline which you can use to jog your memory. This just gives the impact of each sign on the inner personality.

Aries (first)

Lively positive personality. Enthusiastic, self-motivated and outgoing but lacking in patience and consideration for others.

Taurus (second)

Steady type, sorts out what is valuable to him and then hangs on to it. Family person, sensual and musical. Resourceful and materialistic.

Gemini (third)

Communicator, teacher, salesman or travel agent. Usually found on the phone, needs to keep up to date. Mental activity needed, versatile and easily bored.

Cancer (fourth)

Needs a home base and a family around. Good to others but will lean on them. Moody, wants a quiet life. Enjoys travel, novelty. Needs personal security.

Leo (fifth)

Youthful and playful, loyal but dogmatic. Needs to be respected by others. Hard worker especially in a creative field. Likes children.

Virgo (sixth)	Shy inward looking type, dedicated worker, perfectionist. Likes to help others but moans about it. Businesslike, discriminating. Apparently cool emotionally, has strong, but contained, feelings.
Libra (seventh)	Ambitious, determined, also loving. Needs to be surrounded by beauty. Theorizer, may have difficulty putting ideas into practice. Needs partners and companions to complement self and achieve harmony.
Scorpio (eighth)	Steady reliable worker. Determined and independent. Strong, intense but restrained personality. Quick to anger but very caring to those who matter. Can transform self and others.
Sagittarius (ninth)	Restless, but also needing a secure base. Philosophic and broad-minded. Interested in sport, culture and all wide ideas.
Capricorn (tenth)	Ambitious, loyal and caring family person. Career important, good business head. Lacking in confidence, shy, kind. Restrained and self-motivated. Seeks position of authority.
Aquarius (eleventh)	Friendly, humanitarian, politically-minded. Needs family but cannot be confined to the home. Serious-minded, eccentric and detached.
Pisces (twelfth)	Gentle, compassionate, mystical, reclusive. Kind, but can be too self-sacrificing. Religious outlook. Sensitive, vulnerable. Artistic and creative.

CHAPTER 7
Reflections of the Moon

The Dark Side of the Moon

The Moon has a slightly schizophrenic effect on the unconscious aspects of the personality. Just as the Moon is responsible for the ebb and flow of the tides and fluctuations in plant growth, so it seems to be related to some of our innermost inconsistencies. One obvious manifestation of this is the phenomenon of pre-menstrual syndrome in women where every month they become ill, irritable or angry and even find themselves dropping everything on the floor. This situation which is well known in our house, because neither I nor my daughter can keep anything in our hands for a couple of days before each period!

Even men can have lunar mood swings, especially those who have their natal Sun or Moon in water signs. It is well known that mentally ill 'lunatics' are more difficult at the time of the full moon. The police also know that they will have to deal with more violence or thoughtless vandalism at full Moon time than at any other time of the month. Even in the case of perfectly stable people and discounting the pre-menstruals, there is a kind of duality about the Moon in its effect. It can enhance and at the same time confuse and muddle the effects of one of the fixed signs, create an overabundance of cardinality or undermine the dynamic quality of cardinal signs and screw up the mutables until they don't know whether they are on their emotional arms or their elbows!

Reflections

In order to confuse matters further there is the convoluted astrological theory of reflections. The idea is that the Moon 'borrows' some of its nature from the sign which is directly opposite to the sign which it is in! Therefore, a Moon in Virgo would have some characteristics of the sign of Pisces. Here is a list of the opposites.

Aries/Libra
Taurus/Scorpio
Gemini/Sagittarius
Cancer/Capricorn
Leo/Aquarius
Virgo/Pisces

For example, the charming lunar Libran can display considerable Arian aggression when under pressure.

CHAPTER 8
The Ascendant and the Houses

—How to Find Your Ascendant and Houses—

If you really have no idea of the degree, or even the sign which was rising at the time of your birth then I suggest that you try one of the following ideas. *Whatever you do please find out as accurately as you can the date, place and time of your birth!*

1. Find a friendly local astrologer and get him or her to work out your birthchart for you and make up a list of the planets and houses for you.

2. Send for an astrology chart to be made up, the fee for this will be very small as long as you don't ask to have the chart interpreted. There are many people offering this kind of service either by computer or manually, either way will do, it's the chart which matters. All astrology magazines will have details of people offering this kind of service.

3. Apply to: The Foundation of Holistic Consciousness, 25b South Norwood Hill, London SE25. Remember to send a stamped addressed envelope and your birth details. Also, please send £3.00 which is the fee for this service.

The Speedy do-it-yourself Ascendant Finder

This will help you to find your Ascendant and therefore, the house your Sun and Moon occupy but you will still need the help of an astrologer if you decide that you need to know the actual degree of the natal Moon.

Place your Sun in the house slot which corresponds to your time of birth and then add the sign of the Zodiac which lies on the cusp line (house division).For example if you were born at 2.30 am on the 14 April, place your Sun in the 2 am slot and put the sign of Aries on the cusp line between the 2 am slot and the 4 am slot. Then place the signs of the Zodiac on the cusp lines around the chart *in an anti-clockwise direction* and in the right order, then place your Moon in the appropriate sign. This will give you your Rising sign (Ascendant) and the house placement of both your Sun and your Moon.

The order of the signs of the Zodiac plus their glyphs

ARIES ♈

TAURUS ♉

GEMINI ♊

CANCER ♋

LEO ♌

VIRGO ♍

LIBRA ♎

SCORPIO ♏

SAGITTARIUS ♐

CAPRICORN ♑

AQUARIUS ♒

PISCES ♓

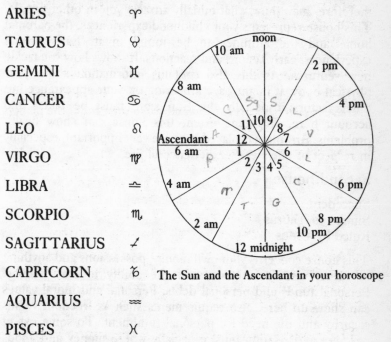

The Sun and the Ascendant in your horoscope

——————The Astrological Houses——————

The first house

Angular
Similar to Aries
Ruled by Mars

This shows how you appear to others, how you present yourself and your normal manner of expressing yourself among people who are new to you. In other words, this is your outermost personality. Obviously this shows the first impressions which you give but also the first impressions which you receive and therefore, may show what initially attracts you in other people. This house represents your childhood experiences, the parental home and the attitudes to be found in it. Early school experiences, early actions and reactions. It shows how you tackle new ventures. As this also contains information about your physical body, it might have a bearing on your appearance but other factors, especially the Sun sign, must be taken into account here. To some extent this house can show health problems. Any planets placed here are very important, especially in respect of one's early experience of life.

Second house

Succedent
Similar to Taurus
Ruled by Venus

This house concerns your own money, possessions and anything of value, also investments and the ability to earn money. Personal funds and personal debts. Personal and moral values can show up here, also requirements such as freedom versus security and the need for personal fulfilment. To some extent partners and relationships, especially where money and goods are involved. Matters related to property, farming, building, gardening and the land. Artistic and musical abilities or interests, if any. To some extent the way you give and receive love, also your attitude to beauty.

Third house

Cadent
Similar to Gemini
Ruled by Mercury

The local environment, matters under negotiation, and in some cases, papers to be signed. Messages, phone calls, correspondence of both a business and private nature. Local journeys, methods of transport. Brothers and sisters, neighbours, colleagues, sometimes nephews, nieces and friends. Business matters related to buying and selling. Education, training and retraining, foreign languages. Some sports and games. The way you think.

Fourth house

Angular
Similar to Cancer
Ruled by the Moon

The home, property and premises of all kinds. Small businesses. Domestic life, roots and background, the basis from which you grew up into adulthood. The mother or any other person of either sex who nurtured you while you were young. The beginning and ending of life, also how you are viewed after your death. Your attitude towards family commitments. Security.

Fifth house

Succedent
Similar to Leo
Ruled by the Sun

Children, young people and their education, even pregnancy. Fun, holidays and leisure pursuits of all kinds. Games of chance, sports, dancing, singing, writing, entertainments and any aspirations to glamour or showbusiness. Creativity and personal projects, even a business of one's own, as long as it offers the possibility of making a personal statement. Also publication, politics and social life — especially if it is influential. Traditional and religious attitudes. Most of all, this house involves *lovers and love affairs*.

Sixth house

Cadent
Similar to Virgo
Ruled by Mercury

Duties and day to day service to others, usually related to work but includes those taking place in the home. Employers and employees, superiors and subordinates. Everything related to health, doctors, hospitals and hygiene. This could apply to the types of health problems you will encounter yourself or among your family. Your clothes and how you wear them. Details and analytical methods, meticulous work, analytical thinking and even changes in your way of thinking. Aunts and uncles. Healthy eating habits. Food and nutrition.

Seventh house

Angular
Similar to Libra
Ruled by Venus

Open partnerships and relationships, husband, wife, live-in lover. Open enemies. The giving and receiving of co-operation. Colleagues one is closely involved with, business partners. Work in a glamorous or attractive field. Creative and artistic endeavours which are done in partnership or a small group. Attraction to places, things and people, therefore, to some extent even sexual attitudes and exploration. The kind of person one looks for to work or live alongside who fill in the gaps in your character. To some extent documents related to partnerships are indicated here. Land, farming and gardening involving co-operation with others.

Eighth house

Succedent
Similar to Scorpio

Ruled by Pluto and Mars

Beginnings and endings. Birth and death. Sexual matters. Money which involves other people e.g. spouse's income, mortgages, taxes, wills, legacies, banking and insurance. Above all partner's assets or lack of them. Shared feelings, feedback of other people's feelings (especially if they are intense). Crime and investigations and the police. Surgeons and surgery, also some illnesses. Hidden assets, secrets. The occult. A sense of commitment to anything or anyone. The things we really need from other people. The ability to regenerate or recycle anything.

Ninth house

Cadent
Similar to Sagittarius
Ruled by Jupiter

Expansion of one's horizons e.g. travel, higher education, new environments. Foreigners, foreign goods and foreign dealings. Legal matters, important legal documents and court cases. Religious and mystical matters, including the philosophical and spiritual side of psychic matters. On the one hand science and on the other hand intuition, dreams and visions. The church and the clergy. Sports and games which are taken fairly seriously. Outdoor pursuits. Gambling (especially on horses). Interest in or work with large animals. Need for personal freedom. Teaching and learning of a high standard also ethics and some aspects of public and political opinion. In-laws and grandchildren.

Tenth house

Angular
Similar to Capricorn
Ruled by Saturn

Aims and aspirations, your goal in life, your professional reputation and standing in the community. This may represent one's career, but also political ambitions, creative aspirations and future success; or lack of it. The ego and its chances of being satisfied. Your employer if your work for a large organization. Authority figures of all kinds including governmental and public authorities. Achievements, fame and personal promotion. The organization of the church or any large organization. The parents, especially father, or father figures. Status, your standing in the world. Responsibilities and visible commitments. Self-promotion.

Eleventh house

Succedent
Similar to Aquarius
Ruled by Uranus and Saturn

Social life, friends and capacity for friendship, clubs and societies. Detached relationships but also love received, even the affection of friends. Intellectual pursuits and hobbies. Hopes, wishes, desires and goals and the chances of achieving them. Conversation, learning for pleasure. Teaching and learning of the usual kind, also instruction at work, political or philosophical training of a specialized kind. Money from one's job, especially if there has been training involved. Eccentricities, unexpected changes and circumstances. Step-children and adopted children.

Twelfth house

Cadent
Similar to Pisces
Ruled by Neptune and Jupiter

One's inner thoughts and feelings also secrets and secret worries. Suffering, sorrows, limitations, frustration and handicaps. This house can show whether you are your own worst enemy or not, it also shows inner resources and inner weaknesses or anything which is too painful to face up to. Hidden talents, hidden thoughts, hidden love, hidden angers.

Also inhibitions, restraints, secret enemies and hidden danger. Any association with hospitals, mental institutions, prisons and other places of confinement, even exile. Any tendency to escapism, or things that we seek to hide from others. Your subconscious mind, plus karmic or spiritual debts. Self-sacrifice, love and help freely given (and possibly received). Also public charity and kindness given and received. Inspiration and insights. Illusions, meditations and daydreams. Hidden friends and enemies. Here is where one could reach the stars — or mess one's life up completely.

If you use the equal house system of chart division, the Moon, of course, will take two-and-a-half years to traverse a house. In all other methods of house division, the periods of time can vary enormously. I usually use the Placidus system, occasionally the topocentric system but if I have to 'slap' a chart together at speed, I still fall back on the equal house system.

CHAPTER 9
The Moon Through the Houses

——The Moon in the Astrological Houses——

The houses are as interesting as the signs although their impact on a birthchart is different. The signs show *what you are* while the houses show *what you do*. In this section we will look at the Moon in each house position, look a little more closely at the areas of life which each house position represents. For the movement of the Moon through the houses, see the chapters on the progressed Moon.

Moon in the first house

You love your home and family and would not be happy to live alone. Your nature may appear quiet and introverted but you have an inner desire to be recognized as a person in your own right. You will do much to help others but you're not prepared to make too many sacrifices on their behalf. Your mother was a strong influence on you and may indeed have been an exceptional woman in *her* own right; you could even find yourself walking in her shadow. The sea calls you so strongly that you may choose to live and work on it. You may be physically restless, finding it hard to sit still, alternatively you could have a love of travel, preferably with your family along for the ride. You may be drawn to hobbies or even work in the field of food and nutrition and could be a vegetarian possibly due to your love of animals. It comes naturally to you to support the underdog wherever you can. This placement suggests a need to work for the public in some way, either before them as some kind of celebrity or, more likely in some kind of humanitarian or welfare capacity. Being finely tuned in to your own body you usually know if you are going down with some illness. You must try not to allow your moods to dominate your personality.

Moon in the second house (accidental exaltation)

Material matters are important to you and you seem to need the security of money and possessions. There is a suggestion that these may be hard to obtain or to keep hold of in some way. Your need for security may result from a materially or emotionally deprived childhood. There is a shrewd and slightly calculating business head on your shoulders but your pleasant approach to others hides this well. Women will be involved in your personal finances in some way and you could be helped by women, possibly by inheritance or through family connections. You will probably take an interest in Taurean pursuits such as cooking, dancing, building, music, the arts, gardening and the creation of beauty.

Moon in the third house

The Moon here shows the need to communicate which could lead you towards a career in travel, the media or education. You are restless and curious but possibly lacking in concentration and easily bored. You pick up knowledge casually from others as you go through life. Your parents might be clever and bookish. Throughout life you will keep learning and then passing on information to others. You have a natural affinity to the telephone and also to vehicles which may, to others, look like an obsession.

Moon in the fourth house (accidental dignity)

This is the natural house of the Moon due to its association with the sign of Cancer which is ruled by the Moon. You prefer to work at home or at least to do your own thing, preferably in your own business. You may be nervous of the big wide world and have a habit of scuttling back home when the going gets rough. You are sympathetic towards those who are weak and helpless and are especially fond of animals. You could be strongly

attached to your parents or on the other hand, separated from
them by circumstances beyond your control. It is possible that
you lack confidence or feel insecure as an adult due to childhood
problems, you need love and affection and should try to avoid
hurting yourself further by forming relationships with destructive types. The past attracts you and this might lead you to work
in the field of antiques or to be a collector of old and valuable
objects. You may have a strong urge to live on or near the sea.

Moon in the fifth house

You are attracted to the world of children which might draw you
to work as an infant school teacher or become involved with
young people's sporting activities. Your emotions are strong and
you seek fulfilment on both a practical and a romantic level in
relationships. You could have a number of affairs if marriage
does not work out for you. You have a good deal of charm and
attractive youthful appearance which is useful to you as you
would take naturally to a rather public type of career such as the
theatre or in marketing and public relations. Be careful not to be
too clinging towards your children. A creative outlet is an
emotional necessity for you. You would make a good teacher,
writer or publisher.

Moon in the sixth house

You have a strong urge to serve the needs of others and may
work in some kind of caring profession, especially medicine.
You could be drawn to a career which involves the production of
food and anything which helps the public to stay in good health.
Your career will have to appeal to you on an emotional level and
you could even walk out of a job if the atmosphere or the people
there didn't suit you. You may be restless and better suited to
having a couple of part-time jobs rather than one full-time one.
You have consideration for others and would yourself be a
rather maternal employer.

Moon in the seventh house

You get on with most people because you need company and
companionship. Where relationships are concerned, you will

bend over backwards to make them work but it may be at quite a price. There is a feeling that while young you are not quite sure who you are and you may feel the need to have your personality and even your opinions validated by others. You prefer to work in co-operation with a partner or in a small group and you may be drawn to work in some kind of caring job like personnel management. You are politically-minded and also have a good grasp of office politics. Glamour appeals to you drawing you towards the world of fashion and music and this could become part of an interesting hobby for you. Your partner may be moody and difficult, but it is possible that *you* could understand him or her where others just don't.

Moon in the eighth house

Women will be instrumental in helping you to gain money or prestige in some way. You could work in trades which cater to women's needs or work mainly among women. You have an interest in psychic matters and you will be drawn to the mediumistic and spiritual side of these things. Your clairvoyance could be prodigious but it will depend upon other factors on the chart as to how this is directed. There is a feeling that love, affection, sensuality and sex are important factors in your chart and you could have your greatest successes in life in partnership with someone who inspires you both mentally and sexually. You can be devious, hurtful and destructive, even to the point of destroying your career or your future chances of success if you feel thwarted. Strange position this, as both the Moon and the house are so involved with instinctive and reactive behaviour.

Moon in the ninth house

Religion and philosophy will be an important part of your life and you will have to go on some kind of inward journey in order to find your way forward. You think deeply and will turn to a consideration of the deeper things of life. You are a natural psychic with the ability to see and feel beyond the boundaries of this Earth. Travel will be an important part of your life as will any dealings with foreigners or foreign goods. You could be a restless roamer who never really touches down for long anywhere; however, you are a natural teacher and instructor of others with a clear view of how to do things. You could find yourself attached to slightly crazy people.

Moon in the tenth house (accidental detriment)
This gives you an inner urge to shine before the public in some way, or to help humanity on a grand scale. There is evidence of an emotionally impoverished childhood during which something went strangely wrong. Your parents (especially you mother) could have been super-achievers whom you seek to emulate. You will change jobs a few times until you find the right road for you. My feelings are that that road will be intensely personal leading to a good deal of acclaim — or even, if the Moon is badly aspected, public scandal and ruin. You are drawn to a career which seeks to supply the needs of women or which is traditionally carried out by women. Sales, marketing, domestic goods and women's literature are a few possibilities. Your standing in the community, especially your career standing, is of paramount importance to you and even to others who are around you. You will be known and remembered by many before your life is done. To some extent this is a compensation for feelings of insecurity deriving from your difficult childhood, and a somewhat arid personal life, but just keep telling yourself that you will one day make it and, somehow you will find the strength to carry on.

Moon in the eleventh house
You enjoy the company of others and could be heavily involved in some kind of club or society. Being extremely independent, you hate to be told what to do. Your family are sometimes left in the dark as to your plans and feelings but there is a possibility that you, yourself may find it hard to know what you really *do* feel at times. Your aims in life may change dramatically from time to time due to circumstances. Friends, especially female ones, are very helpful to you, and you have a strange kind of luck that brings them running to you in times of trouble. You are well

organized and able to manage others, but you can on occasion misjudge people and be taken advantage of by more astute and crafty types.

Moon in the twelfth house

You seek to hide away from the world from time to time and to work in seclusion. Certainly you are happiest doing your own thing and working from you own home. Women will be an important part of any achievement, while men tend to interfere with your life, particularly with your career. You need to get away from time to time to recharge your batteries, too much stress will make you ill. You could be very creative as you have a rich imagination. Your instinctive need to care for others may lead you to work in the field of nursing or with animals. You may be too ready to sacrifice yourself for others. There is a secret side to your life; you may have to keep the secrets of others.

CHAPTER 10

Introduction to the Progressed Moon

—————The Progressed Moon—————

The techniques involved in predictive astrology are complicated to learn and to apply and one really needs to have a good grasp of natal charting before embarking on this. However it is a relatively easy matter to progress the Moon and this will give you some idea of the trends during the coming year. All you have to do is work out how old you are and add as many days as there are years in your age to the date of your birth. Therefore, if you are now twenty-five years old, add twenty-five days to your date of birth. If you are forty-three years old, add forty-three days to your date of birth. Then look up the tables to find the new (progressed) Moon position.

If this looks too difficult for you to do, there are various ways around this. Firstly, if you know a friendly astrologer or someone who runs a computer chart service, you can ask them for help, it wouldn't take them more than a few moments to give you the answer. Secondly, any magazine or other publication which deals with astrology and the occult will be able to help, they might offer a chart service and certainly would have people advertising such a service to the public. As long as you only require data, the costs will be minimal. It is only when you ask for chart interpretations that the costs begin to mount.

When you have established the position of the Moon for the year in question, (that is between your last birthday and the next one) look up the progressed Moon information to see what kind of year you are going to have. If you have sufficient astrological knowledge to know what house your progressed Moon is traversing, then use the house information in conjunction with the relevant sign information. Both the house position and the sign position will apply to you in one way or another. Remember, the *sign* will show the kind of mood or circumstances surrounding you, the *house* will show how you apply yourself and to what ends. For those of you who are really deep into astrology, the progressed data can also be used for lunar transits, these only apply for two-and-a-half days at a time through each sign but can be significant when other events are gathering momentum on a birthchart. An eclipsed Moon, for example, transiting a sore spot on your natal chart can be an unbelievable experience!

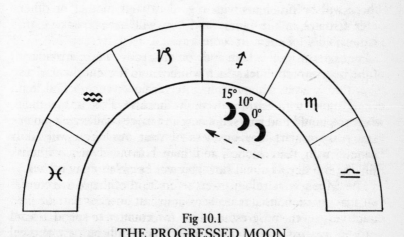

Fig 10.1
THE PROGRESSED MOON

CHAPTER 11

Your Progressed Moon by Sign

Progressed Moon in Aries or in the First House ♈

Aries and the first house is symbolically associated with birth, therefore, with all that is new and fresh. When this progression is in operation you will find that your emotions seem to take on a life of their own, you feel more passionate in every way and even the most placid among you will become excited and enthusiastic about everyone and everything. Being more moody than usual, you could find yourself involved in a series of family arguments, in fact, your home could become something of a battleground which suddenly starts to resemble a nest full of egomaniacs. There will be problems with regard to your mother or other older females in the family and you will have to take extra responsibility for them in some way.

Your energy level is high and you are ready to take advantage of the new opportunities which will begin to present themselves to you now. Even without your intervention, you will find that events move themselves extremely quickly. This is the time when you could find yourself a new and more challenging job or even make a start in a business of your own. You will take chances with your money and may borrow money without thinking too deeply about how you will be able to pay it back.

The Moon in astrology often refers to the home, therefore, you may move house, relocate yourself in another part of the country, or even move right out of the country to spend a few years in another part of the world. There will be new family groupings resulting from marriage, childbirth or divorce, and if you have been sitting in a marriage which has long been worn out, this is the time you will find the courage to do something about leaving. All the familiar patterns of your life will be changing quickly now, both of their own volition and with your help.

You will be able to tackle these new beginnings with a growing confidence in yourself. If you have been assessing your potential and making plans while the Moon was in Pisces or in the twelfth house, you will put those plans into action now. You have to guard against losing your temper in the wrong place at this time. Also guard against letting all the new contacts which you are making now go to waste, or allowing your new enthusiasms to fizzle out. Short-term projects will suit you better than long-term ones but you will need to find a way of expressing yourself and of doing your 'own thing' rather than just following other people's leads.

You may realize that your moods are more changeable and your behaviour more impulsive. The Moon, of course, rules the emotional response, therefore, while it travels through Aries or the first house, the Moon's power will be at a peak. Women may be able to blame their sudden attacks of over-sensitiveness on an increase of pre-menstrual tension, men will have to look for another excuse! You may eat and drink more in order to cope with your extra energies; there is a feeling of Arian greediness for all that life has to offer.

The lunar influence could bring you into a closer connection with the sea or with work which involves liquids, there could also be an interest in mechanical and engineering projects. Women will feature in your life now and may inspire you or encourage you to reach for the stars.

Women who have spent years as housewives may go back to work under this influence; on the other hand those women who view the start of a family as a goal will choose to have their first child now. The general feeling is that you will be taking the initiative, finding new methods and forging ahead with your life. Many of you will make an effort to identify and then to satisfy your own needs rather than only those of others for a change.

Your sexual energies will increase and you may change your outlook and your requirements with regard to sex under this influence. If you meet a new love there will be a strong chemistry between you. If there is a child conceived at this time, it should by all astrological theories, be a boy. Another unproven astrological possibility is that Aries-type people may figure strongly in your life at this time.

Remember the essence of this year is to get you moving and to make a fresh start.

————Progressed Moon in Taurus———— or in the Second House ♉

When the Moon moves into Taurus or the second house your emotions become more settled and comfortable. The projects which were begun in a blaze of enthusiasm while the Moon was in Aries or the first house, should be well under way by now. This is a time of consolidation in all things and of steady and controlled growth.

Material matters move to the top of your priority list now, your attention will be firmly focused upon your personal income and your financial base. This would be a good time to buy a decent property especially if it has a garden as there is a need for you to be seen as a 'man of property'. If you are not buying a new property, you might refurbish the one you're living in. If you have been in the habit of living for the moment you will begin to think ahead, you will no longer allow your credit card debts to get longer and larger. You will be reluctant to lend your money to just anybody, only making loans to those whom you can trust to pay you back in a prompt and orderly manner. If you are challenged about your newly materialistic attitude you will become defensive and awkward whilst at the same time demanding a ten per cent discount! You feel instinctively that this is a good time to put personal savings schemes into operation but a bad time to risk money on nebulous or speculative ventures.

If you buy anything expensive it must be durable, the same

goes for projects which are started at this time. Whenever the Moon is travelling through an earth sign, the prospects are good for long-term projects. Goods, especially luxurious or artistic ones which are bought at this time, will increase in value and business transactions will be carried out in a spirit of pragmatism rather than of overexcited speculation. You will find yourself dealing more with women now and they could become an important part of your financial or working life. There is a danger that there could be too much emphasis on materialism at the expense of other aspects of your life.

This is a good time to form durable business partnerships, especially with women. You could soon find yourself signing leases on premises or land related to your work and there will be a strong connection with people in the building trades.

Emotional partnerships may be formed now but they will not have the explosive chemistry of a meeting when the Moon is in Aries or the first house. Relationships which have been recently formed will become deeper and more reliable, new ones will be based on emotional and possibly also financial security. Your sexual drive will be strong and all your senses will be heightened as Taurus and the second house are so sensual in character. You will be far less changeable emotionally and will be possibly less inclined towards sexual experimentation now, this is a time to settle down in relationships rather than to go on voyages of exploration. Be careful not to become too set in your ways, you don't want to bore your partner to death. You will set the patterns for your future life now, certainly you will be reappraising your values and priorities. If you form a new relationship, your partner will be attractive, quiet and reliable.

You might find yourself involved with the production of food, certainly you will have to do more shopping. This will be a highly developmental time for all artistic or musical interests and you could learn to appreciate art, dancing or music for the first time. All in all, this should be a peaceful and settled period which you can relax into and enjoy.

Remember the essence of a Taurean progression is both literally and metaphorically, to build and consolidate.

————Progressed Moon in Gemini———— or in the Third House ♊

This is going to be a very busy and rather restless year for you. You will be moving around your neighbourhood more than before and if you haven't learned to drive, this is the time to do so because you are going to need the freedom of your own transport. This will also be a year for mental exploration and you could take courses at your local college or at evening classes. The best subjects might be connected with language, communication or computer studies. All studies, whether they are taken for a specific purpose or just for fun will be successful and you shouldn't have much trouble in passing examinations now. You may need to give more attention to your children's education now or to their out-of-school hobbies and interests.

You need all your communication skills now as your work will involve you in activities such as typing, telephone and customer liaison, probably also selling and advertising. There will be more than the usual amount of meetings and discussions with colleagues and there could be some kind of brochure or catalogue to be made up. You will travel around visiting different departments at your place of work and you will deal directly with clients both at your location or at theirs. You might take a series of temporary jobs or travel around your area carrying your skills with you. This will be an especially interesting time in your life as you will be meeting new people and will begin to become known outside your immediate circle. One instance could be that of a youngster taking a job delivering newspapers or groceries on a bicycle for a local firm.

You will have more dealings with neighbours and also with local issues. Although you might want to redecorate or otherwise change the appearance of your home and your garden, this would not be a particularly good time to make major changes or to make a move of house. There will be more visitors to your home than is normal and you will also spend more time visiting friends and family. Party-plan selling with friends and neighbours is a possibility. Gossip and trivial conversations on the phone are all an important part of your life now and you might find other people affecting your thinking in some fairly profound way.

Your own thought processes are more intuitive and instinctive than is usual for you, and in some cases you could find yourself feeling more nervous and jumpy, however when you focus your mind on work or on studies your concentration level will be good. There will be letters and parcels to be sent in the post, also possible are hire-purchase agreements and other minor documents to be signed. There will be more than the usual amount of dealings with females, it is possible that products or services which cater to female requirements or capture the imagination of women could be important in some way. You will be involved with mechanical and inventive ideas and will have to learn new methods, your dexterity will increase now. If you have been away from work for some time, you will return now.

This is not a particularly romantic time but if you do become involved with someone new, you will find that conversation and greater understanding are the keynotes to the relationship. If you are experimenting socially or sexually at this time it would be best if you didn't commit yourself too firmly to one person as your heart will be a little fickle. Romance will involve outings to restaurants, theatres and other local events even to sporting events. You should become involved in some kind of sport or hobby now and this could give you an outlet which will help you to contend with your restlessness and also heighten your tendency to over-analyse and intellectualize your feelings.

The essence of this progression is education and communication.

————Progressed Moon in Cancer———— or in the Fourth House ♋

The Moon rules the sign of Cancer, therefore when it travels through this sign or through the fourth house, one's lunar characteristics will make themselves strongly felt. This may on the one hand make you more moody, emotional and 'Cancerian'

or it may emphasize your own natal lunar position. Regardless of
your basic nature and outlook on life, you will act and react in a
far more emotional manner and will become more interested in
the private and personal aspects of your life.

Your home circumstances are going to play a major part in
your life this year; which may include a move of house, building
work to be done, decorating or buying new furniture and
fittings. The definite domestic slant to this progression will
temporarily anchor you firmly to your home and family. You will
take on more responsibility for relatives, this could be a source
of irritation or a great comfort to you depending, of course, on
the prevailing circumstances. There will be more dealings with
your mother, also other female friends and relatives, especially
those who are older than yourself. Feelings of family loyalty will
strengthen, and you might spend some time researching your
family's history and background. There will be a need to identify
with a specific group on the basis of family, race, religion or
nationality and you will experience some kind of patriotic or
group identity.

You may need to retreat from the outside world and to sink
back into comfort and security, having little desire to meet new
people and preferring to stay close to reliable old friends. You
will want some novelty in your life, but this will come in the form
of new domestic interests or learning how to use new gadgets in
and around the house. You could work from home at this time
or even start a small business from your own back room. The
sign of Cancer is associated with shops, therefore you may take a
job in one or even open a shop of your own. Whatever sex you
are, you will be more concerned with day to day chores and the
reason for this could range from retirement to setting up a
family. Antiques are associated with the sign of Cancer, also
history and genealogy, therefore you could find yourself delving
into the past for a while or even searching for your roots. You
will be over-sensitive, especially over family issues and you
could even become unaccountably possessive towards those
around you. You may feel alienated, neglected and superfluous,
your moods could vacillate between wanting to be alone and

fearing loneliness. Never mind, this will change soon enough when the Moon progresses into Leo or the fifth. Friends could cling to you now, or you could cling to them; old friends that you haven't seen for years could suddenly come back into your life now. Some of you could start to work with liquids. The sea could prove to be a pull, urging you to live and work on or near it. Travel on or over water will be especially pleasant at this time.

Cancerian-type people may influence you at this time and, due to the active femininity of the sign, a child conceived now should, by all accounts, be female.

This time is a time of gradual change where you spend time looking inside yourself and revising your needs and attitudes. Old habits could now be seen as being inappropriate to your present and future way of life.

The essence of this period is to set up or continue to care for a family, to keep your feelings hidden and to deal more frequently with women.

————Progressed Moon in Leo———— or in the Fifth House ♌

During this progression you will be dealing with children and young people. This is often the time when a mother is at the height of her involvement with a growing family. Whoever you are, you will enjoy a more youthful attitude possibly joining in sporting activities and youthful pastimes. The sign of Leo (and the fifth house) is concerned with creativity, therefore you will embark upon projects which are close to your heart. You should develop the ideas and the determination at this time to make something of yourself and to create something which will stand the test of time, but you might have to wait until the Moon progresses into Virgo before you gain the ability to focus your attention and to get on with the job.

Travel will be important now but it might prove something of a trial to you as you may, for instance, have to cart restless and difficult children around with you. Another possibility is that of business travel; this is far harder and less glamorous than it sounds as it is difficult to conduct important negotiations with jet lag and the inevitable touch of Montezuma's revenge.

There might be some connection with work in a glamorous field; indeed you may join some branch of show business. You might take up attractive or amusing hobbies now, skating and dancing are possibilities, also light and interesting sports. This is a good time to give attention to your personal appearance, to keep your figure trim and be prepared to go out and knock 'em in the aisles because it is going to be important for you to look good. This may be the time when you emerge from your shell and find yourself in the limelight; it is even possible that after years of being held back you find yourself breaking out with a vengeance. You may even become the stronger partner in a relationship after years of having been kept down. This is definitely not going to be the time to keep your light under a bushel but to discover the power of your own personality and to enjoy expressing it.

Your feelings will rise to the surface and will be hard to hide and they may even be difficult to control. All your relationships and friendships will be re-evaluated and some changes may be made soon. You could become more aware of and more wrapped up with your own feelings. Sexual feelings will also be high and there might be an affair of the heart (or body) now. None of this may last too long but you will learn a lot about yourself, other people and life generally. You may sometimes appear to be wasting time and energy on frivolities, but this will all be part of the learning process.

The sign of Leo (and the fifth house) is associated with children and you will find yourself dealing with and enjoying the company of children. You might help out the local boy scouts or girl guides, become involved in the activities of the local dancing school or in some other way find yourself in charge of children. You may start your own family now or you may find yourself responsible for someone else's children. All dealings with women will be good, your mood will be generous and happy a good deal of the time and you might gamble a little, either literally or figuratively as this *can* be a time of great gains, but also there may be surprising losses.

All in all this is a time to laugh and enjoy life, also to take a few chances.

————Progressed Moon in Virgo———— or in the Sixth House ♍

Work will be important to you now and you could find that either your normal job becomes more interesting or that you begin to do something new and highly satisfying. You will have to cope with paperwork, bookkeeping, correspondence and record-keeping; computers and word processors might become an important feature of your life now. You will perform precise and delicate tasks whilst analysing and checking your own work carefully; these jobs could include do-it-yourself work, home dressmaking or gardening. You might take a course at your local evening classes. If you do take lessons, these would be in useful and practical subjects such as car maintenance or cookery. Whoever you are, you will be dealing with household chores and, if you are not skilled at these types of job, you will soon learn the ropes. If gardening becomes important now, you will concentrate on producing fruit and vegetables.

You will fall into a sensible routine of work this year and may find yourself following a strict set of directions. This is the time to establish good work habits and you will find reliable and efficient colleagues to work alongside at this time. Women may pose problems on the one hand but they can turn out to be of great benefit as well, perhaps one group of women will give you trouble while another will help enormously. All this talk of duty and effort may seem a bit dull, but the resulting rewards will make it all worthwhile. This is not, strictly speaking, a great time for creative pursuits but writing would work out well, especially if it involves specialized research and analysis.

You may become involved with hospitals now, either because you yourself need treatment or people close to you may be sick. It is possible that you could work in a hospital at this time, but either way, you will take more notice of your own state of health and will try to improve it in any way that you can. You will concentrate on your diet and appearance and could even go a bit overboard by becoming too clean and tidy or by developing hypochondria. There will be some irritating nervous ailments to put up with which, although not dangerous, could make life difficult at times.

Your behaviour under this progression might irritate others as you will try to over-rationalize or over-analyse everything. You must guard against playing the martyr, taking on unnecessary chores and then moaning to everyone about this. Guilty feelings will plague you even though you really have nothing to feel guilty about. You must make time to rest and enjoy life because you will be ill if you don't.

This is hardly the best progression for romance but it is possible that you could meet someone special through your work. Relationships which are formed under this progression should be steady and relatively trouble free, if rather dull. On a brighter note, this is a great time to buy new clothes, perhaps this is a consolation prize result of all that hard work.

All in all this is the year where you should get the work done and attend to all those little details.

————Progressed Moon in Libra———— or in the Seventh House ♎

Partnerships and relationships are going to be of paramount importance to you this year. Whether you are at the dating stage or even contemplating the end of your present partnerships, new relationships made will have an air of freshness and a strangely experimental feel about them. It appears that you will be searching around for the right person rather than making a serious commitment. This doesn't mean that you *won't* settle down with your current date, just that you need to keep your options open now. Not all your relationships will be pleasant as there could be some major confrontations especially with women at this time. The seventh house (and the sign of Libra) are supposed to represent one's first marriage, but I have found this progression to be more concerned with forming and breaking relationships, *including* one's first marriage, rather than settling down for life.

Your emotions will be strong at this time which will cause you to over-react; you will find it particularly hard to be detached and objective. You may require both security and freedom at the same time, wanting your partner to be faithful while you yourself slip off the leash. Hooray for the old double standard! There will be an element of sexual exploration and experimentation too.

You should become drawn into the world of business now, and if you have no business knowledge, you will have to acquire it quickly. The communications side of business will be important, and you will need to keep in touch with current ideas and methods. Although you will not necessarily be directly responsible for the sale of goods and services, you will have to deal with the marketing aspect of sales, which means finding ways to advertise and to present your organization's image in an attractive and modern manner. There will be a good deal of interaction with other business people and also with the general public. Libra is a cardinal sign (the seventh house is a cardinal house) therefore, you will be much more decisive and dynamic now than ever before. You will have to present yourself in a stylish way in front of others, therefore your appearance and manner of dress will become more modern and interesting now.

In your career as in relationships, there will be interesting new beginnings and new working relationships with inspiring and dynamic people. You will spend far more time in cities than in the countryside but you will probably see something of the countryside as you travel through it on business. Your self-esteem will take a few knocks, mainly due to the fact that you will be working in an unfamiliar field and you will inevitably make errors.

There is some evidence that you will find yourself being manipulated in some way and this, when you discover what is going on, could lead you to react angrily or in an uncharacteristically thoughtless manner. In the areas of both your work and in your domestic life you could find that your finances and your financial decisions are inevitably wrapped up with your emotions.

The essence of this progression is that you will experiment

with new people, methods and ideas which will lead to some kind of change and renewal of your partnership situation.

————Progressed Moon in Scorpio———— or in the Eighth House ♏

This is where you will reach out and make the changes which will set the pattern of your life for many years to come. If you have been experimenting with friendships and relationships during the past couple of years, you may settle into marriage now; on the other hand, if you have been travelling towards a potential divorce, this is when you might bring it about. There will be major beginnings and endings which might include setting up a home or dismantling one. You could start a family now or, equally possibly, find yourself at the stage when your children are growing into adults in their own right. Your children may soon start their own families, or there may be births around you in other branches of your family or among your friends. Unfortunately, a time of births is also, astrologically speaking, a time of deaths and there could well be a funeral or two to attend.

You will either make a fresh commitment to your present job or make a change for one which will stand you in good stead in the future. A young woman for example, may give up work for a couple of years in order to stay at home with children. Whichever way this progression works for you it will mean transformation, rebirth and a redefinition of your goals both within and outside the home. You may become interested in conservation, especially re-cycling of used objects, certainly you will be spending money on your surroundings now.

Work changes could take you into the farming or food production industries; another possibility is some kind of professional contact with the police, private detectives or hospitals. Health or legal matters might enter your private life too. You will be more aware of the mystical and psychic elements of life and you might have some kind of psychic experience, possibly for the first time in your life. This progression will make your intuition and hunches strong and you might even go as far as to develop mediumistic qualities.

Financial matters which involve other people's money will become important now also their attitude to financial matters. This could include alimony, legacies, mortgages, taxes, joint accounts and business finances. You must guard against too great an emotional response to legal and financial matters. Joint properties and joint possessions can be sorted out at this time, but you must guard against feelings of greed and covetousness. There may be family or business wrangles, especially over property. These problems would be typical of a divorce situation, the ending of a business partnership or as a result of a death in the family. The structure of your life will be transformed in some way.

Some activities will be deeply satisfying and these could fulfil a variety of instinctual needs. These could include almost anything that makes you happy but I would have to put sex pretty high on the list plus, perhaps, settling into a happy home or a more comfortable way of life. New habits will be formed, probably resulting from a new understanding of your inner needs. Your instinctive side will overshadow your logical mind and you could experience an almost compulsive pursuit of your objectives.

There are some mighty awful problems which could emerge under this progression, the intensity of your intense feelings could spill over into jealousy and passion of a particularly lustful or obsessive kind. You could become trapped or manipulated into a situation which under normal circumstances you would avoid, or conversely, you may seek to possess or manipulate another. The abnormal over-emotional response will take some living with and could cause you to act in a manner which is totally out of character. This would be the right time to delve into the bottom of a long-standing mess and finally sort out the reasons for it, even if it means bringing a few skeletons out of the cupboard. You might feel as if you are in an emotional killing field now but you will emerge at the end of it as if reborn, salvaged from destruction.

————Progressed Moon in Sagittarius———— or in the Ninth House ⟋

The key notion behind this progression is the expansion of your
personal horizons. You might travel overseas for the first time or
you could take the time to really investigate a particular part of
the world which you have always fancied knowing better. Your
work could take you away and you might enter into a business
venture which involves overseas goods, services or property. You
may have to sell to foreigners, thereby learning about them and
their way of living. Your family may move to another country or
there may be people entering the family who are themselves
from a different cultural background and this could be the cause
of some of your long distance journeys. Some of you will fall in
love with a person who comes from a different country or a
different cultural background now and this may cause you to
review your own religious or philosophical outlook.

You may be subjected to economic or cultural changes in
conditions around you which would affect your private or your
business life. There is even a chance that you will have to deal
with people whose views are biased or even bigoted regarding
race and religion.

There might be increased dealings with institutions such as
schools, colleges and churches either personally or as a matter of
business. You could go back into training or just study for fun at
this time. The subjects which you choose will be of a
philosophical or mind-broadening type rather than of a purely
practical nature; however, you may learn a foreign language as a
means of meeting a larger range of interesting people or in order
to progress in your career. You will find ways to overcome
mental stagnation and boredom at this time. School connections
may take you into teaching or training others and you may have
to give lectures on a special subject. Another career possibility is
in the realm of publishing, certainly you could be writing
brochures or trade journals for your company and having them
printed now. There is a feeling that the end of a phase in
your working life is on the way now and you could finish this
progression with a determination to do something quite

different. This may be a high point, a culmination of all that you have worked for, alternatively, you may reach the bottom of a pit of unhappiness with regard to your work and decide to change direction for good and all.

You should be able to enjoy life and have some fun. The chances are that you will become enthusiastic about a number of new ideas, hobbies and pastimes; sports could be high on the list. There will be more chance for you to get out into the fresh air, and you may become interested in the world of large animals, especially horses. Gambling on horses is a possibility, or just taking a chance or two on life. This should be a time of increased fun and a sense of adventure. Your level of confidence will be high, maybe too high, but this might just begin to wane as the progression moves towards the cusp of the tenth house.

Sometimes there is an increase of activity concerning legal matters under this progression, but it is usually the tail end of outstanding problems rather than new ones rearing their heads. This may be a detail or two which is still hanging on from a recent divorce settlement, or some kind of family or business matter that has still to be put to rest.

Sagittarius and the ninth house is concerned with second marriages, therefore this may be the time when you meet a second partner or when you decide to marry for the second time.

To sum this progression up, this is when you can expect to expand your life (plus your waistline if you're not careful), move onwards and outwards mentally and physically, also to forget some of your cares and worries and enjoy yourself.

———Progressed Moon in Capricorn——— or in the Tenth House ♑

This is a time of hard work but also of ultimate achievement. This progression may start with a monumental set-back in your life or just a feeling that you cannot go on any longer in the same old way. The chances are that the frustrations and the problems which are affecting your working life will spill over into your personal life as well. You will receive a great deal of useful help from others at work now. Some of those who help you may be in positions of seniority or they may be equipped with some kind of specialized knowledge which they are willing to pass on to you. If you are selling a product or a service, buyers will be more receptive now; one interesting point is that women are likely to be particularly helpful to you.

Business methods will be important even if your work is not strictly in the business world. If you are not used to working in a structured organization, you will learn how to do so; alternatively, you might go from one sort of structure to a completely different one which runs by a different set of rules. It is important that you be honest in all your dealings whether they be in your working or your private life and you should, with luck, be among people who themselves are honest. You will need to be seen as being respectable both in your public and family life as this is a time when secrets and deceptions might emerge in an uncomfortably embarrassing way.

Your work will bring you into contact with the public and you will perform services for people both individually and in large groups. You will need to dress the part of a successful and competent person as both you and your work will be highly visible at this time. Sales and promotional work will be important and you will have to make public appearances, possibly even give lectures or make speeches from time to time.

Colleagues will be more sympathetic to your aims than before and you, in turn, will be more responsive to the needs of others. It is possible that you could be temporarily short of money, maybe because you are investing fairly heavily in a project or because your job offers training and future possibilities rather than present financial rewards.

You will take a sensitive attitude towards those you work with and will be careful not to tread on their egos. There will be responsibility now attached to the work which you do and you may well also be responsible for the efforts of others. This is the time to build a team of juniors or a sensible framework of method and experience which will follow you into the future. Delays and set-backs in your career will be followed by success, good will come out of bad. Your work will need a conventional attitude and old-fashioned skills and there will be the need for a structured and practical outlook. You may find yourself reviving the spirits of a flagging company or institution, which will require you to be responsive to the moods and feelings of groups around you, possibly in the form of union negotiations. Timekeeping will be important, either in the form of working hours or of timetables of one sort or another.

Your professional and personal relationships may become a bit blurred as you could turn towards someone who you work closely with or alternatively, you could begin a work project with someone you love. This is not, truthfully speaking, a romantic time, your feelings may be dampened or you may be forced to keep them on a tight rein, however, if you do meet someone, it is likely that this will happen through your work.

In personal relationships you will be shyer than usual and also very slow to commit yourself. There may be some strangely public displays of emotion either directed towards you or coming from you. Angry scenes could take place where others can see and hear or feelings of loving and caring which you have been keeping dark might also emerge in a somewhat public manner. Domestic life will have to take a back seat now but the work which you are doing will go to make the domestic scene nicer and more comfortable later on.

The basic feeling of this progression is that this is your time for career advancement and a redefinition of aims and goals.

Progressed Moon in Aquarius or in the Eleventh House ≈

This is a time when friends will be extremely important to you, you will have to rely on them to help you and you will in turn, be a good friend to others. There will be an involvement with clubs and societies of one kind or another and you will definitely feel the need to become part of a group. This group identity may be political or work related. There may be spare time activities with a sports team, people who are interested in artistic pursuits, or some kind of intellectual grouping. You will make achievements as part of a group or a team. At work, you will have to work in co-operation with, and possibly in charge of, others; you cannot achieve much on your own now.

Friendships with women will be important and you will become slightly less attached to your family, finding that your time and attention is diverted from them by outside considerations. Even in the realm of friendships there will be changes as you move on to newer, more dynamic type of people. Both you and your associates could try to achieve something which would be of benefit to humanity, your attitude being highly idealistic but possibly rather impractical at times. It would be wise to guard against being drawn into specific and fixed ideologies which don't leave room for differences of opinion.

It will be necessary for you to learn new methods which could arise from your work or as a result of a change in your way of life. If, for instance, you were to move house at this time, you would have to get to grips with decorating or making a garden. You may learn to sew, drive a car or bring your work skills up to date. If you have school-aged children, you will be dealing with educational matters on their behalf and may be drawn into some of their school activities. It is possible that you could return full-time to college to complete a course; you yourself may turn or return to teaching. Retirement at this time would give you an opportunity to learn to ski, play the piano or to learn any one of a million new ideas. You may have to deal with very modern methods or ideas which are out of the ordinary. This may include learning to use a computer or something similar, you could find yourself dealing with electronics, radio or radar, even taking up astrology.

You will redefine your personal goals and ask yourself what you want out of life in general terms. By investigating your own hopes and wishes you will change the direction of your thinking in some radical way. One instance may be a person who has thus far, never wanted children deciding that he or she wants them after all, another person who had always been lazy might suddenly become ambitious. New goals and values will replace outworn ones now.

There can be a surprisingly disruptive element in this progression which could change your outlook or your life completely. You might re-emerge soon with a new career; almost certainly with a new home, possibly even with a new set of personal relationships. This is the time when you could revolutionize your own life or find that it is being revolutionized for you by bringing a complete breakdown in your present status quo. If this is the case, you may react by becoming jealous and possessive in an attempt to hang on too tightly. It all depends upon your circumstances at the time of entering the progression and your particular nature as to how you handle these changes. Others of you who have been through difficult times during the previous progression, will find this a surprisingly good time when money comes your way, gambles come off and your dreams begin to come true. There is no doubt that this is a phase where anything could happen — and frequently does. Try to keep a strong grip on reality as events around you might become tinged with fantasy or even a subtle form of lunacy.

Remember to keep in touch with friends, whether things are good or bad, they will sustain you now.

————Progressed Moon in Pisces———— or in the Twelfth House ♓

This will be a time of reflection, possibly even retreat from the hurly-burly of life, events seem to be in the hands of fate now and there doesn't seem to be much you can do about it. You may have to suppress your own personality for a while, possibly until your progressed Moon crosses over the Ascendant into Aries, and in addition to having to keep a good many of your feelings under wraps, there could be work projects carried on in secret. One example might be of preparing to set up a small business of your own while still carrying on at your usual job. There may, of course, be some kind of secret relationship going on; this doesn't necessarily have to be an 'eternal triangle' situation but may be something much odder, such as keeping in touch with a 'black sheep' relative that the rest of the family ignores. This progression may be a sad, even a depressing time, as you seem to be working through some kind of karmic programme. The outcome will be a change in your consciousness leading to a renewal of life and hope which will sweep you away into a completely new direction.

It is important to keep some kind of hold on reality during this progression as it would be only too easy to slip into a strange state of mental limbo. Some aspect of your life will be insecure, probably on the emotional level, and you may find it hard to face the facts which confront you. It would be easy to slide into a state of disillusion or even despair, worse still, you could try to chase illusion, exacerbating the situation by the use of drugs and drink. It would be best to keep away from opiates at this time, especially sleeping pills.

There is a much more positive side to all this and it is the opportunity for you to learn how to relax, meditate and travel on a series of inward journeys. One way or another, you will be spending much more time alone than you have before and, while you are looking inwards, you may discover talents and abilities which you never knew you possessed. I can remember when my Moon travelled through the twelfth some years ago, I was at home with small children, running a small dressmaking business also studying foreign languages and astrology — and discovering that I had a talent for both. The benefits of this progression tend to be recognized only in retrospect. Artistic and creative abilities will come to the fore now, also you should be able to enjoy quiet pleasures like reading, listening to the radio and gardening. Photography or film-making is a strong possibility now too.

If you are naturally rather moody, this aspect of your personality will be accentuated but you may find yourself on the receiving end of someone else's moodiness at this time. Your intuitive abilities will develop and you should follow any instincts which you feel. Being more sensitive and shyer than usual, you may find others strangely difficult or even unsympathetic to your needs and wants. It is possible that psychic or mediumistic abilities will become noticeable now and you might begin to take a serious interest in these subjects. There could even be a revelation, a kind of 'gateway' which thrusts you forward into spirituality.

Typical Piscean or twelfth house circumstances would be that of a young woman finding herself at home with small children at the very time when her husband is having to make the maximum effort at his job and therefore, is being less supportive than before. Another reason might be the beginning of retirement with its inevitable change of perspective. One unfortunate reason for this situation might be a period of illness, or possibly of having to take care of somebody else who becomes ill or incapacitated. There may well be a connection with hospitals, even mental institutions or prisons at this time, either because you yourself are directly involved or through those close to you. You could even find yourself working in one of these places. You will have an uncanny ability to link with the moods of others and to give real help and understanding to those who need it.

One of the nicer possibilities is of travel. There may be a move or a drift towards water for you now and, depending upon circumstances you could buy property by the sea, rent a holiday villa on the coast or become involved in the world of boats. Some people go cruising when the Moon is in Pisces.

If you are working, you will be better off as a backroom boy now than out in front. You may find it hard to trust others either in your private or your working life. Relations with women could be particularly difficult or even peculiar now, and you may have to face a change in perspective regarding the women in your life at this time, probably due to factors which are outside your control. An easy way to grasp the idea behind this progression is to think of a seed spending the winter lying in the soil waiting to come to life in the spring.

Strange and subconscious forces affect your moods as the axis of your previous way of life subtly shifts. This is truly a time to recharge your inner forces by retreat and reflection in readiness for the 'first house breakout' which will surely, surely come.

The Moon may set but the Sun also rises.

CHAPTER 12
Advanced Techniques of Lunar Progression

The Moon progresses forward at roughly one degree per month. It may travel eleven, twelve, thirteen, or fourteen degrees during the course of a year but most of the time, conveniently for us, it travels at a rate of twelve degrees per year. The method is simple; once you have established the exact degree of the progressed Moon on your last birthday, move it forward a degree for each month as the year goes by. As there are thirty degrees in a sign, one can see that the Moon will spend roughly two-and-a-half years in each sign. It is strange how this two-and-a-half year time scale does seem to affect the lives of many of us. As an astrologer, I am accustomed to people telling me that a particular situation, such as a relationship or a job lasted for about two-and-a-half years.

When looking at the progressed Moon, first look to see whether it has recently changed signs, if it is in the middle of a sign or if it is wending its way to the end of a sign. Sometimes it takes a few months for a new sign to make an impression on one's life but on other occasions, effects are noticeable immediately, even as the Moon draws to the end of the previous sign.

Once you have established the actual degree of the progressed Moon at the time of the reading, then simply move it forward a degree for a month to see what the year (or couple of years) ahead will bring. If the Moon crosses another planet, this will be a conjunction and, although this is going beyond the scope of this book, I have listed the lunar conjunctions here for you. In the case of positive aspects such as the trine or sextile, read the conjunction information but stress the positive sides of it. In the case of the 'hard' aspects such as the square or opposition, the more difficult reactions will probably apply but, don't forget that more can be achieved under a hard aspect than under an easy one.

————Moon/Sun conjunction————

There may be events concerning children, also this is a time of increased self-confidence or even of personal triumph. Fun, holidays, speculation, games, sports, will become part of your life now. You could fall in love with an exciting person and have an affair to remember. There is a possibility that you may buy yourself a holiday home, a house in the sun. There should be some good times with older relatives now. You might find yourself dealing with more than the usual number of Leo type people at this time.

————Moon/Moon conjunction————

Domestic matters come to the fore, there could even be a move of house or you may take out a lease on business premises. Travel is a possibility especially over or near water and you may revisit the place of your birth. There will be some special dealings with females, especially mother figures. Your emotions will be stronger now. There could be a connection with the provision of food or domestic goods. Things which have been kept secret may suddenly be revealed. You may have more dealings with Cancerian people now.

————Moon/Mercury conjunction————

Communications with the family characterize this progression. There may be documents to be dealt with in connection with property and premises. There could be a new vehicle for you now or you may simply change your method of daily commuting. Paperwork will be important. Any education courses which are undertaken now will go well, exams can be passed at this time, as can the driving test. There should be friendly dealings with neighbours, friends and relatives of your own generation or a bit younger. You could take up a new sporting interest in company with others. Groups of friends may begin to meet in your home. You will begin to think about diet and food values and could make plans to alter the appearance of your home. There may also be a rethink about your methods of working and improvements in the methods you use. You may begin to write for publication. You may have more than the usual amount of dealings with Gemini or Virgo people now.

─────Moon/Venus conjunction─────

Family affairs come to the fore, you will get on well with the women of the family. There could be public relations involving women, or even a business partnership with a woman. This is a good time to decorate the house or to have a celebration in the home. Food and catering, diet and appearance will occupy you now. There could be a new romance, certainly you will begin to feel more attractive and more romantic. There may be some involvement with artists and with artistic work at this time. There will be an increase in business opportunities and good new contacts. You may find yourself dealing with more than the usual number of Taurus or Libra people now.

─────Moon/Mars conjunction─────

You will experience a high level of energy and drive, and you could develop sudden enthusiasms for work projects or energetic hobbies. There will be some kind of fresh start now. There could be a working partnership with a young man and you will have a more energetic and youthful attitude to work matters. If you are in a competitive field or are playing in competitive sports you should be able to win. Your ambition level will be high and opportunities will suddenly come your way. This is not a great time for dealing with women and you will have to watch your temper now as all your feelings will run high. You may become ill, feverish or even have an accident (especially in the home). If you change vehicles now, the new one will go faster than the previous one did. Your sex drive will be high but you could also fight over emotional and sexual matters. For women, this transit is almost bound to bring a man into your life; probably young, certainly sexy and energetic. You could be dealing with more than the usual number of Aries or Scorpio people now.

——————Moon/Jupiter conjunction——————

You might rethink your religious and philosophical views now. There will be an interest in travel and dealings with foreigners, possibly in connection with work. There is a feeling of optimism and change for the better although it may not be apparent immediately. You will make new and useful contacts and could have unexpected opportunities at work. Money should become easier to find and doors will open for you. There might be an involvement with legal matters at this time and, if so, you will come out on the winning side, especially if property is involved. This is a good time to deal with women in regard to financial matters, also to invest in property. Domestic matters should go well and you will be given the opportunity to expand your horizons and even to look at yourself in a new way. You may be involved with more than the usual number of Sagittarius or Pisces people now.

——————Moon/Saturn conjunction——————

There will be problems now, these could relate to your home situation, your parents or other elderly relatives. It is possible that you could feel depressed and rather lonely now even though you might be surrounded by people. You will have extra responsibilities and very little time to rest and, apart from feeling down-hearted, you might actually be ill or just over-tired and run down. Life will feel restricted and rather boring at this time and your love life may also be depressing, it is possible that your loved one is living or working at some distance from you at the moment. Business matters will go slowly but plans which are made now will work out well in the long run. Dealings with people in positions of responsibility or with older people may be awkward but should work out well *after* the progression has passed. There could be the need to make far-reaching decisions with regard to your parents. Money may be short, especially in the home but that will also improve soon. A good time to do some long-range thinking and to chat to knowledgeable and responsible people about your plans for the future. You may meet more than the usual number of Capricorn or Aquarius people now.

———Moon/Uranus conjunction———

Sudden changes in mood characterize this progression. This is one of those times when you will suddenly realize that you can no longer bear the job you're in or the person you are living with. This is the kind of situation which brews up slowly possibly for years beforehand and then, *apparently* all of a sudden, changes for good. You may make an unexpected change of house or suddenly decide to tear down and rebuild some part of your home, there could be unexpected family problems or sudden changes with the home set-up. Friends will be more in evidence at this time. You could have some brilliant ideas or you may find answers to questions which have been bothering you for ages. Working life could bring unexpected changes and benefits, almost anything could happen and you will have to study the signs and the houses involved in order to work out all the possibilities. You might even take up astrology! You should have more than the usual number of dealings with Aquarian people at this time.

———Moon/Neptune conjunction———

If you fall in love now you will see your loved one through rose-coloured glasses. There will be a strong element of fantasy in any love affair at this time, therefore you could do most of your loving at a distance or even confine it to the inside of your own head. Old half-buried memories will come back to haunt you and you could find yourself dealing with ancient fears and phobias, possibly facing up to them at last. There will be an increase in your intuition and you could have some interesting psychic experiences. You will be re-examining your philosophical views and religious outlook and could even go so far as to change your religion. You may spend much time daydreaming or you may go in for some inspired forms of meditation. You will feel atmospheres acutely and could well develop clairvoyant and precognitive abilities. Business matters could become confusing and you might find out that you have been dealing with dishonest people. You may have some great ideas but will have to wait until the progression has passed before putting them into practice. There may be travel to the sea or over it for you, and there should be renewed contact with family and friends overseas. You may rearrange the method of water supply in your home or you may become interested in or work with fluids, gasses, oil and photography. There could be increased contacts with mystical people or those born under the sign of Pisces or who have strongly Piscean birthcharts. Love affairs could be wonderful, inspired or they could really screw you up but you will definitely be awash with emotion and hardly able to think straight. You might be involved with hospitals especially in connection with family members. There may be work in a hospital or institution for you at this time.

You may develop a taste for alcohol or develop strange allergic ailments.

————Moon/Pluto conjunction————

This is a transforming progression which could change the whole of your life from now on. It will certainly change your outlook on life and your view of yourself. You will be emotionally wrought up, possibly because you will be coping with some pretty monumental problems. There will be financial matters to sort out and these may stem from a previous divorce, a legacy or some kind of outstanding tax problem. There could be outstanding business finances to sort out and even liquidation is a possibility. You will want to alter a bad family situation and could clear the air with a really terrific argument or you could even walk out for good. There may be dealings with the police, the courts or hospitals at this time and the matters which are involved could be quite serious. There may be literal births and deaths around you now, certainly there will be figurative ones. There is even the possibility that your life could be affected by geological upheavals or by war! There could be a connection with mines and miners or explosives. There may be some rather strange occult and psychic experiences. Any kind of subterranean rumblings of discontent which have been going on in your life could erupt explosively now.

——————Moon/Ascendant conjunction——————

This is a time of new beginnings as the Moon moves from the twelfth house to the first. You will want to come out of the shadows and be noticed. Your personal and domestic affairs will change for the better now although it might be uncomfortable while this progression is in operation. You will probably change your appearance and your attitudes soon.

——————Moon/Mid-heaven conjunction——————

This is the culmination of a phase of your life. You should feel that you have reached as far as you can in your present job and now want to change direction. You could become more involved with the public or find that your status and public image is improving. You may achieve some long-cherished dream regarding your career. Domestic matters will go well, and if you move house, you will make money on the deal and will like your new home. Domestic matters will influence your professional life either indirectly, via changes in your home and family arrangements or directly, as a result of working in industries related to food and household goods. A woman may influence your thinking in regard to your objectives in life.

——————Moon/IC conjunction——————

This could bring you closer to your family, especially your mother, and will bring you closer to your home. You may begin to work from home now. Any lingering emotional or relationship problem in the home can be sorted out for good now.

Moon and nodes

When the Moon crosses the nodes, you may move, redecorate, have interesting visitors or possibly go on holiday to a completely different place than the one you usually visit. You make take up some special project in the home or start working from home. You could re-appraise your direction in life now. You may have some kind of *Karmic* experience at this time.

CHAPTER 13
Personality and Phases of the Moon

Please see explanation and tables from pages 185 – 209 to find *your* natal moon phase.

First quarter

Whatever sign you were born under, wherever your other planets are placed, you will have an underlying sense of youthful enthusiasm, a touch of Aries at the heart of your nature. You probably prefer to take the initiative, especially in romance and you will always be ready to look for new interests in life, new people and new ideas. Your lively outlook and optimistic approach to life is an attractive feature but you have to guard against selfishness. You can see how things can be made to work and how situations can be improved. You will spur others into action but then leave them to finish the project. You could be self-employed. No-one can make you do something if you really don't want to and this may stand in the way of successful relationships. You should get off to a good start and become quite successful when young, other factors on the chart will indicate whether this early promise will be maintained throughout life. You should try not to react too fast or to take others too much by surprise.

Second quarter

You are ambitious and sociable with an underlying touch of Cancer and Leo in your nature, you are locked into your own goals and your strong need to create something which will be seen and remembered by other people. You need a place of your own where you can express your own personality; this may be your home or your workplace. Your rather charismatic personality will always draw others towards you. You try to be helpful to others but can't be called on to make sacrifices on their behalf for very long. You may use others for your own ends; this behaviour is instinctive rather than calculated. You need the status and outlet of a career but one where your face is out in front, possibly in sales or reception work. You draw attention to yourself and while you can achieve much, you may miss some of the needs of others. You should reach considerable heights of success while still young, other factors in your chart will determine whether you maintain that success. You are slow to anger but formidable when you do lose your temper. You hate to be hurried and may be slightly suspicious of methods and ideas which are presented to you as a *fait accompli*. You don't mind hurrying other people as you know that it puts them slightly off balance and tips the odds in your favour.

Third quarter

You are sensitive to the needs of others and you want them to be equally sensitive to your needs. There is an underlying watchfulness with this quarter rather reminiscent of Libra and Scorpio. You need friendships, colleagues and relationships and you relate well to individuals within a group. You like an exciting life but want others to share the excitement. You are aware of what others think of you and may not be entirely sure of yourself unless acceptably reflected in the eyes of others. You are drawn to more active, more successful people and can help them to achieve their aims, this phase of the Moon suggests that you will be a supreme achiever in your own right but you would still need the help and encouragement of others. There is a nerviness about you, a kind of coiled-spring tension which can lend you originality and wit but also a short attention span and a hungry search for new people and new experiences. In some peculiar way, sex could have a special importance to you. It may transform your life in some manner or other. It is said that people who are born just after a full Moon has passed the Mid-heaven on their birthchart will be rich and famous! Your most sucessful time of your life is in your middle years.

Fourth quarter

Whatever else there may be on your chart, there is an underlying feeling of Capricorn or Pisces here. You finish the projects which others start, you reorganize and sort out problems left by others; you may never start projects of your own. You have clairvoyant insight and may follow hunches rather than work things out logically. You are aware of all kinds of undercurrents and can become upset by the demands of others. You have to try to let their feelings flow past you and always trust your basic instincts. You can be too inclined to sit back and let things happen around you. You are probably at your best when helping a group to achieve something beneficial. You can blend in with a large group or work entirely alone. You are probably not too materialistic but you do need job satisfaction. You may be very slow to grow up, happy to sit back and allow things to change around you, however, you are likely to go through some kind of metamorphosis later in life and achieve success in something unusual and completely individual.

Romany tradition and the Moon's phases

A friend passed this piece of Romany wisdom on to me. I had not realized that such minute observations of human behaviour and lifestyle had been made. I tested out the ideas on my family and friends and found that they work well.

Those born between the new Moon and the first quarter.

You will have a long life.

Born in the first twenty-four hours, you will be lucky.

Born on the second day, you will be exceptionally lucky.

Born on the third day, you will have important and influential friends.

Born on the fourth day, up and down life with luck and reverses.

Fifth and sixth day, pride could be your downfall.

Seventh day, you have to hide the wishes that you want to
   come true.

Those born between the first quarter and the full Moon.

You will do better in life than your parents.

   First day, prosperity.

   Second day, easy life.

   Third day, wealth through travel.

   Fourth and fifth days, charm.

   Sixth, easy success.

   Seventh, many friends.

Those born between the full Moon and the last quarter.

You will have difficulties but will overcome them by doggedness.

   First day, you will succeed in another continent.

   Second day, you will do well in business.

   Third day, success as a result of (and probably foreseen by)
      intuition.

   Fourth day, bravery.

   Fifth day, care must be taken with money.

   Sixth and seventh, great strength.

Those born between the last quarter and the new Moon.

You will be affectionate and honest.

   First and second days, you will be happy in your home.

   Third day, you are dependable.

   Fourth day, you are sensitive.

   Fifth day, you will make ideal parents.

   Sixth and seventh days, you will acquire money (or maybe
      non-material wealth) through loyalty.

———————— **An Eclipsed Moon** ————————

Solar Eclipse ☌   ⊕ ☽ — ☉

If the Moon was lying between the Earth and the Sun when

you were born, your inner and outer natures would interact well.
Your emotional reactions will be fast, you would act instinctively
without having to stop to think in a structured and logical
manner. This would enable you to avoid or get out of sticky
situations admirably but it might be hard for you to make plans
and carry them out.

Lunar Eclipse ☌   ⊕ ☉ — ☽
If the Sun was between the Earth and the Moon when you were
born you would be restless, intense and creative. You are apt to
go overboard in relationships as you take everything in life
seriously. You need people and you also have a knack of drawing
them close to you. You may allow your logical mind to override
your instincts, thereby misjudging situations where you might
have been better served by trusting your gut reaction.

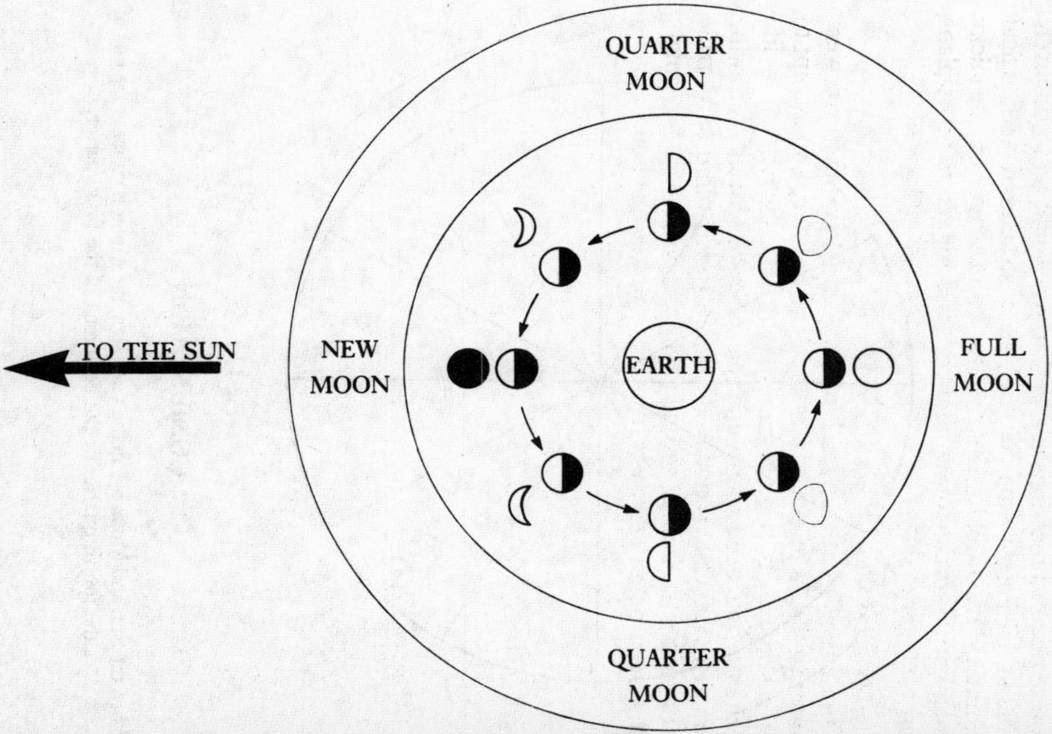

TO THE SUN

FULL MOON

QUARTER MOON

QUARTER MOON

NEW MOON

EARTH

Fig 13.1

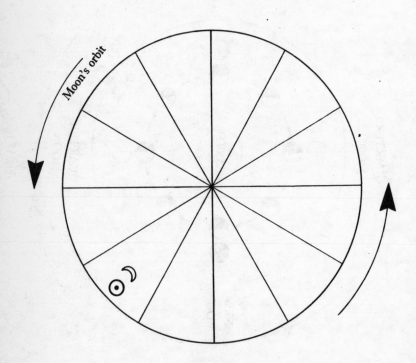

Fig 13.2

CONJUNCTION

When the Sun and Moon are in the same sign, the Moon is either at the end of the fourth quarter or the beginning of the first quarter.

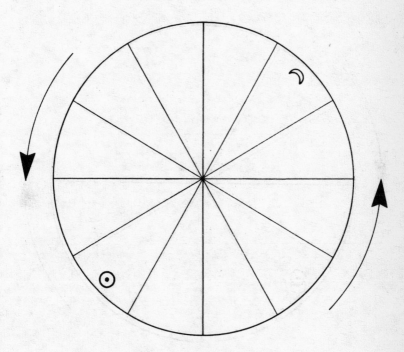

Fig 13.3

OPPOSITION

When the Sun and Moon are in opposite signs, the Moon is full (start of the third quarter)

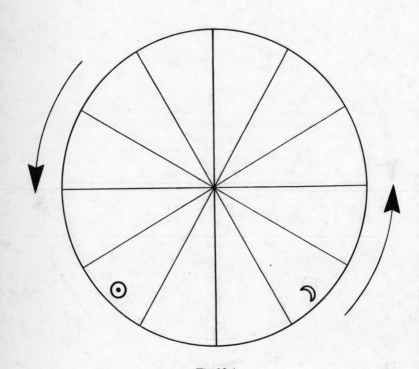

Fig 13.4

SQUARE

A 90° angle shows the Moon at the start of the second quarter.

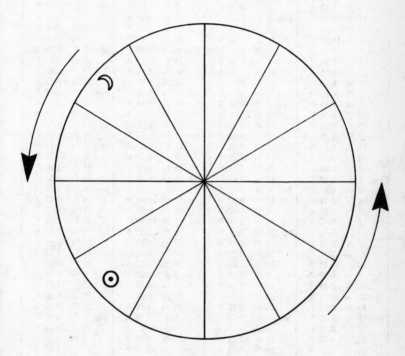

Fig 13.5

SQUARE

A 90° angle shows the Moon at the start of the fourth quarter.

1920	1921	1922	1923
Jan 5 F 9:06 P	Jan 1 ¾ 4:36 A	Jan 6 ¼ 10:25 A	Jan 3 F 2:34 A
13 ¾ 0:09 A	9 N 5:28 A	13 F 2:37 P	10 ¾ 0:55 A
21 N 5:28 A	17 ¼ 6:32 A	20 ¾ 6:01 A	17 N 2:42 A
28 ¼ 3:39 P	23 F 11:08 P	27 N 11:49 P	25 ¼ 4:00 A
Feb 4 F 8:43 A	30 ¾ 8:03 P	Feb 5 ¼ 4:53 A	Feb 1 F 3:54 P
11 ¾ 8:50 P	Feb 8 N 0:38 A	12 F 1:18 A	8 ¾ 9:17 A
19 N 9:35 P	15 ¼ 6:54 P	18 ¾ 6:19 P	15 N 7:08 P
26 ¼ 11:50 P	22 F 9:33 A	26 N 6:49 P	24 ¼ 0:07 A
Mar 4 F 9:13 P	Mar 1 ¾ 2:04 P	Mar 6 ¼ 7:22 P	Mar 3 F 3:24 A
12 ¾ 5:58 P	9 N 6:10 P	13 F 11:15 A	9 ¾ 6:32 P
20 N 10:56 A	17 ¼ 3:50 A	20 ¾ 8:44 A	17 N 0:52 P
27 ¼ 6:46 A	23 F 8:20 P	28 N 1:04 P	25 ¼ 4:42 P
Apr 3 F 10:55 A	31 ¾ 9:14 A	Apr 5 ¼ 5:46 A	Apr 1 F 1:11 P
11 ¾ 1:25 P	Apr 8 N 9:06 A	11 F 8:44 P	8 ¾ 5:23 A
18 N 9:44 P	15 ¼ 10:12 A	19 ¾ 0:55 A	16 N 6:29 A
25 ¼ 1:28 P	22 F 7:50 A	27 N 5:05 A	24 ¼ 5:21 A
May 3 F 1:48 A	30 ¾ 4:10 A	May 4 ¼ 0:56 P	30 F 9:31 P
11 ¾ 5:52 A	May 7 N 9:02 P	11 F 6:07 A	May 7 ¾ 6:19 P
18 N 6:26 A	14 ¼ 3:25 P	18 ¾ 6:18 P	15 N 10:39 P
24 ¼ 9:08 P	21 F 8:16 P	26 N 6:05 P	23 ¼ 2:26 P
Jun 1 F 5:19 P	29 ¾ 9:45 P	Jun 2 ¼ 6:10 P	30 F 5:08 A
9 ¾ 6:59 P	Jun 6 N 6:15 A	9 F 3:59 P	Jun 6 ¾ 9:20 A
16 N 1:42 P	12 ¼ 9:00 P	17 ¾ 0:04 P	14 N 0:43 P
23 ¼ 6:50 A	20 F 9:42 A	25 N 4:20 A	21 ¼ 8:47 P
Jul 1 F 8:42 A	28 ¾ 1:18 P	Jul 1 ¼ 10:53 P	28 F 1:05 P
9 ¾ 5:06 A	Jul 5 N 1:37 P	9 F 3:08 A	Jul 6 ¾ 1:57 A
15 N 8:26 P	12 ¼ 4:16 A	17 ¾ 5:12 A	14 N 0:46 A
22 ¼ 7:21 P	20 F 0:09 A	24 N 0:48 P	21 ¼ 1:33 A
30 F 11:20 P	28 ¾ 2:21 A	31 ¼ 4:22 A	27 F 10:34 P
Aug 7 ¾ 0:51 P	Aug 3 N 8:18 P	Aug 7 F 4:20 P	Aug 4 ¾ 7:23 P
14 N 3:44 A	10 ¼ 2:14 P	15 ¾ 8:47 P	12 N 11:17 A
21 ¼ 10:53 A	18 F 3:29 P	22 N 8:35 P	19 ¼ 6:08 A
29 F 1:04 P	26 ¾ 0:52 P	29 ¼ 11:56 A	26 F 10:30 A
Sep 5 ¾ 7:06 P	Sep 2 N 3:34 A	Sep 6 F 7:48 A	Sep 3 ¾ 0:48 P
12 N 0:52 P	9 ¼ 3:30 A	14 ¾ 10:21 A	10 N 8:54 P
20 ¼ 4:56 A	17 F 7:21 A	21 N 4:39 A	17 ¼ 0:05 P
28 F 1:57 A	24 ¾ 9:18 P	27 ¼ 10:41 P	25 F 1:17 A
Oct 5 ¾ 0:54 A	Oct 1 N 0:27 P	Oct 6 F 0:59 A	Oct 3 ¾ 5:30 A
12 N 0:51 A	8 ¼ 8:13 P	13 ¾ 9:56 P	10 N 6:06 A
20 ¼ 0:30 A	16 F 11:00 P	20 N 1:41 P	16 ¼ 8:54 P
27 F 2:10 P	24 ¾ 4:32 A	27 ¼ 1:27 P	24 F 6:27 P
Nov 3 ¾ 7:36 A	30 N 11:39 P	Nov 4 F 6:37 P	Nov 1 ¾ 8:50 P
10 N 4:06 P	Nov 7 ¼ 3:55 P	12 ¾ 7:53 A	8 N 3:28 P
18 ¼ 8:13 P	15 F 1:40 P	19 N 0:07 A	15 ¼ 9:42 A
26 F 1:43 A	22 ¾ 11:42 P	26 ¼ 8:16 A	23 F 0:59 P
Dec 2 ¾ 4:30 P	29 N 1:26 P	Dec 4 F 11:24 A	Dec 1 ¾ 10:10 A
10 N 10:05 A	Dec 7 ¼ 1:20 P	11 ¾ 4:41 P	8 N 1:31 A
18 ¼ 2:41 P	15 F 2:51 A	18 N 0:21 P	15 ¼ 2:39 A
25 F 0:39 P	21 ¾ 7:55 P	26 ¼ 5:54 A	23 F 7:34 A
	29 N 5:40 A		30 ¾ 9:08 P

1924				1925				1926				1927			
Jan	6	N	0:49 P	Jan	1	¼	11:27 P	Jan	7	¾	7:23 A	Jan	3	N	8:29 P
	13	¼	10:45 P		10	F	2:48 A		14	N	6:36 A		10	¼	2:44 P
	22	F	0:58 A		17	¾	11:34 P		20	¼	10:32 P		17	F	10:28 P
	29	¾	5:54 A		24	N	2:46 P		28	F	9:36 P		26	¾	2:06 A
Feb	5	N	1:39 A		31	¼	4:44 P	Feb	5	¾	11:26 P	Feb	2	N	8:55 A
	12	¼	8:10 P	Feb	8	F	9:50 P		12	N	5:21 P		8	¼	11:55 P
	20	F	4:08 P		16	¾	9:42 A		19	¼	0:37 P		16	F	4:19 P
	27	¾	1:16 P		23	N	2:13 A		27	F	4:52 P		24	¾	8:43 P
Mar	5	N	3:59 P	Mar	2	¼	0:08 P	Mar	7	¾	11:50 A	Mar	3	N	7:26 P
	13	¼	4:51 P		10	F	2:22 P		14	N	3:21 A		10	¼	11:04 A
	21	F	4:31 A		17	¾	5:22 P		21	¼	5:13 A		18	F	10:25 A
	27	¾	8:25 P		24	N	2:04 P		29	F	10:01 A		26	¾	11:36 A
Apr	4	N	7:18 A	Apr	1	¼	8:13 A	Apr	5	¾	8:51 P	Apr	2	N	4:25 A
	12	¼	11:13 A		9	F	3:34 A		12	N	0:57 P		9	¼	0:22 A
	19	F	2:12 P		15	¾	11:41 P		19	¼	11:24 P		17	F	3:36 A
	26	¾	4:29 A		23	N	2:29 A		28	F	0:18 A		24	¾	10:22 P
May	3	N	11:01 P	May	1	¼	3:21 A	May	5	¾	3:14 A	May	1	N	0:41 P
	12	¼	2:15 A		8	F	1:44 P		11	N	10:56 P		8	¼	3:28 P
	18	F	9:53 P		15	¾	5:47 A		19	¼	5:49 P		16	F	7:04 P
	25	¾	2:17 P		22	N	3:49 P		27	F	11:50 A		24	¾	5:35 A
Jun	2	N	2:35 P		30	¼	8:05 P	Jun	3	¾	8:10 A		30	N	9:07 P
	10	¼	1:38 P	Jun	6	F	9:49 P		10	N	10:09 A	Jun	7	¼	7:50 A
	17	F	4:42 A		13	¾	0:45 A		18	¼	11:15 A		15	F	8:20 A
	24	¾	2:17 A		21	N	6:18 A		25	F	9:14 P		22	¾	10:30 A
Jul	2	N	5:36 A		29	¼	9:44 A	Jul	2	¾	1:03 P		29	N	6:33 A
	9	¼	9:47 P	Jul	6	F	4:55 A		9	N	11:07 P	Jul	7	¼	0:53 A
	16	F	11:50 A		12	¾	9:35 P		18	¼	2:56 A		14	F	7:23 P
	23	¾	4:37 P		20	N	9:41 P		25	F	5:14 A		21	¾	2:44 P
	31	N	7:43 P		28	¼	8:24 P		31	¾	7:26 A		28	N	5:37 P
Aug	8	¼	3:42 A	Aug	4	F	12:00 P	Aug	8	N	1:50 P	Aug	5	¼	6:06 P
	14	F	8:20 P		11	¾	9:12 A		16	¼	4:40 P		13	F	4:38 A
	22	¾	9:12 A		19	N	1:16 P		23	F	0:39 P		19	¾	7:55 P
	30	N	8:38 A		27	¼	4:47 A		30	¾	4:41 A		27	N	6:47 A
Sep	6	¼	8:46 A	Sep	2	F	7:54 P	Sep	7	N	5:46 A	Sep	4	¼	10:46 A
	13	F	7:01 A		10	¾	0:13 A		15	¼	4:28 A		11	F	0:55 P
	21	¾	3:36 A		18	N	4:13 A		21	F	8:20 P		18	¾	3:31 A
	28	N	8:17 P		25	¼	11:52 A		28	¾	5:49 P		25	N	10:12 P
Oct	5	¼	2:31 P	Oct	2	F	5:24 A	Oct	6	N	10:14 P	Oct	4	¼	2:03 A
	12	F	8:22 P		9	¾	6:35 P		14	¼	2:29 P		10	F	9:16 P
	20	¾	10:55 P		17	N	6:07 P		21	F	5:16 A		17	¾	2:33 P
	28	N	6:58 A		24	¼	6:39 P		28	¾	10:58 A		25	N	3:39 P
Nov	3	¼	10:19 P		31	F	5:18 P	Nov	5	N	2:35 P	Nov	2	¼	3:17 P
	11	F	0:32 P	Nov	8	¾	3:14 P		12	¼	11:02 P		9	F	6:37 A
	19	¾	5:39 P		16	N	6:59 A		19	F	4:22 P		16	¾	5:29 A
	26	N	5:17 P		23	¼	2:06 A		27	¾	7:16 A		24	N	10:10 A
Dec	3	¼	9:11 A		30	F	8:12 A	Dec	5	N	6:13 A	Dec	2	¼	2:16 A
	11	F	7:05 A	Dec	8	¾	0:12 P		12	¼	6:48 A		8	F	5:33 P
	19	¾	10:12 A		15	N	7:06 P		19	F	6:10 A		16	¾	0:05 A
	26	N	3:46 A		22	¼	11:09 A		27	¾	5:00 A		24	N	4:14 A
					30	F	2:03 A						31	¼	11:23 A

1928			1929			1930			1931		
Jan 7	F	6:09 A	Jan 2	¾	6:45 P	Jan 8	¼	3:12 A	Jan 4	F	1:16 P
14	¾	9:15 P	11	N	0:29 A	14	F	10:22 P	11	¾	5:10 A
22	N	8:20 P	18	¼	3:16 P	21	¾	4:08 P	18	N	6:37 P
29	¼	7:27 P	25	F	7:10 A	29	N	7:08 P	27	¼	0:07 A
Feb 5	F	8:12 P	Feb 1	¾	2:11 P	Feb 6	¼	5:27 P	Feb 3	F	0:27 A
13	¾	7:06 P	9	N	5:56 P	13	F	8:39 A	9	¾	4:11 P
21	N	9:42 A	17	¼	0:23 A	20	¾	8:46 A	17	N	1:12 P
28	¼	3:22 A	23	F	7:00 P	28	N	1:34 P	25	¼	4:43 P
Mar 6	F	11:28 A	Mar 3	¾	11:10 A	Mar 8	¼	4:01 A	Mar 4	F	10:37 A
14	¾	3:21 P	11	N	8:38 A	14	F	6:59 P	11	¾	5:16 A
21	N	8:30 P	18	¼	7:42 A	22	¾	3:14 A	19	N	7:52 A
28	¼	11:55 A	25	F	7:47 A	30	N	5:47 A	27	¼	5:05 A
Apr 5	F	3:39 A	Apr 2	¾	7:30 A	Apr 6	¼	11:26 A	Apr 2	F	8:07 P
13	¾	8:10 A	9	N	8:34 P	13	F	5:50 A	9	¾	8:16 P
20	N	5:25 A	16	¼	2:10 P	20	¾	10:10 P	18	N	1:01 A
26	¼	9:43 P	23	F	9:49 P	28	N	7:10 P	25	¼	1:41 P
May 4	F	8:13 P	May 2	¾	1:27 A	May 5	¼	4:54 P	May 2	F	5:15 A
12	¾	8:51 P	9	N	6:08 A	12	F	5:30 P	9	¾	0:49 P
19	N	1:15 P	15	¼	8:57 P	20	¾	4:23 P	17	N	3:29 P
26	¼	9:13 A	23	F	0:51 P	28	N	5:38 A	24	¼	7:40 P
Jun 3	F	0:15 P	31	¾	4:14 P	Jun 3	¼	9:57 P	31	F	2:34 P
11	¾	5:52 A	Jun 7	N	1:57 P	11	F	6:13 A	Jun 8	¾	6:19 A
17	N	8:43 P	14	¼	5:16 A	19	¾	9:02 A	16	N	3:03 A
24	¼	10:48 P	22	F	4:16 A	26	N	1:48 P	23	¼	0:24 A
Jul 3	F	2:50 A	30	¾	3:55 A	Jul 3	¼	4:04 A	30	F	0:48 A
10	¾	0:17 P	Jul 6	N	8:48 P	10	F	8:02 P	Jul 7	¾	11:53 P
17	N	4:36 A	13	¼	4:06 P	18	¾	11:30 P	15	N	0:21 P
24	¼	2:39 P	21	F	7:22 P	25	N	8:43 P	22	¼	5:17 A
Aug 1	F	3:32 P	29	¾	0:57 P	Aug 1	¼	0:27 P	29	F	0:49 P
8	¾	5:25 P	Aug 5	N	3:41 A	9	F	10:59 A	Aug 6	¾	4:29 P
15	N	1:50 P	12	¼	6:03 A	17	¾	11:32 A	13	N	8:28 P
23	¼	8:22 A	20	F	9:43 A	24	N	3:38 A	20	¼	11:37 A
31	F	2:35 A	27	¾	8:03 P	30	¼	11:58 P	28	F	3:11 A
Sep 6	¾	10:36 P	Sep 3	N	11:48 A	Sep 8	F	2:49 A	Sep 5	¾	7:22 A
14	N	1:21 A	10	¼	10:58 P	15	¾	9:14 P	12	N	4:27 A
22	¼	2:59 A	18	F	11:17 P	22	N	11:43 A	18	¼	8:38 P
29	F	0:44 P	26	¾	2:08 A	29	¼	2:59 P	26	F	7:46 P
Oct 6	¾	5:07 A	Oct 2	N	10:20 P	Oct 7	F	6:57 P	Oct 4	¾	8:16 P
13	N	3:57 P	10	¼	6:06 P	15	¾	5:13 A	11	N	1:07 P
21	¼	9:07 P	18	F	0:07 P	21	N	9:49 P	18	¼	9:21 A
28	F	10:44 P	25	¾	8:22 A	29	¼	9:23 A	26	F	1:35 P
Nov 4	¾	2:07 P	Nov 1	N	0:02 P	Nov 6	F	10:29 A	Nov 3	¾	7:19 A
12	N	9:37 A	9	¼	2:11 P	13	¾	0:28 P	9	N	10:56 P
20	¼	1:37 P	17	F	0:15 A	20	N	10:22 A	17	¼	2:15 A
27	F	9:06 A	23	¾	4:05 P	28	¼	6:19 A	25	F	7:11 A
Dec 4	¾	2:33 A	Dec 1	N	4:50 A	Dec 6	F	0:41 A	Dec 2	¾	4:51 P
12	N	5:07 A	9	¼	9:43 A	12	¾	8:08 P	9	N	10:17 A
20	¼	3:44 A	16	F	11:39 A	20	N	1:25 A	16	¼	10:44 P
26	F	7:56 P	23	¾	2:28 A	28	¼	4:00 A	24	F	11:25 P
			30	N	11:43 P						

1932

Date	Phase	Time
Jan 1	¾	1:24 A
7	N	11:30 P
15	¼	8:56 P
23	F	1:45 P
30	¾	9:33 A
Feb 6	N	2:46 P
14	¼	6:17 P
22	F	2:08 A
28	¾	6:04 P
Mar 7	N	7:45 A
15	¼	0:42 P
22	F	0:38 P
29	¾	3:45 A
Apr 6	N	1:22 A
14	¼	3:17 A
20	F	9:28 P
27	¾	3:15 P
May 5	N	6:13 P
13	¼	2:03 P
20	F	5:09 A
27	¾	4:56 A
Jun 4	N	9:17 A
11	¼	9:40 P
18	F	0:39 P
25	¾	8:37 P
Jul 3	N	10:21 P
11	¼	3:08 A
17	F	9:07 P
25	¾	1:43 P
Aug 2	N	9:43 A
9	¼	7:42 A
16	F	7:43 A
24	¾	7:23 A
31	N	7:56 P
Sep 7	¼	0:50 P
14	F	9:07 P
23	¾	0:48 A
30	N	5:31 A
Oct 6	¼	8:06 P
14	F	1:19 P
22	¾	5:15 P
29	N	2:57 P
Nov 5	¼	6:52 A
13	F	7:29 A
21	¾	7:59 A
28	N	0:44 A
Dec 4	¼	9:46 P
13	F	2:22 A
20	¾	8:23 P
27	N	11:23 A

1933

Date	Phase	Time
Jan 3	¼	4:25 P
11	F	8:37 P
19	¾	6:16 A
25	N	11:21 P
Feb 2	¼	1:17 P
10	F	1:02 P
17	¾	2:09 P
24	N	0:45 P
Mar 4	¼	10:24 A
12	F	2:47 A
18	¾	9:06 P
26	N	3:21 A
Apr 3	¼	5:58 A
10	F	1:39 P
17	¾	4:19 A
24	N	6:39 P
May 2	¼	10:40 P
9	F	10:05 P
16	¾	0:51 P
24	N	10:08 A
Jun 1	¼	11:54 A
8	F	5:06 A
14	¾	11:27 P
23	N	1:23 A
30	¼	9:41 P
Jul 7	F	11:52 A
14	¾	0:25 P
22	N	4:04 P
30	¼	4:45 A
Aug 5	F	7:33 P
13	¾	3:51 A
21	N	5:49 A
28	¼	10:14 A
Sep 4	F	5:05 A
11	¾	9:31 P
19	N	6:22 P
26	¼	3:37 P
Oct 3	F	5:09 P
11	¾	4:47 P
19	N	5:46 A
25	¼	10:22 P
Nov 2	F	8:00 A
10	¾	0:19 P
17	N	4:25 P
24	¼	7:40 A
Dec 2	F	1:32 A
10	¾	6:25 A
17	N	2:54 A
23	¼	8:10 P
31	F	8:55 P

1934

Date	Phase	Time
Jan 8	¾	9:37 P
15	N	1:38 P
22	¼	11:51 A
30	F	4:33 P
Feb 7	¾	9:23 A
14	N	0:44 A
21	¼	6:06 A
Mar 1	F	10:27 A
8	¾	6:07 P
15	N	0:09 P
23	¼	1:46 A
31	F	1:16 A
Apr 7	¾	0:50 A
13	N	11:58 P
21	¼	9:22 P
29	F	0:47 P
May 6	¾	6:42 A
13	N	0:31 P
21	¼	3:21 P
28	F	9:42 P
Jun 4	¾	0:54 P
12	N	2:13 A
20	¼	6:38 A
27	F	5:09 A
Jul 3	¾	8:29 P
11	N	5:07 P
19	¼	6:54 P
26	F	0:10 P
Aug 2	¾	6:28 A
10	N	8:47 A
18	¼	4:34 A
24	F	7:38 P
31	¾	7:41 P
Sep 9	N	0:21 A
16	¼	0:27 P
23	F	4:20 A
30	¾	0:30 P
Oct 8	N	3:06 P
15	¼	7:30 P
22	F	3:02 P
30	¾	8:23 A
Nov 7	N	4:45 A
14	¼	2:40 A
21	F	4:27 A
29	¾	5:40 A
Dec 6	N	5:26 P
13	¼	10:53 A
20	F	8:55 P
29	¾	2:09 A

1935

Date	Phase	Time
Jan 5	N	5:21 A
11	¼	8:56 P
19	F	3:45 P
27	¾	8:00 P
Feb 3	N	4:28 P
10	¼	9:26 A
18	F	11:18 A
26	¾	10:15 A
Mar 5	N	2:41 A
12	¼	0:31 A
20	F	5:33 A
27	¾	8:52 P
Apr 3	N	0:12 P
10	¼	5:43 P
18	F	9:11 P
26	¾	4:22 A
May 2	N	9:37 P
10	¼	11:55 A
18	F	9:58 A
25	¾	9:45 A
Jun 1	N	7:53 A
9	¼	5:51 A
16	F	8:21 P
23	¾	2:22 P
30	N	7:46 P
Jul 8	¼	10:29 P
16	F	5:01 A
22	¾	7:43 P
30	N	9:34 A
Aug 7	¼	1:24 A
14	F	0:45 P
21	¾	3:19 A
29	N	1:02 A
Sep 6	¼	2:27 A
12	F	8:19 P
19	¾	2:24 P
27	N	5:31 P
Oct 5	¼	1:41 P
12	F	4:40 A
19	¾	5:38 A
27	N	10:17 A
Nov 3	¼	11:13 P
10	F	2:43 P
18	¾	0:37 A
26	N	2:37 A
Dec 3	¼	7:29 A
10	F	3:11 A
17	¾	9:59 P
25	N	5:51 P

1936	1937	1938	1939
Jan 1 ¼ 3:16 P	Jan 4 ¾ 2:23 P	Jan 1 N 6:59 P	Jan 5 F 9:31 P
8 F 6:16 P	12 N 4:48 P	9 ¼ 2:14 P	12 ¾ 1:12 P
16 ¾ 7:42 P	19 ¼ 8:03 P	16 F 5:54 A	20 N 1:28 P
24 N 7:19 A	26 F 5:16 P	23 ¾ 8:10 A	28 ¼ 3:01 P
30 ¼ 11:37 P	Feb 3 ¾ 0:06 P	31 N 1:36 P	Feb 4 F 7:56 A
Feb 7 F 11:20 A	11 N 7:35 A	Feb 8 ¼ 0:34 A	11 ¾ 4:13 A
15 ¾ 3:47 P	18 ¼ 3:51 A	14 F 5:16 P	19 N 8:29 A
22 N 6:43 P	25 F 7:44 A	22 ¾ 4:26 A	27 ¼ 3:27 A
29 ¼ 9:29 A	Mar 5 ¾ 9:18 A	Mar 2 N 5:41 A	Mar 5 F 6:02 P
Mar 8 F 5:15 A	12 N 7:33 P	9 ¼ 8:36 A	12 ¾ 9:38 P
16 ¾ 8:36 A	19 ¼ 11:47 A	16 F 5:16 A	21 N 1:51 A
23 N 4:14 A	26 F 11:13 P	24 ¾ 1:07 A	28 ¼ 0:17 P
29 ¼ 9:23 P	Apr 4 ¾ 3:54 A	31 N 6:53 P	Apr 4 F 4:19 A
Apr 6 F 10:48 P	11 N 5:11 A	Apr 7 ¼ 3:11 P	11 ¾ 4:13 P
14 ¾ 9:22 P	17 ¼ 8:35 P	14 F 6:22 P	19 N 4:36 P
21 N 0:34 P	25 F 3:25 P	22 ¾ 8:16 P	26 ¼ 6:26 P
28 ¼ 11:17 A	May 3 ¾ 6:38 P	30 N 5:29 A	May 3 F 3:16 P
May 6 F 3:02 P	10 N 1:18 P	May 6 ¼ 9:25 P	11 ¾ 10:41 A
14 ¾ 6:13 A	17 ¼ 6:51 A	14 F 8:40 A	19 N 4:26 A
20 N 8:36 P	25 F 7:39 A	22 ¾ 0:37 P	25 ¼ 11:21 P
28 ¼ 2:47 A	Jun 2 ¾ 5:25 A	29 N 2:01 P	Jun 2 F 3:12 A
Jun 5 F 5:24 A	8 N 8:44 P	Jun 5 ¼ 4:33 A	10 ¾ 4:08 A
12 ¾ 0:06 P	15 ¼ 7:04 P	12 F 11:48 P	17 N 1:38 P
19 N 5:15 A	23 F 11:01 P	21 ¾ 1:53 A	24 ¼ 4:36 A
26 ¼ 7:24 P	Jul 1 ¾ 1:04 P	27 N 9:11 P	Jul 1 F 4:17 P
Jul 4 F 5:36 P	8 N 4:14 A	Jul 4 ¼ 1:48 P	9 ¾ 7:50 P
11 ¾ 4:29 P	15 ¼ 9:38 A	12 F 3:06 P	16 N 9:04 P
18 N 3:20 P	23 F 0:47 P	20 ¾ 0:20 P	23 ¼ 11:35 A
26 ¼ 0:37 P	30 ¾ 6:48 P	27 N 3:54 A	31 F 6:38 A
Aug 3 F 3:48 A	Aug 6 N 0:38 P	Aug 3 ¼ 2:01 A	Aug 8 ¾ 9:19 A
9 ¾ 9:00 P	14 ¼ 2:30 A	11 F 5:58 A	15 N 3:54 A
17 N 3:22 A	22 F 0:48 A	18 ¾ 8:31 P	21 ¼ 9:22 P
25 ¼ 5:50 A	28 ¾ 11:56 P	25 N 11:18 A	29 F 10:10 P
Sep 1 F 0:38 P	Sep 4 N 10:55 P	Sep 1 ¼ 5:29 P	Sep 6 ¾ 8:26 P
8 ¾ 3:15 A	12 ¼ 8:58 P	9 F 8:09 P	13 N 11:23 A
15 N 5:43 P	20 F 11:34 A	17 ¾ 3:13 A	20 ¼ 10:35 A
23 ¼ 10:14 P	27 ¾ 5:44 A	23 N 8:35 P	28 F 2:28 P
30 F 9:02 P	Oct 4 N 11:59 A	Oct 1 ¼ 11:46 A	Oct 6 ¾ 5:29 A
Oct 7 ¾ 0:29 P	12 ¼ 3:48 P	9 F 9:38 A	12 N 8:31 P
15 N 10:22 A	19 F 9:49 P	16 ¾ 9:25 A	20 ¼ 3:26 A
23 ¼ 0:55 P	26 ¾ 1:27 P	23 N 8:43 A	28 F 6:43 A
30 F 5:59 A	Nov 3 N 4:17 A	31 ¼ 7:46 A	Nov 4 ¾ 1:13 P
Nov 6 ¾ 1:30 A	11 ¼ 9:35 A	Nov 7 F 10:25 P	11 N 7:55 A
14 N 4:43 A	18 F 8:10 A	14 ¾ 4:21 P	18 ¼ 11:22 P
22 ¼ 1:20 A	25 ¾ 0:05 A	22 N 0:06 A	26 F 9:56 P
28 F 4:13 P	Dec 2 N 11:12 P	30 ¼ 4:01 A	Dec 3 ¾ 8:41 P
Dec 5 ¾ 6:21 P	11 ¼ 1:14 A	Dec 7 F 10:23 A	10 N 9:47 P
13 N 11:26 P	17 F 6:54 P	14 ¾ 1:18 A	18 ¼ 9:05 P
21 ¼ 11:31 A	24 ¾ 2:21 P	21 N 6:08 P	26 F 11:30 A
28 F 4:01 A		29 ¼ 10:54 P	

1940	1941	1942	1943
Jan 2 ¾ 4:57 A	Jan 5 ¼ 1:41 P	Jan 2 F 3:43 P	Jan 6 N 0:39 P
9 N 1:54 P	13 F 11:05 A	10 ¾ 6:06 A	13 ¼ 7:50 A
17 ¼ 6:22 P	20 ¾ 10:03 A	16 N 9:33 P	21 F 10:49 A
24 F 11:23 P	27 N 11:04 A	24 ¼ 6:37 A	29 ¾ 8:14 A
31 ¾ 2:48 P	Feb 4 ¼ 11:44 A	Feb 1 F 9:13 A	Feb 4 N 11:30 P
Feb 8 N 7:46 A	12 F 0:28 A	8 ¾ 2:53 P	12 ¼ 0:41 A
16 ¼ 0:57 P	18 ¾ 6:08 P	15 N 10:04 A	20 F 5:46 A
23 F 9:56 A	26 N 3:03 A	23 ¼ 3:41 A	27 ¾ 6:24 P
Mar 1 ¾ 2:36 A	Mar 6 ¼ 7:44 A	Mar 3 F 0:21 a	Mar 6 N 10:35 A
9 N 2:24 A	13 F 11:48 A	9 ¾ 10:02 P	13 ¼ 7:31 P
17 ¼ 3:26 A	20 ¾ 2:53 A	16 N 11:51 P	21 F 10:09 A
23 F 7:34 P	27 N 8:15 P	25 ¼ 0:02 A	29 ¾ 1:53 A
30 ¾ 4:21 P	Apr 5 ¼ 0:13 A	Apr 1 F 0:33 P	Apr 4 N 9:54 P
Apr 7 N 8:20 P	11 F 9:16 P	8 ¾ 4:44 A	12 ¼ 3:05 P
15 ¼ 1:47 P	18 ¾ 1:04 P	15 N 2:35 P	20 F 11:12 A
22 F 4:38 A	26 N 1:24 A	23 ¼ 6:11 P	27 ¾ 7:52 A
29 ¾ 7:50 A	May 4 ¼ 0:50 P	30 F 10:01 P	May 4 N 9:44 A
May 7 N 0:08 P	11 F 5:16 A	May 7 ¾ 0:14 P	12 ¼ 9:54 A
14 ¼ 8:52 P	18 ¾ 1:18 A	15 N 5:46 A	19 F 9:14 P
21 F 1:34 P	26 N 5:20 A	23 ¼ 9:12 A	26 ¾ 1:35 P
29 ¾ 0:42 A	Jun 2 ¼ 9:57 P	30 F 5:30 A	Jun 2 N 10:34 P
Jun 6 N 1:06 A	9 F 0:35 P	Jun 5 ¾ 9:27 P	11 ¼ 2:37 A
13 ¼ 2:00 A	16 ¾ 3:46 P	13 N 9:03 P	18 F 5:15 A
19 F 11:03 P	24 N 7:23 P	21 ¼ 8:46 P	24 ¾ 8:09 P
27 ¾ 6:14 P	Jul 2 ¼ 4:25 A	28 F 0:10 P	Jul 2 N 0:45 P
Jul 5 N 11:29 A	8 F 8:19 P	Jul 5 ¾ 8:59 A	10 ¼ 4:30 P
12 ¼ 6:36 A	16 ¾ 8:09 A	13 N 0:04 P	17 F 0:23 P
19 F 9:57 A	24 N 7:40 A	21 ¼ 5:14 A	24 ¾ 4:40 A
27 ¾ 11:31 A	31 ¼ 9:20 A	27 F 7:15 P	Aug 1 N 4:08 A
Aug 3 N 8:10 P	Aug 7 F 5:40 A	Aug 3 ¾ 11:05 P	9 ¼ 3:37 A
10 ¼ 0:01 P	15 ¾ 1:41 A	12 N 2:29 A	15 F 7:35 P
17 F 11:04 P	22 N 6:35 P	19 ¼ 11:32 A	22 ¾ 4:05 P
26 ¾ 3:34 A	29 ¼ 2:05 P	26 F 3:47 A	30 N 8:01 P
Sep 2 N 4:16 A	Sep 5 F 5:37 P	Sep 2 ¾ 3:43 P	Sep 7 ¼ 0:34 P
8 ¼ 7:33 P	13 ¾ 7:32 P	10 N 3:54 P	14 F 3:41 A
16 F 2:42 P	21 N 4:40 A	17 ¼ 4:58 P	21 ¾ 7:07 A
24 ¾ 5:48 P	27 ¼ 8:10 P	24 F 2:35 P	29 N 11:31 A
Oct 1 N 0:42 P	Oct 5 F 8:34 A	Oct 2 ¾ 10:28 A	Oct 6 ¼ 8:11 P
8 ¼ 6:19 A	13 ¾ 0:53 P	10 N 4:07 A	13 F 1:24 P
16 F 8:16 A	20 N 2:21 P	16 ¼ 10:59 P	21 ¾ 1:43 A
24 ¾ 6:05 A	27 ¼ 5:05 P	24 F 4:07 A	29 N 2:00 A
30 N 10:04 P	Nov 4 F 2:01 A	Nov 1 ¾ 6:19 A	Nov 5 ¼ 3:23 A
Nov 6 ¼ 9:09 P	12 ¾ 4:55 A	8 N 3:20 P	12 F 1:28 A
15 F 2:25 A	19 N 0:05 A	15 ¼ 6:58 A	19 ¾ 10:44 P
22 ¾ 4:37 P	25 ¼ 5:54 P	22 F 8:26 P	27 N 3:24 P
29 N 8:43 A	Dec 3 F 8:52 P	Dec 1 ¾ 1:38 A	Dec 4 ¼ 11:05 A
Dec 6 ¼ 4:02 P	11 ¾ 6:49 P	8 N 2:00 A	11 F 4:26 P
14 F 7:39 P	18 N 10:19 A	14 ¼ 5:48 P	19 ¾ 8:05 P
22 ¾ 1:46 A	25 ¼ 10:45 A	22 F 3:04 P	27 N 3:51 A
28 N 8:57 P		30 ¾ 6:38 P	

1944	1945	1946	1947
Jan 2 ¼ 8:05 P	Jan 6 ¾ 0:49 P	Jan 3 N 0:31 P	Jan 7 F 4:48 A
10 F 10:11 A	14 N 5:08 A	10 ¼ 8:28 P	14 ¾ 2:57 A
18 ¾ 3:33 P	20 ¼ 11:49 P	17 F 2:48 P	22 N 8:36 A
25 N 3:25 P	28 F 6:42 A	25 ¾ 5:01 A	30 ¼ 0:08 A
Feb 1 ¼ 7:09 A	Feb 5 ¾ 9:57 A	Feb 2 N 4:44 A	Feb 5 F 3:52 P
9 F 5:31 A	12 N 5:34 P	9 ¼ 4:29 A	12 ¾ 9:59 P
17 ¾ 7:43 A	19 ¼ 8:39 A	16 F 4:29 A	21 N 2:01 A
24 N 2:00 A	27 F 0:08 A	24 ¾ 2:38 A	28 ¼ 9:13 A
Mar 1 ¼ 8:41 P	Mar 7 ¾ 4:31 A	Mar 3 N 6:03 P	Mar 7 F 3:16 A
10 F 0:29 A	14 N 3:52 A	10 ¼ 0:04 P	14 ¾ 6:29 P
17 ¾ 8:06 P	20 ¼ 7:13 P	17 F 7:12 P	22 N 4:35 P
24 N 11:37 A	28 F 5:46 P	25 ¾ 10:39 P	29 ¼ 4:16 P
31 ¼ 0:36 P	Apr 5 ¾ 7:20 P	Apr 2 N 4:38 A	Apr 5 F 3:30 P
Apr 8 F 5:23 P	12 N 0:31 P	8 ¼ 8:05 P	13 ¾ 2:25 P
16 ¾ 5:00 A	19 ¼ 7:48 A	16 F 10:48 A	21 N 4:20 A
22 N 8:45 P	27 F 10:34 A	24 ¾ 3:20 P	27 ¼ 10:19 P
30 ¼ 6:08 A	May 5 ¾ 6:03 A	May 1 N 1:17 P	May 5 F 4:55 A
May 8 F 7:29 A	11 N 8:23 P	8 ¼ 5:15 A	13 ¾ 8:09 A
15 ¾ 11:13 A	18 ¼ 10:13 P	16 F 2:54 A	20 N 1:45 P
22 N 6:14 A	27 F 1:50 A	24 ¾ 4:03 A	27 ¼ 4:37 A
30 ¼ 0:08 A	Jun 3 ¾ 1:16 P	30 N 8:51 P	Jun 3 F 7:28 P
Jun 6 F 6:59 P	10 N 4:27 A	Jun 6 ¼ 4:08 P	11 ¾ 10:59 P
13 ¾ 3:58 P	17 ¼ 2:07 P	14 F 6:43 P	18 N 9:27 P
20 N 5:01 P	25 F 3:09 P	22 ¾ 1:13 P	25 ¼ 0:26 P
28 ¼ 5:28 P	Jul 2 ¾ 6:14 P	29 N 4:07 A	Jul 3 F 10:40 A
Jul 6 F 4:28 A	9 N 1:36 P	Jul 6 ¼ 5:17 A	11 ¾ 10:56 A
12 ¾ 8:40 P	17 ¼ 7:02 A	14 F 9:24 A	18 N 4:16 A
20 N 5:44 A	25 F 2:27 A	21 ¾ 7:53 P	24 ¼ 10:55 P
28 ¼ 9:25 A	31 ¾ 10:31 P	28 N 11:55 A	Aug 2 F 1:51 A
Aug 4 F 0:40 P	Aug 8 N 0:33 A	Aug 4 ¼ 8:57 P	9 ¾ 8:23 P
11 ¾ 2:53 A	16 ¼ 0:28 A	12 F 10:27 P	16 N 11:14 A
18 N 8:26 P	23 F 0:04 P	20 ¾ 1:18 A	23 ¼ 0:41 P
26 ¼ 11:40 P	30 ¾ 3:46 A	26 N 9:09 P	31 F 4:35 P
Sep 2 F 8:22 P	Sep 6 N 1:45 P	Sep 3 ¼ 2:50 P	Sep 8 ¾ 3:58 A
9 ¾ 0:04 P	14 ¼ 5:40 P	11 F 10:01 A	14 N 7:29 P
17 N 0:38 P	21 F 8:47 P	18 ¾ 6:46 A	22 ¼ 5:43 A
25 ¼ 0:08 P	28 ¾ 11:25 A	25 N 8:46 A	30 F 6:42 A
Oct 2 F 4:23 A	Oct 6 N 5:24 A	Oct 3 ¼ 9:55 A	Oct 7 ¾ 10:30 A
9 ¾ 1:13 A	14 ¼ 9:39 A	10 F 8:42 P	14 N 6:11 A
17 N 5:36 A	21 F 5:33 A	17 ¾ 1:29 P	22 ¼ 1:12 A
24 ¼ 10:49 P	27 ¾ 10:31 P	24 N 11:33 P	29 F 8:08 P
31 F 1:37 P	Nov 4 N 11:12 P	Nov 2 ¼ 4:42 A	Nov 5 ¾ 5:05 P
Nov 7 ¾ 6:30 P	12 ¼ 11:35 P	9 F 7:11 A	12 N 8:02 P
15 N 10:31 P	19 F 3:14 P	15 ¾ 10:36 P	20 ¼ 9:45 P
23 ¼ 7:54 A	26 ¾ 1:29 P	23 N 5:25 P	28 F 8:46 A
30 F 0:53 A	Dec 4 N 6:08 P	Dec 1 ¼ 9:49 P	Dec 5 ¾ 0:56 A
Dec 7 ¾ 2:58 P	12 ¼ 11:06 A	8 F 5:53 P	12 N 0:55 P
15 N 2:36 P	19 F 2:18 A	15 ¾ 10:58 A	20 ¼ 5:45 P
22 ¼ 3:55 P	26 ¾ 8:02 A	23 N 1:07 P	27 F 8:28 P
29 F 2:39 P		31 ¼ 0:24 P	

1948	1949	1950	1951
Jan 3 ¾ 11:14 A	Jan 7 ¼ 11:53 A	Jan 4 F 7:48 A	Jan 1 ¾ 5:12 A
11 N 7:46 A	14 F 10:01 P	11 ¾ 10:32 A	7 N 8:11 P
19 ¼ 11:33 A	21 ¾ 2:09 P	18 N 8:00 A	15 ¼ 0:23 A
26 F 7:12 A	29 N 2:44 A	26 ¼ 4:40 A	23 F 4:48 A
Feb 2 ¾ 0:33 A	Feb 6 ¼ 8:07 A	Feb 2 F 10:17 P	30 ¾ 3:14 P
10 N 3:03 A	13 F 9:09 A	9 ¾ 6:33 P	Feb 6 N 7:54 P
18 ¼ 1:56 A	20 ¾ 0:44 A	16 N 10:53 P	13 ¼ 8:56 P
24 F 5:17 P	27 N 8:56 P	25 ¼ 1:53 P	21 F 9:13 P
Mar 2 ¾ 4:37 P	Mar 8 ¼ 0:43 A	Mar 4 F 10:34 A	28 ¾ 11:00 P
10 N 9:16 P	14 F 7:04 P	11 ¾ 2:39 A	Mar 7 N 8:51 P
18 ¼ 0:28 P	21 ¾ 1:12 P	18 N 3:21 P	15 ¼ 5:40 P
25 F 3:11 A	29 N 3:12 P	26 ¼ 8:10 P	23 F 10:50 A
Apr 1 ¾ 10:26 A	Apr 6 ¼ 1:03 P	Apr 2 F 8:49 P	30 ¾ 5:35 A
9 N 1:18 P	13 F 4:09 A	9 ¾ 11:43 A	Apr 6 N 10:52 A
16 ¼ 7:43 P	20 ¾ 3:29 A	17 N 8:26 A	14 ¼ 0:56 P
23 F 1:30 P	28 N 8:04 A	25 ¼ 10:40 A	21 F 9:31 P
May 1 ¾ 4:50 A	May 5 ¼ 9:34 P	May 2 F 5:20 A	28 ¾ 0:18 P
9 N 2:31 A	12 F 0:52 P	8 ¾ 10:32 P	May 6 N 1:36 A
16 ¼ 0:56 A	19 ¾ 7:23 P	17 N 0:55 A	14 ¼ 5:32 A
23 F 0:38 A	27 N 10:25 P	24 ¼ 9:29 P	21 F 5:45 A
30 ¾ 10:44 P	Jun 4 ¼ 3:28 A	31 F 0:44 P	27 ¾ 8:17 P
Jun 7 N 0:57 P	10 F 9:47 P	Jun 7 ¾ 11:36 A	Jun 4 N 4:41 P
14 ¼ 5:41 A	18 ¾ 0:31 P	15 N 3:53 P	12 ¼ 6:52 P
21 F 0:55 P	26 N 10:03 A	23 ¼ 5:13 A	19 F 0:37 P
29 ¾ 3:24 P	Jul 3 ¼ 8:09 A	29 F 7:59 P	26 ¾ 6:22 A
Jul 6 N 9:10 P	10 F 7:42 A	Jul 7 ¾ 2:54 A	Jul 4 N 7:49 A
13 ¼ 11:31 A	18 ¾ 6:03 A	15 N 5:06 A	12 ¼ 4:57 A
21 F 2:32 A	25 N 7:34 P	22 ¼ 10:51 A	18 F 7:18 A
29 ¾ 6:13 A	Aug 1 ¼ 0:59 P	29 F 4:18 A	25 ¾ 7:00 P
Aug 5 N 4:14 A	8 F 7:35 P	Aug 5 ¾ 7:56 P	Aug 2 N 10:40 P
11 ¼ 7:41 P	16 ¾ 11:00 P	13 N 4:49 P	10 ¼ 0:23 P
19 F 5:33 P	24 N 4:00 A	20 ¼ 3:36 P	17 F 3:00 A
27 ¾ 6:47 P	30 ¼ 7:18 P	27 F 2:52 P	24 ¾ 10:21 A
Sep 3 N 11:22 A	Sep 7 F 10:01 A	Sep 4 ¾ 1:54 P	Sep 1 N 0:50 P
10 ¼ 7:06 A	15 ¾ 2:30 P	12 N 3:29 A	8 ¼ 6:17 P
18 F 9:44 A	22 N 0:22 P	18 ¼ 8:55 P	15 F 0:39 P
26 ¾ 5:08 A	29 ¼ 4:20 A	26 F 4:22 A	23 ¾ 4:14 A
Oct 2 N 7:43 P	Oct 7 F 2:54 A	Oct 4 ¾ 7:54 A	Oct 1 N 1:57 A
9 ¼ 10:12 P	15 ¾ 4:07 A	11 N 1:34 P	8 ¼ 0:01 A
18 F 2:25 A	21 N 9:24 P	18 ¼ 4:18 A	15 F 0:52 P
25 ¾ 1:43 P	28 ¼ 5:06 P	25 F 8:47 P	22 ¼ 11:56 P
Nov 1 N 6:04 A	Nov 5 F 9:10 P	Nov 3 ¾ 1:01 A	30 N 1:55 P
8 ¼ 4:48 P	13 ¾ 3:49 P	9 N 11:26 P	Nov 6 ¼ 6:59 A
16 F 6:33 P	20 N 7:30 A	16 ¼ 3:07 P	13 F 3:53 P
23 ¾ 9:23 P	27 ¼ 10:03 A	24 F 3:15 P	21 ¾ 8:02 P
30 N 6:46 P	Dec 5 F 3:15 P	Dec 2 ¾ 4:22 P	29 N 1:01 A
Dec 8 ¼ 1:59 A	13 ¾ 1:49 A	9 N 9:29 P	Dec 5 ¼ 4:21 P
16 F 9:12 A	19 N 6:57 P	16 ¼ 5:57 A	13 F 9:31 A
23 ¾ 5:13 A	27 ¼ 6:33 A	24 F 10:24 A	21 ¾ 2:38 P
30 N 9:46 A			28 N 11:44 A

1952	1953	1954	1955
Jan 4 ¼ 4:43 A	Jan 8 ¾ 10:10 A	Jan 5 N 2:22 A	Jan 1 ¼ 8:29 P
12 F 4:56 A	15 N 2:09 P	12 ¼ 0:22 A	8 F 0:45 P
20 ¾ 6:10 A	22 ¼ 5:43 A	19 F 2:37 A	15 ¾ 10:14 P
26 N 10:27 P	29 F 11:45 P	27 ¾ 3:29 A	24 N 1:07 A
Feb 2 ¼ 8:02 P	Feb 7 ¾ 4:10 A	Feb 3 N 3:56 P	31 ¼ 5:06 A
11 F 0:29 A	14 N 1:11 A	10 ¼ 8:30 A	Feb 7 F 1:43 A
18 ¾ 6:02 P	20 ¼ 5:45 A	17 F 7:18 P	14 ¾ 7:40 P
25 N 9:16 A	28 F 6:59 P	25 ¾ 11:30 P	22 N 3:55 P
Mar 3 ¼ 1:44 P	Mar 8 ¾ 6:27 P	Mar 5 N 3:12 A	Mar 1 ¼ 0:41 P
11 F 6:15 P	15 N 11:05 A	11 ¼ 5:52 P	8 F 3:42 P
19 ¾ 2:40 A	22 ¼ 8:11 A	19 F 0:43 P	16 ¾ 4:37 P
25 N 8:13 P	30 F 0:55 P	27 ¾ 4:14 P	24 N 3:43 A
Apr 2 ¼ 8:49 A	Apr 7 ¾ 4:59 A	Apr 3 N 0:25 P	30 ¼ 8:10 P
10 F 8:54 A	13 N 8:10 P	10 ¼ 5:06 A	Apr 7 F 6:36 A
17 ¾ 9:08 A	21 ¼ 0:41 A	18 F 5:49 A	15 ¾ 11:01 A
24 N 7:28 A	29 F 4:21 A	26 ¾ 4:58 A	22 N 1:07 P
May 2 ¼ 3:58 A	May 6 ¾ 0:21 P	May 2 N 8:23 P	29 ¼ 4:24 A
9 F 8:16 P	13 N 5:06 A	9 ¼ 6:18 P	May 6 F 10:15 P
16 ¾ 2:40 P	20 ¼ 6:21 P	17 F 9:48 P	15 ¾ 1:43 A
23 N 7:28 P	28 F 5:04 P	25 ¾ 1:50 P	21 N 8:59 P
31 ¼ 9:47 P	Jun 4 ¾ 5:36 P	Jun 1 N 4:03 A	28 ¼ 2:02 P
Jun 8 F 5:07 A	11 N 2:55 P	8 ¼ 9:14 A	Jun 5 F 2:09 P
14 ¾ 8:28 P	19 ¼ 0:02 P	16 F 0:06 P	13 ¾ 0:38 P
22 N 8:46 P	27 F 3:30 A	23 ¾ 7:46 P	20 N 4:12 A
30 ¼ 1:12 P	Jul 3 ¾ 10:04 A	30 N 0:26 P	27 ¼ 1:45 A
Jul 7 F 0:34 P	11 N 2:29 A	Jul 8 ¼ 1:34 A	Jul 5 F 5:29 A
14 ¾ 3:43 A	19 ¼ 4:48 A	16 F 0:30 A	12 ¾ 8:31 P
21 N 11:31 P	26 F 0:21 P	23 ¾ 0:14 A	19 N 11:35 A
30 ¼ 1:52 A	Aug 2 ¾ 3:17 A	29 N 10:20 P	26 ¼ 4:00 P
Aug 5 F 7:41 P	9 N 4:11 P	Aug 6 ¼ 6:51 P	Aug 3 F 7:31 P
12 ¾ 1:28 P	17 ¼ 8:09 P	14 F 11:04 P	11 ¾ 2:33 A
20 N 3:21 P	24 F 8:21 P	23 ¾ 4:52 A	17 N 7:59 P
28 ¼ 0:04 P	31 ¾ 10:47 A	28 N 10:21 A	25 ¼ 8:52 A
Sep 4 F 3:20 A	Sep 8 N 7:49 A	Sep 5 ¼ 0:29 P	Sep 2 F 8:00 A
11 ¾ 2:37 A	16 ¼ 9:50 A	12 F 8:20 P	9 ¾ 8:00 A
19 N 7:22 A	23 F 4:16 A	19 ¾ 11:12 A	16 N 6:20 A
26 ¼ 8:31 P	29 ¾ 9:52 P	27 N 0:51 A	24 ¼ 3:41 A
Oct 3 F 0:16 P	Oct 8 N 0:41 A	Oct 5 ¼ 5:32 A	Oct 1 F 7:18 P
10 ¾ 7:33 P	15 ¼ 9:45 P	12 F 5:10 A	8 ¾ 2:04 P
18 N 10:43 P	22 F 0:56 P	18 ¾ 8:31 A	15 N 7:33 P
26 ¼ 4:05 A	29 ¾ 1:10 P	26 N 5:48 P	23 ¼ 11:05 P
Nov 1 F 11:10 P	Nov 6 N 5:58 P	Nov 3 ¼ 8:55 P	31 F 6:04 A
9 ¾ 3:44 P	14 ¼ 7:53 A	10 F 2:30 P	Nov 6 ¾ 9:57 P
17 N 0:56 P	20 F 11:13 P	17 ¾ 9:33 A	14 N 0:02 P
24 ¼ 11:35 A	28 ¾ 8:17 A	25 N 0:31 P	22 ¼ 5:30 P
Dec 1 F 0:42 P	Dec 6 N 10:49 A	Dec 3 ¼ 9:57 A	29 F 4:51 P
9 ¾ 1:22 P	13 ¼ 4:31 P	10 F 0:57 A	Dec 6 ¾ 8:36 A
17 N 2:03 A	20 F 11:44 A	17 ¾ 2:22 A	14 N 7:08 A
23 ¼ 7:52 P	28 ¾ 5:44 A	25 N 7:34 A	22 ¼ 9:40 A
31 F 5:06 A			29 F 3:44 A

1956

Jan 4 ¾ 10:42 P
13 N 3:02 A
20 ¼ 10:59 P
27 F 2:41 P
Feb 3 ¾ 4:09 P
11 N 9:38 P
19 ¼ 9:22 A
26 F 1:42 A
Mar 4 ¾ 11:54 A
12 N 1:37 P
19 ¼ 5:14 P
26 F 1:12 P
Apr 3 ¾ 8:07 A
11 N 2:39 A
17 ¼ 11:29 P
25 F 1:41 A
May 3 ¾ 2:56 A
10 N 1:05 P
17 ¼ 5:16 A
24 F 3:27 P
Jun 1 ¾ 7:14 P
8 N 9:30 P
15 ¼ 11:57 A
23 F 6:14 A
Jul 1 ¾ 8:41 A
8 N 4:38 A
14 ¼ 8:47 P
22 F 9:30 P
30 ¾ 7:32 P
Aug 6 N 11:25 A
13 ¼ 8:46 A
21 F 0:38 P
29 ¾ 4:13 A
Sep 4 N 6:58 P
12 ¼ 0:14 A
20 F 3:20 A
27 ¾ 11:26 A
Oct 4 N 4:25 A
11 ¼ 6:45 P
19 F 5:25 P
26 ¾ 6:03 A
Nov 2 N 4:44 P
10 ¼ 3:10 P
18 F 6:45 A
25 ¾ 1:13 A
Dec 2 N 8:13 A
10 ¼ 11:52 A
17 F 7:07 P
24 ¾ 10:10 A

1957

Jan 1 N 2:14 A
9 ¼ 7:07 A
16 F 6:22 A
22 ¾ 9:48 P
30 N 9:26 P
Feb 7 ¼ 11:24 P
14 F 4:39 P
21 ¾ 0:19 P
Mar 1 N 4:13 P
9 ¼ 11:51 A
16 F 2:22 A
23 ¾ 5:05 A
31 N 9:20 A
Apr 7 ¼ 8:33 P
14 F 0:10 P
21 ¾ 11:01 P
29 N 11:54 P
May 7 ¼ 2:30 A
13 F 10:35 P
21 ¾ 5:04 P
29 N 11:40 A
Jun 5 ¼ 7:10 A
12 F 10:03 A
20 ¾ 10:23 A
27 N 8:54 P
Jul 4 ¼ 0:10 P
11 F 10:50 P
20 ¾ 2:18 A
27 N 4:29 A
Aug 2 ¼ 6:56 P
10 F 1:09 P
18 ¾ 4:17 P
25 N 11:33 A
Sep 1 ¼ 4:35 A
9 F 4:56 A
17 ¾ 4:03 A
23 N 7:19 P
30 ¼ 5:50 P
Oct 8 F 9:43 P
16 ¾ 1:45 P
23 N 4:44 A
30 ¼ 10:49 A
Nov 7 F 2:33 P
14 ¾ 10:00 P
21 N 4:20 P
29 ¼ 6:58 A
Dec 7 F 6:16 A
14 ¾ 5:46 A
21 N 6:12 A
29 ¼ 4:53 A

1958

Jan 5 F 8:09 P
12 ¾ 2:02 P
19 N 10:09 P
28 ¼ 2:17 A
Feb 4 F 8:06 A
10 ¾ 11:34 P
18 N 3:39 P
26 ¼ 8:52 P
Mar 5 F 6:29 P
12 ¾ 10:48 A
20 N 9:51 A
28 ¼ 11:19 A
Apr 4 F 3:45 A
10 ¾ 11:51 P
19 N 3:24 A
26 ¼ 9:36 P
May 3 F 0:24 P
10 ¾ 2:38 P
18 N 7:01 P
26 ¼ 4:39 A
Jun 1 F 8:56 P
9 ¾ 7:00 A
17 N 8:00 A
24 ¼ 9:45 A
Jul 1 F 6:05 A
9 ¾ 0:22 A
16 N 6:34 P
23 ¼ 2:20 P
30 F 4:48 P
Aug 7 ¾ 5:50 P
15 N 3:34 A
21 ¼ 7:45 P
29 F 5:54 A
Sep 6 ¾ 10:25 A
13 N 0:03 P
20 ¼ 3:18 A
27 F 9:45 P
Oct 6 ¾ 1:21 A
12 N 8:53 P
19 ¼ 2:08 P
27 F 3:41 P
Nov 4 ¾ 2:20 P
11 N 6:34 A
18 ¼ 5:00 A
26 F 10:18 A
Dec 4 ¾ 1:25 A
10 N 5:24 P
17 ¼ 11:53 P
26 F 3:55 A

1959

Jan 2 ¾ 10:51 A
9 N 5:34 A
16 ¼ 9:27 P
24 F 7:33 P
31 ¾ 7:07 P
Feb 7 N 7:23 P
15 ¼ 7:21 P
23 F 8:54 A
Mar 2 ¾ 2:55 A
9 N 10:52 A
17 ¼ 3:11 P
24 F 8:03 P
31 ¾ 11:07 A
Apr 8 N 3:30 A
16 ¼ 7:33 A
23 F 5:14 A
29 ¾ 8:39 P
May 7 N 8:12 P
15 ¼ 8:10 P
22 F 0:57 P
29 ¾ 8:14 A
Jun 6 N 11:54 A
14 ¼ 5:23 A
20 F 8:00 P
27 ¾ 10:13 P
Jul 6 N 2:01 A
13 ¼ 0:02 P
20 F 3:34 A
27 ¾ 2:23 P
Aug 4 N 2:34 P
11 ¼ 5:10 P
18 F 0:51 P
26 ¾ 8:04 A
Sep 3 N 1:56 A
9 ¼ 10:08 P
17 F 0:52 A
25 ¾ 2:23 A
Oct 2 N 0:31 P
9 ¼ 4:23 A
16 F 3:59 P
24 ¾ 8:22 P
31 N 10:42 P
Nov 7 ¼ 1:24 P
15 F 9:42 A
23 ¾ 1:04 P
30 N 8:46 A
Dec 7 ¼ 2:12 A
15 F 4:50 A
23 ¾ 3:29 A
29 N 7:10 P

1960	1961	1962	1963
Jan 5 ¼ 6:54 P	Jan 1 F 11:07 P	Jan 6 N 0:36 P	Jan 3 ¼ 1:02 A
13 F 11:51 P	10 ¾ 3:03 A	13 ¼ 5:02 A	9 F 11:09 P
21 ¾ 3:01 P	16 N 9:31 P	20 F 6:17 P	17 ¾ 8:35 P
28 N 6:16 A	23 ¼ 4:14 P	28 ¾ 11:37 P	25 N 1:43 P
Feb 4 ¼ 2:27 P	31 F 6:47 P	Feb 5 N 0:11 A	Feb 1 ¼ 8:51 A
12 F 5:25 P	Feb 8 ¾ 4:50 P	11 ¼ 3:43 P	8 F 2:52 P
19 ¾ 11:48 P	15 N 8:11 A	19 F 1:19 P	16 ¾ 5:39 P
26 N 6:24 P	22 ¼ 8:35 A	27 ¾ 3:50 P	24 N 2:06 A
Mar 5 ¼ 11:06 A	Mar 2 F 1:35 P	Mar 6 N 10:31 A	Mar 2 ¼ 5:18 P
13 F 8:26 A	10 ¾ 2:58 A	13 ¼ 4:39 A	10 F 7:49 A
20 ¾ 6:41 A	16 N 6:51 P	21 F 7:56 A	18 ¾ 0:08 P
27 N 7:38 A	24 ¼ 2:49 A	29 ¾ 4:12 A	25 N 0:10 P
Apr 4 ¼ 7:05 A	Apr 1 F 5:48 A	Apr 4 N 7:46 P	Apr 1 ¼ 3:15 A
11 F 8:28 A	8 ¾ 10:16 A	11 ¼ 7:51 P	9 F 0:58 A
18 ¾ 0:57 P	15 N 5:38 A	20 F 0:34 A	17 ¾ 2:53 A
25 N 9:45 P	22 ¼ 9:50 P	27 ¾ 1:00 P	23 N 8:29 P
May 4 ¼ 1:01 A	30 F 6:41 P	May 4 N 4:25 A	30 ¼ 3:08 P
11 F 5:43 A	May 7 ¾ 3:58 A	11 ¼ 0:45 P	May 8 F 5:24 P
17 ¾ 7:55 P	14 N 4:55 P	19 F 2:33 P	16 ¾ 1:37 P
25 N 0:27 P	22 ¼ 4:19 A	26 ¾ 7:06 P	23 N 4:00 A
Jun 2 ¼ 4:02 P	30 F 4:38 A	Jun 2 N 1:27 P	30 ¼ 4:56 A
9 F 1:02 P	Jun 5 ¾ 9:19 P	10 ¼ 6:22 A	Jun 7 F 8:31 A
16 ¾ 4:36 A	13 N 5:17 A	18 F 2:03 A	14 ¾ 8:54 P
24 N 3:28 A	21 ¼ 9:02 A	24 ¾ 11:43 P	21 N 11:46 A
Jul 2 ¼ 3:49 A	28 F 0:38 P	Jul 1 N 11:53 P	28 ¼ 8:24 P
8 F 7:37 P	Jul 5 ¾ 3:33 A	9 ¼ 11:40 P	Jul 6 F 9:56 P
15 ¾ 3:43 P	12 N 7:12 P	17 F 11:41 A	14 ¾ 1:58 A
23 N 6:31 P	20 ¼ 11:14 P	24 ¾ 4:19 A	20 N 8:43 P
31 ¼ 0:39 P	27 F 7:51 P	31 N 0:24 P	28 ¼ 1:14 P
Aug 7 F 2:41 A	Aug 3 ¾ 11:48 A	Aug 8 ¼ 3:56 P	Aug 5 F 9:31 A
14 ¾ 5:37 A	11 N 10:37 A	15 F 8:10 P	12 ¾ 6:22 A
22 N 9:16 A	19 ¼ 10:52 A	22 ¾ 10:27 A	19 N 7:35 A
29 ¼ 7:23 P	26 F 3:14 A	30 N 3:10 A	27 ¼ 6:55 A
Sep 5 F 11:19 A	Sep 1 ¾ 11:06 P	Sep 7 ¼ 6:45 A	Sep 3 F 7:34 P
12 ¾ 10:20 P	10 N 2:50 A	14 F 4:12 A	10 ¾ 11:43 A
20 N 11:13 P	17 ¼ 8:24 P	20 ¾ 7:36 P	17 N 8:51 P
28 ¼ 1:13 A	24 F 11:34 A	28 N 7:40 P	26 ¼ 0:39 A
Oct 4 F 10:17 P	Oct 1 ¾ 2:11 P	Oct 6 ¼ 7:55 P	Oct 3 F 4:44 A
12 ¾ 5:26 P	9 N 6:53 P	13 F 0:34 P	9 ¾ 7:28 P
20 N 0:03 P	17 ¼ 4:35 A	20 ¾ 8:48 A	17 N 0:43 P
27 ¼ 7:34 A	23 F 9:31 P	28 N 1:06 P	25 ¼ 5:21 P
Nov 3 F 11:58 A	31 ¾ 8:59 A	Nov 5 ¼ 7:15 A	Nov 1 F 1:56 P
11 ¾ 1:48 P	Nov 8 N 9:59 A	11 F 10:04 P	8 ¾ 6:37 A
18 N 11:47 P	15 ¼ 0:13 P	19 ¾ 2:10 A	16 N 6:51 A
25 ¼ 3:42 P	22 F 9:44 A	27 N 6:30 A	24 ¼ 7:56 A
Dec 3 F 4:25 A	30 ¾ 6:19 A	Dec 4 ¼ 4:49 P	30 F 11:55 P
11 ¾ 9:39 A	Dec 7 N 11:52 P	11 F 9:28 A	Dec 7 ¾ 9:35 P
18 N 10:47 A	14 ¼ 8:06 P	18 ¾ 10:43 P	16 N 2:07 A
25 ¼ 2:30 A	22 F 0:43 A	26 N 11:00 P	23 ¼ 7:55 P
	30 ¾ 3:58 A		30 F 11:04 A

1964	1965	1966	1967
Jan 6 ¾ 3:59 P	Jan 2 N 9:07 P	Jan 7 F 5:17 A	Jan 3 ¾ 2:20 P
14 N 8:44 P	10 ¼ 9:00 P	13 ¾ 8:00 P	10 N 6:07 P
22 ¼ 5:29 A	17 F 1:38 P	21 N 3:47 P	18 ¼ 7:42 P
28 F 11:23 P	24 ¾ 11:08 A	29 ¼ 7:49 P	26 F 6:41 A
Feb 5 ¾ 0:43 P	Feb 2 N 4:36 P	Feb 5 F 3:59 P	Feb 1 ¾ 11:04 P
13 N 1:02 P	9 ¼ 8:53 A	12 ¾ 8:53 A	9 N 10:45 A
20 ¼ 1:25 P	16 F 0:27 A	20 N 10:49 A	17 ¼ 3:57 P
27 F 0:40 P	23 ¾ 5:40 A	28 ¼ 10:16 A	24 F 5:44 P
Mar 6 ¾ 10:01 A	Mar 3 N 9:56 A	Mar 7 F 1:46 A	Mar 3 ¾ 9:11 A
14 N 2:14 A	10 ¼ 5:53 P	14 ¾ 0:20 A	11 N 4:30 A
20 ¼ 8:40 P	17 F 11:24 A	22 N 4:47 A	19 ¼ 8:32 A
28 F 2:49 A	25 ¾ 1:37 A	29 ¼ 8:44 P	26 F 3:21 A
Apr 5 ¾ 5:46 A	Apr 2 N 0:21 A	Apr 5 F 11:14 A	Apr 1 ¾ 8:59 P
12 N 0:38 P	9 ¼ 0:40 A	12 ¾ 5:29 P	9 N 10:21 P
19 ¼ 4:10 A	15 F 11:03 P	20 N 8:36 P	17 ¼ 8:48 P
26 F 5:50 P	23 ¾ 9:07 P	28 ¼ 3:50 A	24 F 0:04 P
May 4 ¾ 10:20 P	May 1 N 11:56 A	May 4 F 9:01 P	May 1 ¾ 10:33 A
11 N 9:02 P	8 ¼ 6:20 A	12 ¾ 11:20 A	9 N 2:56 P
18 ¼ 0:43 P	15 F 11:53 A	20 N 9:43 A	17 ¼ 5:18 A
26 F 9:30 A	23 ¾ 2:41 P	27 ¼ 8:51 A	23 F 8:23 P
Jun 3 ¾ 11:08 A	30 N 9:13 P	Jun 3 F 7:41 A	31 ¾ 1:53 A
10 N 4:23 A	Jun 6 ¼ 0:12 P	11 ¾ 4:59 A	Jun 8 N 5:14 A
16 ¼ 11:02 P	14 F 2:00 A	18 N 8:09 P	15 ¼ 11:12 A
25 F 1:09 A	22 ¾ 5:37 A	25 ¼ 1:23 P	22 F 4:58 A
Jul 2 ¾ 8:31 P	29 N 4:53 A	Jul 2 F 7:37 P	29 ¾ 6:40 P
9 N 11:31 A	Jul 5 ¼ 7:37 P	10 ¾ 9:43 P	Jul 7 N 5:01 P
16 ¼ 11:48 A	13 F 5:03 P	18 N 4:31 A	14 ¼ 3:54 P
24 F 3:59 P	21 ¾ 5:54 A	24 ¼ 7:00 P	21 F 2:40 P
Aug 1 ¾ 3:30 A	28 N 11:45 A	Aug 1 F 9:06 A	29 ¾ 0:15 P
7 N 7:17 P	Aug 4 ¼ 5:48 A	9 ¾ 0:56 P	Aug 6 N 2:49 A
15 ¼ 3:20 A	12 F 8:23 A	16 N 11:48 A	12 ¼ 8:45 P
23 F 5:26 A	20 ¾ 3:51 A	23 ¼ 3:02 A	20 F 2:27 A
30 ¾ 9:16 A	26 N 6:51 P	31 F 0:15 A	28 ¾ 5:36 A
Sep 6 N 4:34 A	Sep 2 ¼ 7:28 P	Sep 8 ¾ 2:08 A	Sep 4 N 11:38 A
13 ¼ 9:24 P	10 F 11:33 P	14 N 7:14 P	11 ¼ 3:06 A
21 F 5:31 P	18 ¾ 11:59 A	21 ¼ 2:25 P	18 F 5:00 P
28 ¾ 3:02 P	25 N 3:18 A	29 F 4:48 P	26 ¾ 9:44 P
Oct 5 N 4:20 P	Oct 2 ¼ 0:38 P	Oct 7 ¾ 1:09 P	Oct 3 N 8:25 P
13 ¼ 4:57 P	10 F 2:14 P	14 N 3:52 A	10 ¼ 0:12 P
21 F 4:46 A	17 ¾ 7:00 P	21 ¼ 5:35 A	18 F 10:12 A
27 ¾ 9:59 P	24 N 2:12 P	29 F 10:01 A	26 ¾ 0:04 P
Nov 4 N 7:17 A	Nov 1 ¼ 8:27 A	Nov 5 ¾ 10:19 P	Nov 2 N 5:49 A
12 ¼ 0:21 P	9 F 4:16 A	12 N 2:27 P	9 ¼ 1:00 A
19 F 3:44 P	16 ¾ 1:54 A	20 ¼ 0:21 A	17 F 4:53 A
26 ¾ 7:11 A	23 N 4:11 A	28 F 2:41 A	25 ¾ 0:24 A
Dec 4 N 1:19 A	Dec 1 ¼ 5:25 A	Dec 5 ¾ 6:23 A	Dec 1 N 4:10 P
12 ¼ 6:02 A	8 F 5:22 P	12 N 3:14 A	8 ¼ 5:58 P
19 F 2:42 A	15 ¾ 9:52 A	19 ¼ 9:42 P	16 F 11:22 P
25 ¾ 7:28 P	22 N 9:04 P	27 F 5:44 P	24 ¾ 10:49 A
	31 ¼ 1:47 A		31 N 3:39 A

1968	1969	1970	1971
Jan 7 ¼ 2:23 P	Jan 3 F 6:28 P	Jan 7 N 8:36 P	Jan 4 ¼ 4:56 A
15 F 4:12 P	11 ¾ 2:01 P	14 ¼ 1:19 P	11 F 1:21 P
22 ¾ 7:39 P	18 N 4:59 A	22 F 0:57 P	19 ¾ 6:09 P
29 N 4:30 P	25 ¼ 8:24 A	30 ¾ 2:39 P	26 N 10:56 P
Feb 6 ¼ 0:21 P	Feb 2 F 0:57 P	Feb 6 N 7:13 A	Feb 2 ¼ 2:31 P
14 F 6:44 A	10 ¾ 0:09 P	13 ¼ 4:11 A	10 F 7:42 A
21 ¾ 3:28 A	16 N 4:26 A	21 F 8:20 A	18 ¾ 0:14 A
28 N 6:56 A	24 ¼ 4:31 A	Mar 1 ¾ 2:34 A	25 N 9:49 A
Mar 7 ¼ 9:21 A	Mar 4 F 5:18 A	7 N 5:43 P	Mar 4 ¼ 2:02 A
14 F 6:53 P	11 ¾ 7:45 A	14 ¼ 9:16 P	12 F 2:34 A
21 ¾ 11:08 A	18 N 4:52 A	23 F 1:53 A	20 ¾ 2:31 A
28 N 10:49 P	26 ¼ 0:49 A	30 ¾ 11:05 A	26 N 7:24 P
Apr 6 ¼ 3:28 A	Apr 2 F 6:46 P	Apr 6 N 4:10 A	Apr 2 ¼ 3:47 P
13 F 4:52 A	9 ¾ 1:59 P	13 ¼ 3:44 P	10 F 8:11 P
19 ¾ 7:36 P	16 N 6:17 P	21 F 4:22 P	18 ¾ 0:59 P
27 N 3:22 P	24 ¼ 7:45 P	28 ¾ 5:19 P	25 N 4:02 A
May 5 ¼ 5:55 P	May 2 F 5:14 A	May 5 N 2:52 P	May 2 ¼ 7:35 A
12 F 1:05 P	8 ¾ 8:12 P	13 ¼ 10:26 A	10 F 11:24 A
19 ¾ 5:45 A	16 N 8:27 A	21 F 3:38 A	17 ¾ 8:16 P
27 N 7:30 A	24 ¼ 0:16 P	27 ¾ 10:32 P	24 N 0:33 P
Jun 4 ¼ 4:47 A	31 F 1:19 P	Jun 4 N 2:22 A	Jun 1 ¼ 0:43 A
10 F 8:14 P	Jun 7 ¾ 3:40 A	12 ¼ 4:07 A	9 F 0:04 A
17 ¾ 6:14 P	14 N 11:09 P	19 F 0:28 P	16 ¾ 1:25 A
25 N 10:25 P	23 ¼ 1:45 A	26 ¾ 4:02 A	22 N 9:58 P
Jul 3 ¼ 0:42 P	29 F 8:04 P	Jul 3 N 3:19 P	30 ¼ 6:11 P
10 F 3:18 A	Jul 6 ¾ 1:18 P	11 ¼ 7:44 P	Jul 8 F 10:37 A
17 ¾ 9:12 A	14 N 2:12 P	18 F 7:59 P	15 ¾ 5:47 A
25 N 11:50 A	22 ¼ 0:10 P	25 ¾ 11:00 A	22 N 9:16 A
Aug 1 ¼ 6:35 P	29 F 2:46 A	Aug 2 N 5:59 A	30 ¼ 11:08 A
8 F 11:33 A	Aug 5 ¾ 1:39 A	10 ¼ 8:51 A	Aug 6 F 7:43 P
16 ¾ 2:14 A	13 N 5:17 A	17 F 3:16 A	13 ¾ 10:56 A
23 N 11:57 P	20 ¼ 8:04 P	23 ¾ 8:35 P	20 N 10:54 P
30 ¼ 11:35 P	27 F 10:33 A	31 N 10:02 P	29 ¼ 2:57 A
Sep 6 F 10:08 P	Sep 3 ¾ 4:59 P	Sep 8 ¼ 7:39 P	Sep 5 F 4:03 A
14 ¾ 8:32 P	11 N 7:57 P	15 F 11:10 A	11 ¾ 6:24 P
22 N 11:09 A	19 ¼ 2:25 A	22 ¾ 9:43 A	19 N 2:43 P
29 ¼ 5:07 A	25 F 8:22 P	30 N 2:32 P	27 ¼ 5:18 P
Oct 6 F 11:47 A	Oct 3 ¾ 11:06 A	Oct 8 ¼ 4:44 A	Oct 4 F 0:20 P
14 ¾ 3:06 P	11 N 9:40 A	14 F 8:22 P	11 ¾ 5:30 A
21 N 9:45 P	18 ¼ 8:32 A	22 ¾ 2:48 A	19 N 8:00 A
28 ¼ 0:40 P	25 F 8:45 A	30 N 6:29 A	27 ¼ 5:55 A
Nov 5 F 4:26 A	Nov 2 ¾ 7:15 A	Nov 6 ¼ 0:48 P	Nov 2 F 9:20 P
13 ¾ 8:54 A	9 N 10:12 P	13 F 7:29 A	9 ¾ 8:52 P
20 N 8:02 A	16 ¼ 3:46 P	20 ¾ 11:14 P	18 N 1:47 A
26 ¼ 11:31 P	23 F 11:55 P	26 N 9:15 P	25 ¼ 4:38 P
Dec 4 F 11:08 P	Dec 2 ¾ 3:51 A	Dec 5 ¼ 8:36 P	Dec 2 F 7:49 A
13 ¾ 0:50 A	9 N 9:43 A	12 F 9:04 P	9 ¾ 4:03 P
19 N 6:19 P	16 ¼ 1:10 A	20 ¾ 9:10 P	17 N 7:04 P
26 ¼ 2:15 P	23 F 5:36 P	28 N 10:43 A	25 ¼ 1:36 A
	31 ¾ 10:53 P		31 F 8:20 P

1972	1973	1974	1975
Jan 8 ¾ 1:32 P	Jan 4 N 3:43 P	Jan 1 ¼ 6:07 P	Jan 4 ¾ 7:05 P
16 N 10:53 A	12 ¼ 5:28 A	8 F 0:37 P	12 N 10:21 A
23 ¼ 9:30 A	18 F 9:29 P	15 ¾ 7:05 A	20 ¼ 3:15 P
30 F 10:59 A	26 ¾ 6:06 A	23 N 11:03 A	27 F 3:10 P
Feb 7 ¾ 11:12 A	Feb 3 N 9:24 A	31 ¼ 7:40 A	Feb 3 ¾ 6:24 A
15 N 0:30 A	10 ¼ 2:06 P	Feb 6 F 11:25 P	11 N 5:18 A
21 ¼ 5:21 P	17 F 10:08 A	14 ¾ 0:05 A	19 ¼ 7:40 A
29 F 3:13 A	25 ¾ 3:12 A	22 N 5:35 A	26 F 1:15 A
Mar 8 ¾ 7:06 A	Mar 5 N 0:08 A	Mar 1 ¼ 6:03 P	Mar 4 ¾ 8:21 P
15 N 11:35 A	11 ¼ 9:26 P	8 F 10:04 A	12 N 11:48 P
22 ¼ 2:13 A	18 F 11:34 P	15 ¾ 7:16 P	20 ¼ 8:05 P
29 F 8:06 P	26 ¾ 11:47 P	23 N 9:25 P	27 F 10:37 A
Apr 6 ¾ 11:45 P	Apr 3 N 11:46 A	31 ¼ 1:45 A	Apr 3 ¾ 0:26 P
13 N 8:32 P	10 ¼ 4:29 A	Apr 6 F 9:01 P	11 N 4:40 P
20 ¼ 0:46 P	17 F 1:52 P	14 ¾ 2:59 P	19 ¼ 4:42 A
28 F 0:45 P	25 ¾ 6:00 P	22 N 10:17 A	25 F 7:56 P
May 6 ¾ 0:27 P	May 2 N 8:56 P	29 ¼ 7:40 A	May 3 ¾ 5:45 A
13 N 4:09 A	9 ¼ 0:07 P	May 6 F 8:55 A	11 N 7:06 A
20 ¼ 1:17 A	17 F 4:59 A	14 ¾ 9:30 A	18 ¼ 10:30 A
28 F 4:28 A	25 ¾ 8:41 A	21 N 8:35 P	25 F 5:51 A
Jun 4 ¾ 9:22 P	Jun 1 N 4:35 A	28 ¼ 1:04 P	Jun 1 ¾ 11:24 P
11 N 11:31 A	7 ¼ 9:12 P	Jun 4 F 10:11 P	9 N 6:50 P
18 ¼ 3:42 P	15 F 8:36 P	13 ¾ 1:46 A	16 ¼ 2:59 P
26 F 6:47 P	23 ¾ 7:46 A	20 N 4:56 A	23 F 4:55 P
Jul 4 ¾ 3:26 A	30 N 11:39 A	26 ¼ 7:21 P	Jul 1 ¾ 4:38 P
10 N 7:40 P	Jul 7 ¼ 8:27 A	Jul 4 F 0:41 P	9 N 4:11 A
18 ¼ 7:47 A	15 F 11:57 A	12 ¾ 3:29 P	15 ¼ 7:48 P
26 F 7:24 A	23 ¾ 3:58 A	19 N 0:07 P	23 F 5:29 A
Aug 2 ¾ 8:03 A	29 N 7:00 P	26 ¼ 3:52 A	31 ¾ 8:49 A
9 N 5:27 A	Aug 5 ¼ 10:28 P	Aug 3 F 3:58 A	Aug 7 N 11:58 A
17 ¼ 1:10 A	14 F 2:17 A	11 ¾ 2:47 A	14 ¼ 2:24 A
24 F 6:23 P	21 ¾ 10:23 A	17 N 7:02 P	21 F 7:49 P
31 ¾ 0:49 P	28 N 3:26 A	24 ¼ 3:39 P	29 ¾ 11:20 P
Sep 7 N 5:29 P	Sep 4 ¼ 3:23 P	Sep 1 F 7:26 A	Sep 5 N 7:20 P
15 ¼ 7:14 P	12 F 3:17 P	9 ¾ 0:02 P	12 ¼ 0:00 P
23 F 4:08 A	19 ¾ 4:11 P	16 N 2:46 A	20 F 11:51 A
29 ¾ 7:17 P	26 N 1:55 P	23 ¼ 7:09 A	28 ¾ 11:47 A
Oct 7 N 8:09 A	Oct 4 ¼ 10:33 A	Oct 1 F 10:39 A	Oct 5 N 3:24 A
15 ¼ 0:56 P	12 F 3:10 A	8 ¾ 7:46 P	12 ¼ 1:16 A
22 F 1:26 P	18 ¾ 10:33 P	15 N 0:26 P	20 F 5:07 A
29 ¾ 4:42 A	26 N 3:17 A	23 ¼ 1:54 A	27 ¾ 10:08 P
Nov 6 N 1:22 A	Nov 3 ¼ 6:30 A	31 F 1:20 A	Nov 3 N 1:06 P
14 ¼ 5:02 A	10 F 2:28 P	Nov 7 ¾ 2:48 A	10 ¼ 6:22 P
20 F 11:07 P	17 ¾ 6:35 A	14 N 0:54 A	18 F 10:29 P
27 ¾ 5:45 P	24 N 7:56 P	21 ¼ 10:40 P	26 ¾ 6:53 A
Dec 5 N 8:25 P	Dec 3 ¼ 1:30 A	29 F 3:11 P	Dec 3 N 0:51 A
13 ¼ 6:36 P	10 F 1:35 A	Dec 6 ¾ 10:11 A	10 ¼ 2:40 P
20 F 9:46 A	16 ¾ 5:13 P	13 N 4:26 P	18 F 2:40 P
27 ¾ 10:28 A	24 N 3:08 P	21 ¼ 7:44 P	25 ¾ 2:53 P
		29 F 3:52 A	

1976	1977	1978	1979
Jan 1 N 2:41 P	Jan 5 F 0:11 P	Jan 2 ¾ 0:08 P	Jan 5 ¼ 11:16 A
9 ¼ 0:40 P	12 ¾ 7:56 P	9 N 4:00 A	13 F 7:10 A
17 F 4:48 A	19 N 2:12 P	16 ¼ 3:04 A	21 ¾ 11:24 A
23 ¾ 11:05 P	27 ¼ 5:13 A	24 F 7:57 A	28 N 6:20 A
31 N 6:21 A	Feb 4 F 3:57 A	31 ¾ 11:52 P	Feb 4 ¼ 0:37 A
Feb 8 ¼ 10:06 A	11 ¾ 4:08 A	Feb 7 N 2:55 P	12 F 2:40 A
15 F 4:44 P	18 N 3:38 A	14 ¼ 10:12 P	20 ¾ 1:18 A
22 ¾ 8:17 A	26 ¼ 2:51 A	23 F 1:27 A	26 N 4:46 P
29 N 11:26 P	Mar 5 F 5:14 P	Mar 2 ¾ 8:35 A	Mar 5 ¼ 4:24 P
Mar 9 ¼ 4:39 A	12 ¾ 11:36 A	9 N 2:37 A	13 F 9:15 P
16 F 2:53 A	19 N 6:34 P	16 ¼ 6:22 P	21 ¾ 11:23 A
22 ¾ 6:55 P	27 ¼ 10:27 P	24 F 4:21 P	28 N 3:00 A
30 N 5:09 P	Apr 4 F 4:10 A	31 ¾ 3:12 P	Apr 4 ¼ 9:58 A
Apr 7 ¼ 7:03 P	10 ¾ 7:15 P	Apr 7 N 3:16 P	12 F 1:16 P
14 F 11:50 A	18 N 10:36 A	15 ¼ 1:57 P	19 ¾ 6:31 P
21 ¾ 7:15 A	26 ¼ 2:43 P	23 F 4:12 A	26 N 1:16 P
29 N 10:20 A	May 3 F 1:04 P	29 ¾ 9:03 P	May 4 ¼ 4:27 P
May 7 ¼ 5:18 A	10 ¾ 4:09 A	May 7 N 4:48 A	12 F 2:02 A
13 F 8:05 P	18 N 2:52 A	15 ¼ 7:41 A	18 ¾ 11:58 P
20 ¾ 9:23 P	26 ¼ 3:21 A	22 F 1:18 P	26 N 0:01 A
29 N 1:48 A	Jun 1 F 8:32 P	29 ¾ 3:31 A	Jun 2 ¼ 10:38 P
Jun 5 ¼ 0:21 P	8 ¾ 3:08 P	Jun 5 N 7:02 P	10 F 11:56 A
12 F 4:16 A	16 N 6:24 P	13 ¼ 10:45 P	17 ¾ 5:02 A
19 ¾ 1:16 P	24 ¼ 0:45 P	20 F 8:32 P	24 N 11:59 A
27 N 2:51 P	Jul 1 F 3:25 A	27 ¾ 11:45 A	Jul 2 ¼ 3:25 P
Jul 4 ¼ 5:29 P	8 ¾ 4:40 A	Jul 5 N 9:52 A	9 F 8:00 P
11 F 1:10 P	16 N 8:37 A	13 ¼ 10:50 A	16 ¾ 11:00 A
19 ¾ 6:30 A	23 ¼ 7:39 P	20 F 3:06 A	24 N 1:42 A
27 N 1:39 A	30 F 10:53 A	26 ¾ 10:32 P	Aug 1 ¼ 5:58 A
Aug 2 ¼ 10:07 P	Aug 6 ¾ 8:41 P	Aug 4 N 1:02 A	8 F 3:22 A
9 F 11:44 P	14 N 9:32 P	11 ¼ 8:07 P	14 ¾ 7:03 P
18 ¾ 0:14 A	22 ¼ 1:05 A	18 F 10:15 A	22 N 5:11 P
25 N 11:01 A	28 F 8:11 P	25 ¾ 0:19 P	30 ¼ 6:10 A
Sep 1 ¼ 3:36 A	Sep 5 ¾ 2:34 P	Sep 2 N 4:10 P	Sep 6 F 10:59 A
8 F 0:53 P	13 N 9:24 A	10 ¼ 3:21 A	13 ¾ 6:16 A
16 ¾ 5:21 P	20 ¼ 6:19 A	16 F 7:02 P	21 N 9:48 A
23 N 7:56 P	27 F 8:18 A	24 ¾ 5:09 A	29 ¼ 4:21 A
30 ¼ 11:13 A	Oct 5 ¾ 9:22 A	Oct 2 N 6:42 A	Oct 5 F 7:36 P
Oct 8 F 4:56 A	12 N 8:32 P	9 ¼ 9:39 A	12 ¾ 9:25 P
16 ¾ 9:00 A	19 ¼ 0:47 P	16 F 6:10 A	21 N 2:24 A
23 N 5:10 A	26 F 11:36 P	24 ¾ 0:35 A	28 ¼ 1:07 P
29 ¼ 10:06 P	Nov 4 ¾ 3:59 A	31 N 8:07 P	Nov 4 F 5:48 A
Nov 6 F 11:16 P	11 N 7:10 A	Nov 7 ¼ 4:19 P	11 ¾ 4:25 P
14 ¾ 10:40 P	17 ¼ 9:53 P	14 F 8:01 P	19 N 6:05 P
21 N 3:12 P	25 F 5:32 P	22 ¾ 9:25 P	26 ¼ 9:09 P
28 ¼ 1:00 P	Dec 3 ¾ 9:17 P	30 N 8:20 A	Dec 3 F 6:09 P
Dec 6 F 6:16 P	10 N 5:34 P	Dec 7 ¼ 0:35 A	11 ¾ 2:00 P
14 ¾ 10:15 A	17 ¼ 10:38 A	14 F 0:32 P	19 N 8:24 A
21 N 2:09 A	25 F 0:50 P	22 ¾ 5:42 P	26 ¼ 5:12 A
28 ¼ 7:49 A		29 N 7:37 P	

1980	1981	1982	1983
Jan 2 F 9:03 A	Jan 6 N 7:25 A	Jan 3 ¼ 4:47 A	Jan 6 ¾ 4:01 A
10 ¾ 11:51 A	13 ¼ 10:11 A	9 F 7:54 P	14 N 5:09 A
17 N 9:20 P	20 F 7:40 A	16 ¾ 11:59 P	22 ¼ 5:35 A
24 ¼ 1:59 P	28 ¾ 4:20 A	25 N 4:57 A	28 F 10:27 P
Feb 1 F 2:22 P	Feb 4 N 10:15 P	Feb 1 ¼ 2:29 P	Feb 4 ¾ 7:18 P
9 ¾ 7:36 A	11 ¼ 5:50 P	8 F 7:58 P	13 N 0:33 A
16 N 8:52 A	18 F 10:59 P	15 ¾ 8:22 P	20 ¼ 5:33 P
23 ¼ 0:15 A	27 ¾ 1:15 A	23 N 9:14 P	27 F 8:59 A
Mar 1 F 9:01 P	Mar 6 N 10:32 A	Mar 2 ¼ 10:16 P	Mar 6 ¾ 1:17 P
9 ¾ 11:50 P	13 ¼ 1:51 A	9 F 8:46 P	14 N 5:44 P
16 N 6:57 P	20 F 3:23 P	17 ¾ 5:16 P	22 ¼ 2:26 A
23 ¼ 0:32 P	28 ¾ 7:35 P	25 N 10:19 A	28 F 7:28 P
Apr 8 F 3:15 P	Apr 4 N 8:20 P	Apr 1 ¼ 5:09 A	Apr 5 ¾ 8:39 A
15 ¾ 0:07 P	11 ¼ 11:11 A	8 F 10:19 A	13 N 7:59 A
22 N 3:47 A	19 F 8:00 A	16 ¾ 0:43 P	20 ¼ 8:59 A
30 ¼ 3:00 A	27 ¾ 10:16 A	23 N 8:30 P	27 F 6:32 A
May 7 F 7:36 A	May 4 N 4:20 A	30 ¼ 0:08 P	May 5 ¾ 3:44 A
14 ¾ 8:51 P	10 ¼ 10:23 P	May 8 F 0:46 A	12 N 7:26 P
21 N 0:01 P	19 F 0:05 A	16 ¾ 5:12 A	19 ¼ 2:18 P
29 ¼ 7:17 P	26 ¾ 9:01 P	23 N 4:41 A	26 F 6:49 P
Jun 6 F 9:29 P	Jun 2 N 11:32 A	29 ¼ 8:07 P	Jun 3 ¾ 9:08 P
12 ¾ 2:54 A	9 ¼ 11:34 A	Jun 6 F 4:00 P	11 N 4:38 P
20 N 8:39 P	17 F 3:05 P	14 ¾ 6:07 P	17 ¼ 7:47 P
28 ¼ 0:33 P	25 ¾ 4:26 A	21 N 11:53 A	25 F 8:33 A
Jul 5 F 9:03 A	Jul 1 N 7:04 P	28 ¼ 5:57 A	Jul 3 ¾ 0:13 P
12 ¾ 7:28 A	9 ¼ 2:40 A	Jul 6 F 7:33 A	10 N 0:19 P
20 N 6:47 A	17 F 4:40 A	14 ¾ 3:48 A	17 ¼ 2:51 A
27 ¼ 5:52 A	24 ¾ 9:41 A	20 N 6:58 P	24 F 11:28 P
Aug 3 F 6:55 P	31 N 3:53 A	27 ¼ 6:23 P	Aug 2 ¾ 0:53 A
10 ¾ 0:01 P	Aug 7 ¼ 7:27 P	Aug 4 F 10:35 P	8 N 7:19 P
18 N 7:10 P	15 F 4:38 P	12 ¾ 11:09 A	15 ¼ 0:48 P
26 ¼ 10:29 P	22 ¾ 2:17 P	19 N 2:46 A	23 F 3:00 P
Sep 1 F 3:43 A	29 N 2:45 P	26 ¼ 9:51 A	31 ¾ 11:23 A
9 ¾ 6:08 P	Sep 6 ¼ 1:27 P	Sep 3 F 0:29 P	Sep 7 N 2:36 A
17 N 10:01 A	14 F 3:10 A	10 ¾ 5:20 P	14 ¼ 2:25 A
24 ¼ 1:55 P	20 ¾ 7:48 P	17 N 0:10 P	22 F 6:37 A
Oct 1 F 0:09 P	28 N 4:08 A	25 ¼ 4:08 A	29 ¾ 8:06 P
9 ¾ 3:19 A	Oct 6 ¼ 7:46 A	Oct 3 F 1:09 A	Oct 6 N 11:17 A
17 N 2:51 A	13 F 0:50 P	9 ¾ 11:27 P	13 ¼ 7:43 P
23 ¼ 3:48 A	20 ¾ 3:42 A	17 N 0:05 A	21 F 9:54 P
30 F 8:53 P	27 N 8:15 P	25 ¼ 0:09 A	29 ¾ 3:38 P
Nov 7 ¾ 4:34 P	Nov 5 ¼ 1:10 A	Nov 1 F 0:58 P	Nov 4 N 10:22 P
15 N 8:44 P	11 F 10:28 P	8 ¾ 6:39 A	12 ¼ 3:50 P
22 ¼ 3:48 P	18 ¾ 2:55 P	15 N 3:11 P	20 F 0:30 P
29 F 6:40 A	26 N 2:40 P	23 ¼ 8:07 P	27 ¾ 10:51 A
Dec 7 ¾ 10:00 A	Dec 4 ¼ 4:23 P	Dec 1 F 0:22 A	Dec 4 N 0:27 P
15 N 2:36 P	11 F 8:42 A	7 ¾ 3:54 P	12 ¼ 1:10 P
21 ¼ 1:48 A	18 ¾ 5:48 A	15 N 9:19 A	20 F 2:01 A
29 F 6:09 P	26 N 10:11 A	23 ¼ 2:18 P	26 ¾ 6:53 P
¾ 6:33 A		30 F 11:34 A	

1984	1985	1986	1987
Jan 3 N 5:17 A	Jan 7 F 2:17 A	Jan 3 ¾ 7:48 P	Jan 6 ¼ 10:36 P
11 ¼ 9:49 A	13 ¾ 11:28 P	10 N 0:23 P	15 F 2:32 A
18 F 2:06 P	21 N 2:29 A	17 ¼ 10:14 P	22 ¾ 10:46 P
25 ¾ 4:49 A	29 ¼ 3:30 A	26 F 0:32 A	29 N 1:46 P
Feb 1 N 11:47 P	Feb 5 F 3:20 P	Feb 2 ¾ 4:42 A	Feb 5 ¼ 4:22 P
10 ¼ 4:01 A	12 ¾ 7:58 A	9 N 0:56 A	13 F 8:59 P
17 F 0:42 A	19 N 6:44 P	16 ¼ 7:56 P	21 ¾ 8:57 A
23 ¾ 5:13 P	27 ¼ 11:42 P	24 F 3:03 P	28 N 0:52 A
Mar 2 N 6:32 P	Mar 7 F 2:14 A	Mar 3 ¾ 0:18 P	Mar 7 ¼ 11:59 A
10 ¼ 6:28 P	13 ¾ 5:35 P	10 N 2:53 P	15 F 1:14 P
17 F 10:11 A	21 N 0:00 P	18 ¼ 4:40 P	22 ¾ 4:23 P
24 ¾ 7:59 A	29 ¼ 4:12 P	26 F 3:03 A	29 N 0:47 P
Apr 1 N 0:11 P	Apr 5 F 11:33 A	Apr 1 ¾ 7:31 P	Apr 6 ¼ 7:49 A
9 ¼ 4:52 A	12 -¾ 4:43 A	9 N 6:09 A	14 F 2:32 A
15 F 7:12 P	20 N 5:23 A	17 ¼ 10:36 A	20 ¾ 10:16 P
23 ¾ 0:27 A	28 ¼ 4:26 A	24 F 0:47 P	28 N 1:35 A
May 1 N 3:47 A	May 4 F 7:54 P	May 1 ¾ 3:23 A	May 6 ¼ 2:27 A
8 ¼ 11:51 A	11 ¾ 5:35 P	8 N 10:11 P	13 F 0:51 P
15 F 4:30 A	19 N 9:42 P	17 ¼ 1:01 A	20 ¾ 4:03 A
22 ¾ 5:46 P	27 ¼ 0:57 P	23 F 8:46 P	27 N 3:15 P
30 N 4:49 P	Jun 3 F 3:51 A	30 ¾ 0:56 P	Jun 4 ¼ 6:54 P
Jun 6 ¼ 4:42 P	10 ¾ 8:20 A	Jun 7 N 2:01 P	11 F 8:50 P
13 F 2:43 P	18 N 11:59 A	15 ¼ 0:01 P	18 ¾ 11:04 A
21 ¾ 11:11 A	25 ¼ 6:54 P	22 F 3:43 A	26 N 5:38 A
29 N 3:19 A	Jul 2 F 0:09 P	29 ¾ 0:54 A	Jul 4 ¼ 8:35 A
Jul 5 ¼ 9:05 P	10 ¾ 0:51 A	Jul 7 N 4:56 A	11 F 3:34 A
13 F 2:21 A	17 N 11:57 P	14 ¼ 8:11 P	17 ¾ 8:18 P
21 ¾ 4:02 A	24 ¼ 11:40 P	21 F 10:41 P	25 N 8:39 P
28 N 11:52 A	31 F 9:42 P	28 ¾ 3:35 P	Aug 2 ¼ 7:25 P
Aug 4 ¼ 2:34 A	Aug 8 ¾ 6:29 P	Aug 5 N 6:37 P	9 F 10:18 A
11 F 3:44 P	16 N 10:07 A	13 ¼ 2:22 A	16 ¾ 8:26 A
19 ¾ 7:42 P	23 ¼ 4:37 A	19 F 6:55 A	24 N 0:00 P
26 N 7:27 P	30 F 9:28 A	27 ¾ 8:40 A	Sep 1 ¼ 3:49 A
Sep 2 ¼ 10:31 A	Sep 7 ¾ 0:17 P	Sep 4 N 7:11 A	7 F 6:14 P
10 F 7:02 A	14 N 7:21 P	11 ¼ 7:42 A	14 ¾ 11:46 P
18 ¾ 9:32 A	21 ¼ 11:04 A	18 F 5:35 A	23 N 3:09 A
25 N 3:12 A	29 F 0:10 A	26 ¾ 3:19 A	30 ¼ 10:40 A
Oct 1 ¼ 9:53 P	Oct 7 ¾ 5:05 A	Oct 3 N 6:56 P	Oct 7 F 4:13 A
9 F 11:59 P	14 N 4:34 A	10 ¼ 1:29 P	14 ¾ 6:07 P
17 ¾ 9:15 P	20 ¼ 8:14 P	17 F 7:23 P	22 N 5:29 P
24 N 0:09 P	28 F 5:39 P	25 ¾ 10:27 P	29 ¼ 5:11 P
31 ¼ 1:09 P	Nov 5 ¾ 8:07 P	Nov 2 N 6:03 A	Nov 5 F 4:47 P
Nov 8 F 5:44 P	12 N 2:21 P	8 ¼ 9:12 P	13 ¾ 2:39 P
16 ¾ 7:00 A	19 ¼ 9:05 A	16 F 0:13 P	21 N 6:34 A
22 N 10:58 P	27 F 0:43 P	24 ¾ 4:51 P	28 ¼ 0:38 A
30 ¼ 8:02 A	Dec 5 ¾ 9:02 A	Dec 1 N 4:44 P	Dec 5 F 8:02 A
Dec 8 F 10:54 A	12 N 0:55 A	8 ¼ 8:03 A	13 ¾ 11:42 A
15 ¾ 3:26 P	19 ¼ 1:59 A	16 F 7:06 A	20 N 6:26 A
22 N 11:48 A	27 F 7:31 A	24 ¾ 9:18 A	27 ¼ 10:02 A
30 ¼ 5:29 A		31 N 3:11 A	

1988	1989	1990	1991
Jan 4 F 1:42 A	Jan 7 N 7:23 P	Jan 4 ¼ 10:41 A	Jan 7 ¾ 6:36 P
12 ¾ 7:05 A	14 ¼ 1:59 P	11 F 4:58 A	15 N 11:51 P
19 N 5:26 A	21 F 9:35 P	18 ¾ 9:18 P	23 ¼ 2:23 P
25 ¼ 9:54 P	30 ¾ 2:03 A	26 N 7:21 P	30 F 6:11 A
Feb 2 F 8:53 P	Feb 6 N 7:38 A	Feb 2 ¼ 6:33 P	Feb 6 ¾ 1:53 P
10 ¾ 11:02 P	12 ¼ 11:16 P	9 F 7:17 P	14 N 5:33 P
17 N 3:55 P	20 F 3:33 P	17 ¾ 6:49 P	21 ¼ 10:59 P
24 ¼ 0:16 P	28 ¾ 8:09 P	25 N 8:55 A	28 F 6:26 P
Mar 3 F 4:02 P	Mar 7 N 6:20 P	Mar 4 ¼ 2:06 A	Mar 8 ¾ 10:33 A
11 ¾ 10:57 A	14 ¼ 10:12 A	11 F 11:00 A	16 N 8:12 A
18 N 2:03 A	22 F 9:59 A	19 ¾ 2:32 P	23 ¼ 6:04 A
25 ¼ 4:43 A	30 ¾ 10:23 A	26 N 7:49 P	30 F 7:18 A
Apr 2 F 9:22 A	Apr 6 N 3:33 A	Apr 2 ¼ 10:25 A	Apr 7 ¾ 6:47 A
9 ¾ 7:22 P	12 ¼ 11:14 P	10 F 3:20 A	14 N 7:39 P
16 N 0:01 P	21 F 3:14 A	18 ¾ 7:04 A	21 ¼ 0:40 P
23 ¼ 10:33 P	28 ¾ 8:47 P	25 N 4:28 A	28 F 9:00 P
May 1 F 11:42 P	May 5 N 11:47 A	May 1 ¼ 8:19 P	May 7 ¾ 0:47 A
9 ¾ 1:24 A	12 ¼ 2:21 P	9 F 7:32 P	14 N 4:37 A
15 N 10:12 P	20 F 6:17 P	17 ¾ 7:46 A	20 ¼ 7:47 P
23 ¼ 4:50 P	28 ¾ 4:02 A	24 N 11:48 A	28 F 11:38 A
31 F 10:54 A	Jun 3 N 7:54 P	31 ¼ 8:12 A	Jun 5 ¾ 3:31 P
Jun 7 ¾ 6:23 A	11 ¼ 7:00 A	Jun 8 F 11:02 A	12 N 0:07 P
14 N 9:15 A	19 F 6:58 A	16 ¾ 4:49 A	19 ¼ 4:20 A
22 ¼ 10:24 A	26 ¾ 9:10 A	22 N 6:56 P	27 F 3:00 A
29 F 7:47 P	Jul 3 N 5:00 A	29 ¼ 10:09 P	Jul 5 ¾ 2:51 A
Jul 6 ¾ 11:37 A	11 ¼ 0:20 A	Jul 8 F 1:25 A	11 N 7:07 P
13 N 9:54 P	18 F 5:43 P	15 ¾ 11:05 A	18 ¼ 3:12 P
22 ¼ 2:15 A	25 ¾ 1:32 P	22 N 2:55 A	26 F 6:26 P
29 F 3:26 A	Aug 1 N 4:07 P	29 ¼ 2:03 P	Aug 3 ¾ 11:27 A
Aug 4 ¾ 6:23 P	9 ¼ 5:30 P	Aug 6 F 2:21 P	10 N 2:29 A
12 N 0:32 P	17 F 3:08 A	13 ¾ 3:55 P	17 ¼ 5:02 A
20 ¼ 3:53 P	23 ¾ 6:41 P	20 N 0:40 P	25 F 9:08 A
27 F 10:57 A	31 N 5:46 A	28 ¼ 7:35 A	Sep 1 ¾ 6:18 P
Sep 3 ¾ 3:51 A	Sep 8 ¼ 9:50 A	Sep 5 F 1:47 A	8 N 11:02 A
11 N 4:50 A	15 F 11:52 A	11 ¾ 8:54 P	15 ¼ 10:03 P
19 ¼ 3:19 A	22 ¾ 2:11 A	19 N 0:47 A	23 F 10:41 P
25 F 7:08 A	29 N 9:48 P	27 ¼ 2:07 A	Oct 1 ¾ 0:31 A
Oct 2 ¾ 4:59 P	Oct 8 ¼ 0:53 A	Oct 4 F 0:03 P	7 N 9:40 P
10 N 9:50 P	14 F 8:33 P	11 ¾ 3:32 A	15 ¼ 5:34 P
18 ¼ 1:02 P	21 ¾ 1:20 P	18 N 3:38 P	23 F 11:09 A
25 F 4:36 A	29 N 3:28 P	26 ¼ 8:28 P	30 ¾ 7:12 A
Nov 1 ¾ 10:13 A	Nov 6 ¼ 2:12 P	Nov 2 F 9:49 P	Nov 6 N 11:12 A
9 N 2:21 P	13 F 5:52 A	9 ¾ 1:03 P	14 ¼ 2:03 P
16 ¼ 9:36 P	20 ¾ 4:45 A	17 N 9:06 A	21 F 10:57 P
23 F 3:54 P	28 N 9:42 A	25 ¼ 1:13 P	28 ¾ 3:22 P
Dec 1 ¾ 6:51 A	Dec 6 ¼ 1:27 A	Dec 2 F 7:50 A	Dec 6 N 3:57 A
9 N 5:37 A	12 F 4:31 P	9 ¾ 2:05 A	14 ¼ 9:33 A
16 ¼ 5:41 A	19 ¾ 11:56 P	17 N 4:23 A	21 F 10:24 A
23 F 5:30 A	28 N 3:21 A	25 ¼ 3:17 A	28 ¾ 1:56 A
31 ¾ 4:58 A		31 F 6:36 P	

1992				1993				1994				1995			
Jan	4	N	11:11 P	Jan	1	¼	3:40 A	Jan	5	¾	0:02 A	Jan	1	N	10:57 A
	13	¼	2:33 A		8	F	0:38 P		11	N	11:11 P		8	¼	3:47 P
	19	F	9:29 P		15	¾	4:02 A		19	¼	8:28 P		16	F	8:28 P
	26	¾	3:28 P		22	N	6:28 P		27	F	1:24 P		24	¾	4:59 A
Feb	3	N	7:01 P		30	¼	11:21 P	Feb	3	¾	8:07 A		30	N	10:49 P
	11	¼	4:16 P	Feb	6	F	11:56 P		10	N	2:31 P	Feb	7	¼	0:55 P
	18	F	8:05 A		13	¾	2:58 P		18	¼	5:48 P		15	F	0:17 P
	25	¾	7:57 A		21	N	1:06 P		26	F	1:16 A		22	¾	1:05 P
Mar	4	N	1:23 P	Mar	1	¼	3:47 P	Mar	4	¾	4:54 P	Mar	1	N	11:49 A
	12	¼	2:37 A		8	F	9:47 A		12	N	7:06 A		9	¼	10:15 A
	18	F	6:19 P		15	¾	4:18 A		20	¼	0:15 P		17	F	1:27 A
	26	¾	2:31 A		23	N	7:16 A		27	F	11:10 A		23	¾	8:11 P
Apr	3	N	5:02 A		31	¼	4:11 A	Apr	3	¾	2:56 A		31	N	2:10 A
	10	¼	10:07 A	Apr	6	F	6:44 P		11	N	0:18 A	Apr	8	¼	5:36 A
	17	F	4:43 A		13	¾	7:40 P		19	¼	2:35 A		15	F	0:09 P
	24	¾	9:41 P		21	N	11:50 P		25	F	7:46 P		22	¾	3:19 A
May	2	N	5:46 P		29	¼	0:42 P	May	2	¾	2:34 P		29	N	5:38 P
	9	¼	3:45 A	May	6	F	3:35 A		10	N	5:08 P	May	7	¼	9:45 P
	16	F	4:04 P		13	¾	0:21 P		18	¼	0:51 P		14	F	8:49 P
	24	¾	3:54 P		21	N	2:08 P		25	F	3:40 P		21	¾	11:37 A
Jun	1	N	3:58 A		28	¼	6:22 P	Jun	1	¾	4:04 A		29	N	9:29 A
	7	¼	8:48 P	Jun	4	F	1:03 P		9	N	8:28 A	Jun	6	¼	10:27 A
	15	F	4:51 A		12	¾	5:37 A		16	¼	7:58 P		13	F	4:04 A
	23	¾	8:12 A		20	N	1:54 A		23	F	11:34 A		19	¾	10:02 P
	30	N	0:19 P		26	¼	10:44 P		30	¾	7:32 P		28	N	0:51 A
Jul	7	¼	2:45 A	Jul	3	F	11:46 P	Jul	8	N	9:39 P	Jul	5	¼	8:04 P
	14	F	7:07 P		11	¾	10:50 P		16	¼	1:13 A		12	F	10:50 A
	22	¾	10:13 P		19	N	11:25 A		22	F	8:17 P		19	¾	11:11 A
	29	N	7:36 P		26	¼	3:26 A		30	¾	0:41 P		27	N	3:14 P
Aug	5	¼	11:00 A	Aug	2	F	0:11 P	Aug	7	N	8:46 A	Aug	4	¼	3:17 A
	13	F	10:28 A		10	¾	3:21 P		14	¼	5:58 A		10	F	6:17 P
	21	¾	10:02 A		17	N	7:29 P		21	F	6:48 A		18	¾	3:05 A
	28	N	2:43 A		24	¼	9:59 A		29	¾	6:42 A		26	N	4:32 A
Sep	3	¼	10:40 P	Sep	1	F	2:34 A	Sep	5	N	6:34 P	Sep	2	¼	9:04 A
	12	F	2:18 A		9	¾	6:28 A		12	¼	11:35 A		9	F	3:38 A
	19	¾	7:54 A		16	N	3:11 A		19	F	8:02 P		16	¾	9:11 P
	26	N	10:41 A		22	¼	7:33 P		28	¾	0:25 A		24	N	4:56 P
Oct	3	¼	2:13 P		30	F	6:55 P	Oct	5	N	3:56 A	Oct	1	¼	2:37 P
	11	F	6:04 P	Oct	8	¾	7:36 P		11	¼	7:18 P		8	F	3:53 P
	19	¾	4:13 A		15	N	11:37 A		19	F	0:19 P		16	¾	4:27 P
	25	N	8:35 P		22	¼	8:53 A		27	¾	4:45 P		24	N	4:37 A
Nov	2	¼	9:12 A		30	F	0:39 P	Nov	3	N	1:37 P		30	¼	9:18 P
	10	F	9:21 A	Nov	7	¾	6:37 A		10	¼	6:15 A	Nov	7	F	7:22 A
	17	¾	11:40 A		13	N	9:35 P		18	F	6:58 A		15	¾	11:41 A
	24	N	9:12 A		21	¼	2:05 A		26	¾	7:05 A		22	N	3:44 P
Dec	2	¼	6:18 A		29	F	6:32 A	Dec	2	N	11:55 P		29	¼	6:29 A
	9	F	11:42 P	Dec	6	¾	3:50 A		9	¼	9:07 P	Dec	7	F	1:28 A
	16	¾	7:14 P		13	N	9:28 A		18	F	2:18 A		15	¾	5:32 A
	24	N	0:44 A		20	¼	10:27 P		25	¾	7:07 P		22	N	2:23 A
					28	F	11:06 P						28	¼	7:08 P

1996	1997	1998	1999
Jan 5 F 8:52 P	Jan 2 ¾ 1:46 A	Jan 5 ¼ 2:19 P	Jan 2 F 2:51 A
13 ¾ 8:46 P	9 N 4:27 A	12 F 5:25 P	9 ¾ 2:23 P
20 N 0:52 P	15 ¼ 8:03 P	20 ¾ 7:41 P	17 N 3:47 P
27 ¼ 11:15 A	23 F 3:12 P	28 N 6:02 A	24 ¼ 7:16 P
Feb 4 F 3:59 P	31 ¾ 7:41 P	Feb 3 ¼ 10:55 P	31 F 4:08 P
12 ¾ 8:38 A	Feb 7 N 3:07 P	11 F 10:24 A	Feb 8 ¾ 11:59 A
18 N 11:31 P	14 ¼ 8:59 A	19 ¾ 3:28 P	16 N 6:40 A
26 ¼ 5:54 A	22 F 10:28 A	26 N 5:27 P	23 ¼ 2:44 A
Mar 5 F 9:24 A	Mar 2 ¾ 9:39 A	Mar 5 ¼ 8:42 A	Mar 2 F 7:00 A
12 ¾ 5:16 P	9 N 1:16 A	13 F 4:36 A	10 ¾ 8:42 A
19 N 10:46 A	16 ¼ 0:07 A	21 ¾ 7:39 A	17 N 6:49 P
27 ¼ 1:32 A	24 F 4:47 A	28 N 3:15 A	24 ¼ 10:19 A
Apr 4 F 0:08 A	31 ¾ 7:39 P	Apr 3 ¼ 8:20 P	31 F 10:50 P
10 ¾ 11:37 P	Apr 7 N 11:03 A	11 F 10:25 P	Apr 9 ¾ 2:52 A
17 N 10:50 P	14 ¼ 5:01 P	19 ¾ 7:54 P	16 N 4:23 A
25 ¼ 8:41 P	22 F 8:35 P	26 N 11:42 A	22 ¼ 7:03 P
May 3 F 11:49 A	30 ¾ 2:38 A	May 3 ¼ 10:05 A	30 F 2:56 P
10 ¾ 5:05 A	May 6 N 8:48 P	11 F 2:31 P	May 8 ¾ 5:30 P
17 N 11:47 P	14 ¼ 10:56 A	19 ¾ 4:37 A	15 N 0:06 P
25 ¼ 2:14 P	22 F 9:15 A	25 N 7:33 P	22 ¼ 5:35 A
Jun 1 F 8:48 P	29 ¾ 7:53 A	Jun 2 ¼ 1:46 A	30 F 6:41 A
8 ¾ 11:07 A	Jun 5 N 7:05 A	10 F 4:20 A	Jun 7 ¾ 4:21 A
16 N 1:37 A	13 ¼ 4:53 A	17 ¾ 10:39 A	13 N 7:04 P
24 ¼ 5:25 A	20 F 7:10 P	24 N 3:51 A	20 ¼ 6:14 P
Jul 1 F 3:59 A	27 ¾ 0:43 P	Jul 1 ¼ 6:44 P	28 F 9:39 P
7 ¾ 6:56 P	Jul 4 N 6:41 P	9 F 4:02 P	Jul 6 ¾ 11:58 A
15 N 4:16 P	12 ¼ 9:45 P	16 ¾ 3:15 P	13 N 2:25 A
23 ¼ 5:50 P	20 F 3:21 A	23 N 1:45 P	20 ¼ 9:01 A
30 F 10:36 A	26 ¾ 6:29 P	31 ¼ 0:06 P	28 F 11:26 A
Aug 6 ¾ 5:26 A	Aug 3 N 8:15 A	Aug 8 F 2:11 A	Aug 4 ¾ 5:26 P
14 N 7:35 A	11 ¼ 0:44 P	14 ¾ 7:50 P	11 N 11:10 A
22 ¼ 3:38 A	18 F 10:56 A	22 N 2:04 A	19 ¼ 1:48 A
28 F 5:53 P	25 ¾ 2:25 A	30 ¼ 5:08 A	26 F 11:49 P
Sep 4 ¾ 7:07 P	Sep 1 N 11:53 P	Sep 6 F 11:22 A	Sep 2 ¾ 10:18 P
12 N 11:08 P	10 ¼ 1:32 A	13 ¾ 1:59 A	9 N 10:04 P
20 ¼ 11:24 A	16 F 6:51 P	20 N 5:03 P	17 ¼ 8:07 P
27 F 2:52 A	23 ¾ 1:36 P	28 ¼ 9:12 P	25 F 10:52 A
Oct 4 ¾ 0:05 P	Oct 1 N 4:53 P	Oct 5 F 8:13 P	Oct 2 ¾ 4:03 A
12 N 2:16 P	9 ¼ 0:23 P	12 ¾ 11:12 A	9 N 11:36 A
19 ¼ 6:10 P	16 F 3:47 A	20 N 10:11 A	17 ¼ 3:01 P
26 F 2:12 P	23 ¾ 4:50 A	28 ¼ 11:47 A	24 F 9:04 P
Nov 3 ¾ 7:52 A	31 N 10:02 A	Nov 4 F 5:19 A	31 ¾ 0:05 P
11 N 4:17 A	Nov 7 ¼ 9:45 P	11 ¾ 0:29 A	Nov 8 N 3:54 A
18 ¼ 1:10 A	14 F 2:13 P	19 N 4:28 A	16 ¼ 9:04 A
25 F 4:11 A	21 ¾ 11:59 P	27 ¼ 0:24 A	23 F 7:05 A
Dec 3 ¾ 5:07 A	30 N 2:15 A	Dec 3 F 3:20 P	29 ¾ 11:20 P
10 N 4:57 P	Dec 7 ¼ 6:10 A	10 ¾ 5:55 P	Dec 7 N 10:33 P
17 ¼ 9:32 A	14 F 2:38 A	18 N 10:44 P	16 ¼ 0:51 A
24 F 8:42 P	21 ¾ 9:44 P	26 ¼ 10:47 A	22 F 5:33 P
	29 N 4:58 P		29 ¾ 2:06 P

CHAPTER 14

A Brief Introduction to Chart Synthesis

1. When you have discovered the degree and sign of your Ascendant, place it on the left-hand side of the chart.

2. Place the other eleven glyphs round the chart in an *anti-clockwise* direction.

3. Place the Sun and the Moon in their respective positions.

4. Look at the chart and work out how many masculine and feminine features there are. If all three Sun, Moon and Ascendant are in masculine/positive signs, the personality will be extrovert, confident, possibly sporty and energetic. If all three are in feminine signs, the subject will be introverted, domestically inclined, gentle and possibly a little shy with strangers.

5. Give the same treatment to the elements and triplicities. There is no need to make heavy weather of this, just make a note of the elements to see whether there is some kind of imbalance e.g. two features in fire signs or none in cardinal signs. This will give you a quick clue to the character of the subject.

6. Now look to see what signs the Sun and Moon occupy, this will really reveal the subject's character for you.

7. Finally, and most importantly take a look at the houses the Sun and Moon occupy to see *where* the subject's energies are directed, what he does and what he is trying to achieve.

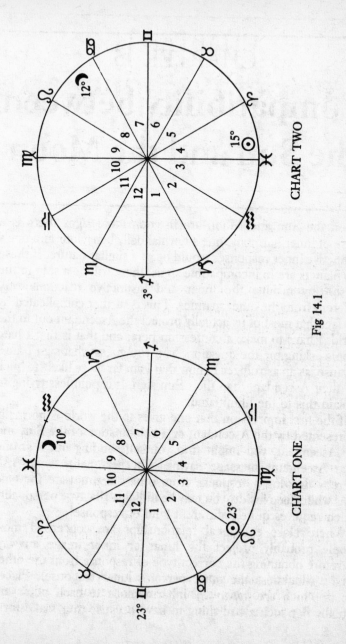

CHART ONE

CHART TWO

Fig 14.1

CHAPTER 15

Compatibility between the Sun and the Moon

When the Sun and Moon are in compatible signs there is a sense of inner harmony, one's normal daily behaviour and one's instinctive inner responses would be of a similar nature. If these two planets are in incompatible signs, there will be a split in the personality making the inner and instinctive reactions very different from the outer manner. This is further complicated by the fact that most of us actually project the Ascendant out to the world. I have to make a confession here, and that is that I hate people asking me the question, 'can you guess what sign I am?' because, as an astrologer I know that I am far more likely to 'pick up' their Ascendant than their Sun sign. It is pointless trying to explain this to the uninitiated.

If the first impression that one gives to the world is normally represented by the Ascendant or a combination of the Sun and the Ascendant, you might find yourself sending out a strong solar/Ascendant message saying 'I'm personality type AA', thereby drawing a response from others appropriate for type 'AA' while deep inside, you may be hiding a 'BB' type personality which requires quite a different kind of response!

Where close emotional relationships are concerned most people probably project the lunar or inner image anyway, therefore obtaining the correct type of response from the other person (doubtless the other person's lunar response). Placements which are *apparently* inharmonious to each other are actually not such a bad thing to have because they make for a more rounded personality. The thinking which lies behind this concept can be explained by a mixture of astrology and psychology or from pure astrological theory.

——Elements, Triplicities and Aspects——

If we look at this purely from the astrological view, it is a matter of breaking each sign down into its elements and triplicities plus the astrological aspects. Therefore planets which are in the same element (air, fire, earth or water) have something in common; planets in the same triplicity (cardinal, fixed, mutable) also have something in common. The only time two planets are in complete harmony is when thay are in the same sign, otherwise there are mixtures of harmony and inharmony in most planetary aspects. This concept is very advanced and very complicated but I have broken it down in order to explain it for you.

1. Planets in the same element have something in common.
    Sun in Aries   – fire
    Moon in Leo   – fire
    These planets are in TRINE aspect.

2. Planets in the same triplicity have something in common.
    Sun in Aries   – cardinal
    Moon in Cancer   – cardinal
    These planets are in SQUARE aspect.

    Sun in Aries   – cardinal
    Moon in Libra   – cardinal
    These planets are in OPPOSITION to each other.

3. Planets of the same gender have something in common.
    Sun in Aries   – masculine
    Moon in Gemini   – masculine
    These planets are in SEXTILE aspect.

4. Generally speaking, air and fire get on fairly well together as do earth and water, but air plus water/earth are different in nature as are fire plus earth/water etc. The really awkward aspects are the semi-sextile and the inconjunct because, in

both cases, neither the elements nor the triplicities are harmonious. In the case of the semi-sextile, at least the signs are adjacent to one another and adjacent signs *do* have a little in common with each other but planets which are inconjunct to each other have nothing at all in common.

Sun in Aries   – fire, cardinal
Moon in Taurus   – earth, fixed
This is a SEMI-SEXTILE aspect.

Sun in Aries   – fire, cardinal
Moon in Virgo   – earth, mutable
This is an INCONJUNCT aspect.

Standard astrological theory tells us that conjunctions (planets in the same sign) are a strong force for good or ill, sextiles and trines are easy placements while squares and oppositions cause tension. Semi-sextiles don't usually have much effect either way but inconjuncts can be a real pain. Figure 15.2 shows the geometric shape of these aspects.

Psychologically speaking, the apparently super-harmonious situation of Sun plus Moon in the same sign may be a *little too much* of a good thing. The effect of having one's most important planets in the same sign may make the personality too one-sided. An interesting exercise for an absolute beginner would be to combine the effects of the Sun and Moon in your own personality and see how they blend. First look at Figure 15.1 to see how they blend astrologically and then look up the list to see how they work together in practice.

SUN/MOON COMPATIBILITY CHART

LOCATE YOUR SUN POSITION ALONG HERE

L O C A T E Y O U R M O O N P O S I T I O N H E R E		Ar	Ta	Ge	Cn	Le	Vi	Li	Sc	Sg	Cp	Aq	Pi
	Ar	*	0	=	=	=	0	=	0	=	=	=	0
	Ta	0	*	0	=	=	=	0	=	0	=	=	=
	Ge	=	0	*	0	=	=	=	0	=	0	=	=
	Cn	=	=	0	*	0	=	=	=	0	=	0	=
	Le	=	=	=	0	*	0	=	=	=	0	=	0
	Vi	0	=	=	=	0	*	0	=	=	=	0	=
	Li	=	0	=	=	=	0	*	0	=	=	=	0
	Sc	0	=	0	=	=	=	0	*	0	=	=	=
	Sg	=	0	=	0	=	=	=	0	*	0	=	=
	Cp	=	=	0	=	0	=	=	=	0	*	0	=
	Aq	=	=	=	0	=	0	=	=	=	0	*	0
	Pi	0	=	=	=	0	=	0	=	=	=	0	*

*   Harmonious
0   Inharmonious
=   Reasonable

Figure 15.1

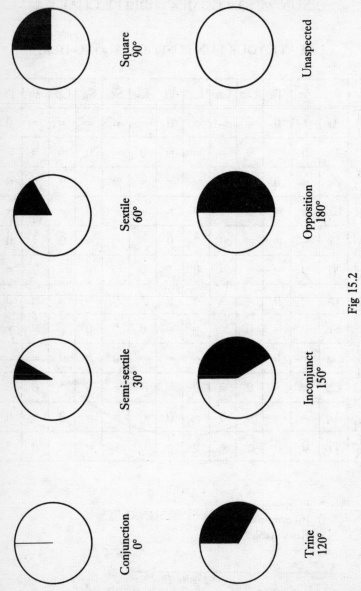

Fig 15.2

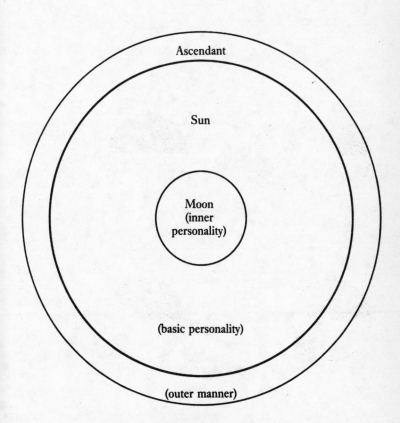

Fig 15.3

LAYERS OF PERSONALITY

CHAPTER 16
Sun/Moon Combinations

Sun Aries, Moon Aries ☉ ♈ ☽ ♈
An extrovert and self-starter with an endless supply of enthusiasm, quick to think and act. You lack patience and may be too self-centred.

Sun Aries, Moon Taurus ☉ ♈ ☽ ♉
Confident, enthusiastic and lovable, good builder, architect or gardener with an artistic eye. Could be dogmatic.

Sun Aries, Moon Gemini ☉ ♈ ☽ ♊
Dextrous, good engineer or draftsman, full of bright ideas. Clever with words but sharp and sarcastic at times. You may leave tasks for others to finish off.

Sun Aries, Moon Cancer ☉ ♈ ☽ ♋
Very determined, a good business head on your shoulders and a pleasant manner. Home life is very important to you. Sensitive but you hide it from others.

Sun Aries, Moon Leo ☉ ♈ ☽ ♌
A real go-getter, you need the limelight. Enthusiastic and optimistic you may be bossy and domineering. Very creative, but blind to underlying influences at times.

Sun Aries, Moon Virgo ☉ ♈ ☽ ♍
Probing, analytical and clever. Very efficient and clever worker, shy in personal matters. Good writer, harsh critic, may be too fond of nit-picking details.

Sun Aries, Moon Libra ☉ ♈ ☽ ♎

Outwardly confident and ebullient, inwardly calmer. Sensitive to others also loving and passionate. Good business sense but may be overambitious.

Sun Aries, Moon Scorpio ☉ ♈ ☽ ♏

An excellent soldier or surgeon, good concentration level. Single-minded, intense and passionate about everything; you may be too much for anyone to handle for long. Try to relax and let others do the same.

Sun Aries, Moon Sagittarius ☉ ♈ ☽ ♐

Restless and energetic, you are a born explorer on both the physical and mental level. You can fill others with a zest for life and idealism. Tactless and sarcastic.

Sun Aries, Moon Capricorn ☉ ♈ ☽ ♑

Determined, unstoppable, must reach the top but this could be at the expense of your personal life. You seek to dominate others by force of your personality.

Sun Aries, Moon Aquarius ☉ ♈ ☽ ♒

Humanitarian and enthusiastic, you would make a wonderful sports coach or teacher, but you must be careful not to hurt others by thoughtlessly sarcastic remarks.

Sun Aries, Moon Pisces ☉ ♈ ☽ ♓

Outwardly enthusiastic, inwardly shy and lacking in confidence. Kind and well-meaning but could be apt to preach. You need to get away from others from time to time.

Sun Taurus, Moon Aries ☉ ♉ ☽ ♈

Outwardly calm, inwardly ambitious and determined. Could be very creative in a practical way. You may be too fond of your own opinions. Good engineer and builder, artistic too.

Sun Taurus, Moon Taurus ☉ ♉ ☽ ♉

Stubborn, fixed in your views and materialistic but also creative and artistic with a love of music. You will make things that stand the test of time. Loyal in love.

Sun Taurus, Moon Gemini ☉ ♉ ☽ ♊
Artistic and perceptive, a good media worker or marketing expert. Home-loving but occasional outbursts of restlessness. Affectionate but not too sensual.

Sun Taurus, Moon Cancer ☉ ♉ ☽ ♋
A real homemaker and family person. You can motivate others to achieve a great deal but you hold back from the limelight. Your imagination can be successfully harnessed.

Sun Taurus, Moon Leo ☉ ♉ ☽ ♌
Very fixed opinions and a definite personality, you find it hard to adapt to change. You love children and are intensely loyal to others. You could be a good singer or dancer.

Sun Taurus, Moon Virgo ☉ ♉ ☽ ♍
A careful worker who can combine detail and artistry. Good family person, can learn and teach wordy or musical skills. Don't be too critical or pessimistic. A strong interest in nutrition.

Sun Taurus, Moon Libra ☉ ♉ ☽ ♎
Very sensual and also artistic with a good business head. Maybe too lazy to achieve much but when motivated, can reach the top. Lovable and kind but selfish too.

Sun Taurus, Moon Scorpio ☉ ♉ ☽ ♏
Artistic and sensual you can achieve much. Your opinions are fixed and your nature stubborn. Very loyal and persistent, could be a good sales person, also strongly independent.

Sun Taurus, Moon Sagittarius ☉ ♉ ☽ ♐
Outwardly steady, inwardly restless. Could be an armchair traveller. Traditional religion interests you, don't be too old-fashioned or quick to judge others.

Sun Taurus, Moon Capricorn ☉ ♉ ☽ ♑
Determined and ambitious with a strong need for security. A shrewd and practical business head but inwardly shy and nervous in personal situations. Very loyal and loving.

Sun Taurus, Moon Aquarius ☉ ♉ ☽ ≈

Innovative and artistic you are good company and a hard worker. You need freedom but will insist on others toeing the line. Good concentration and high level of confidence.

Sun Taurus, Moon Pisces ☉ ♉ ☽ ♓

Dreamy and patient, highly artistic you may have difficulty in getting projects off the ground. Your sympathy may land you with the care of lame ducks. Sensual and loving.

Sun Gemini, Moon Aries ☉ ♊ ☽ ♈

Very sharp mind and a great deal of enthusiasm which can carry you away. Good media type, interesting friend but a touch too sarcastic for comfort.

Sun Gemini, Moon Taurus ☉ ♊ ☽ ♉

You have good ideas and the patience to finish what you start. A good homemaker and parent. You need communication and comfort in a relationship and work in a mentally artistic field.

Sun Gemini, Moon Gemini ☉ ♊ ☽ ♊

You have dozens of bright ideas but difficulty in completing anything. Very clever and dextrous but could be a bit unfeeling. Tension is your problem, try to relax and feel.

Sun Gemini, Moon Cancer ☉ ♊ ☽ ♋

Friendly and chatty, usually on the phone. You love travel and novelty plus family life. Don't be put upon by stronger characters. You can make a happy home for others, your memory is good.

Sun Gemini, Moon Leo ☉ ♊ ☽ ♌

Lively, friendly and good looking you will always be popular. You need to express your ideas creatively. Good with children as you will never quite grow up yourself.

Sun Gemini, Moon Virgo ☉ ♊ ☽ ♍

Inventive, versatile and full of ideas but lacking in confidence. Your nerves sometimes get the better of you. Good researcher, writer, secretary.

Sun Gemini, Moon Libra ☉ ♊ ☽ ♎

You are full of ideas which may not always get off the ground. Diplomatic and fun you can be a bit too restless. Flirtatious and fun but inclined to be long-winded.

Sun Gemini, Moon Scorpio ☉ ♊ ☽ ♏

Brilliant and perceptive mind. Outwardly a cool-hearted loner but burning with secret passions also emotionally vulnerable. Very creative writer, musician, doctor or spy. Clever with words, sarcastic.

Sun Gemini, Moon Sagittarius ☉ ♊ ☽ ♐

Restless, good sportsman or adventurous traveller. Good scholar and teacher. Might need to get in touch with your own feelings and those of others.

Sun Gemini, Moon Capricorn ☉ ♊ ☽ ♑

Clever and ambitious, literate, would succeed in the media. Relationships may bring suffering, you must try to be warmer to others. Capable and businesslike.

Sun Gemini, Moon Aquarius ☉ ♊ ☽ ♒

Broad-minded, good scholar and teacher. Wide-ranging ideas, perceptive. May fear emotional display or even own feelings. Detachment sought, good journalist or traveller.

Sun Gemini, Moon Pisces ☉ ♊ ☽ ♓

Hidden depths to personality, good with children, also sports and dancing. Imaginative writer but too ready to explain all to others. Bubbly personality but lacking in confidence, nervous and incapable if under severe stress.

Sun Cancer, Moon Aries ☉ ♋ ☽ ♈

Capable and competitive type with a good business head and the ability to understand others. Would need a good home but easily bored if spending too much time on it. A strange mixture of caring and impatience.

Sun Cancer, Moon Taurus ☉ ♋ ☽ ♉

Kind, caring and cuddly. You love your home and family, you

also have a good head for business. Artistic, musical and rather lazy, inclined to brood.

Sun Cancer, Moon Gemini ☉ ♋ ☽ ♊

Clever and businesslike, pleasant and successful. You appear slow but can be quick and cunning. Good politician, terrific traveller. Could have sporting abilities.

Sun Cancer, Moon Cancer ☉ ♋ ☽ ♋

Strong emotions, strong attachment to family. You tend to be moody and to cut off from other people. Kind-hearted, aware of the needs of others. Attached to the past, good historian.

Sun Cancer, Moon Leo ☉ ♋ ☽ ♌

Caring and compassionate, very loving towards your family and friends. Emotionally vulnerable. You have high standards and can cut off your nose to spite your face.

Sun Cancer, Moon Virgo ☉ ♋ ☽ ♍

Good placement for a nurse or doctor, caring in a practical way. Good with details, excellent memory. Will cut off from others when hurt. Good business head, rather dogged, good salesperson. A worrier.

Sun Cancer, Moon Libra ☉ ♋ ☽ ♎

Good business head on your shoulders. Ambitious for self and your family. Love of beauty and harmony, probably artistic. May have difficulty in putting ideas into practice.

Sun Cancer, Moon Scorpio ☉ ♋ ☽ ♏

Strongly intuitive and probably very moody. You would be difficult to ignore. Try to keep a positive outlook on life and avoid being too pessimistic.

Sun Cancer, Moon Sagittarius ☉ ♋ ☽ ♐

This combination makes you a family person who needs emotional freedom. You are idealistic and lovable but you may ask more from life than you could reasonably expect to obtain.

Sun Cancer, Moon Capricorn ☉ ♋ ☽ ♑

You have a very good head for business, you are shrewd and

intuitive. You can succeed as long as you don't try to cut corners or to save money in silly ways.

Sun Cancer, Moon Aquarius ☉ ♋ ☽ ♒

A clever politician with a quirky mind which operates behind a placid façade. You can put your point of view across well. You keep your eye firmly fixed on the main chance.

Sun Cancer, Moon Pisces ☉ ♋ ☽ ♓

Very sensitive and intuitive, you are so tuned in to others that you can forget your own needs. You may prefer to work in a field where you can care for less fortunate people (or animals).

Sun Leo, Moon Aries ☉ ♌ ☽ ♈

You have courage, verve and enthusiasm but you must learn not to ride roughshod over others. If you can see beyond your own needs, you can go far.

Sun Leo, Moon Taurus ☉ ♌ ☽ ♉

You are kind reliable, dedicated to your family and highly practical but you may be too obstinate for your own good. Traditional outlook on life.

Sun Leo, Moon Gemini ☉ ♌ ☽ ♊

You like to be busy and your mind works overtime. You are independent, creative and clever with good leadership qualities but your sarcasm might be a bit too much for some people.

Sun Leo, Moon Cancer ☉ ♌ ☽ ♋

A real family person with strong need to mother people. Your emotions may overtake you at times. You like the past and tradition. Very caring and kind.

Sun Leo, Moon Leo ☉ ♌ ☽ ♌

Dramatic and outgoing, you need to dazzle others. You are funny and entertaining but might be a bit too self-centred for comfort. Try to cope with details rather than ignore them.

Sun Leo, Moon Virgo ☉ ♌ ☽ ♍

You could be an excellent employer as you can delegate and also work in a logical manner. Your sharp tongue might be a bit hard to live with. You are very honest and basically kind natured.

Sun Leo, Moon Libra ☉ ♌ ☽ ♎

Very affectionate and probably very sexy, you have a great sense of style. You also have a good head for business but you may be too fond of having things your own way.

Sun Leo, Moon Scorpio ☉ ♌ ☽ ♏

Very intense and strong personality, possibly too dramatic. You are very loyal and may be rather possessive but your colleagues will respect you for your honesty and your capacity for work.

Sun Leo, Moon Sagittarius ☉ ♌ ☽ ♐

Very adventurous, you cannot be tied down. You are loyal, proud and kind-hearted. You have high personal standards but will have to curb your sarcasm and also think before committing yourself.

Sun Leo, Moon Capricorn ☉ ♌ ☽ ♑

Very organized and ambitious, you are destined to succeed in some traditional field of work. Don't ride roughshod over others or cover up your softness too much.

Sun Leo, Moon Aquarius ☉ ♌ ☽ ♒

You have strong opinions and can throw yourself into a cause. You are loyal, faithful and have a well developed sense of fair play. Try to develop practicality and a flexible outlook.

Sun Leo, Moon Pisces ☉ ♌ ☽ ♓

A dreamer and mystic who can bring dreams to life. It is hard for you to turn away from those who need your help and strength. Don't become down-hearted if all your plans don't work out. Creative and kind-hearted.

Sun Virgo, Moon Aries ☉ ♍ ☽ ♈

Your mind is sharp and so is your tongue. Being quick and clever you can succeed at many jobs. Self-expression in the form of writing is essential for you.

Sun Virgo, Moon Taurus ☉ ♍ ☽ ♉

Interested in the growing and preparing of food, creative in a structured way and kind. You may lack the confidence to get things off the ground. Sensible, helpful and practical outlook.

Sun Virgo, Moon Gemini ☉ ♍ ☽ ♊

You are very quick and clever, your mind and tongue are rarely still. You can gather and analyse information but your intellect may prevent you from getting in touch with your own and other people's feelings.

Sun Virgo, Moon Cancer ☉ ♍ ☽ ♋

Very caring, interested in food and nutrition. Could be a good business person in a small way. You worry about your family and can be a bit too fussy and moody for comfort.

Sun Virgo, Moon Leo ☉ ♍ ☽ ♌

Caring, conscientious and organized, you can be relied upon to get things done. You may work with children. Your personal standards are very high but you lack confidence.

Sun Virgo, Moon Virgo ☉ ♍ ☽ ♍

Lack of confidence partly due to an unhappy childhood. You may pay too much attention to details and worry too much about small matters. Honest and kind, you always try to help others and do your duty in every way.

Sun Virgo, Moon Libra ☉ ♍ ☽ ♎

You are neat and tidy, you enjoy organizing. Could be a good mediator or co-operative worker. Good thinker but slow to make decisions. A good cook.

Sun Virgo, Moon Scorpio ☉ ♍ ☽ ♏

Clever and critical you would make a very good doctor or nurse. You need to get to the bottom of things but may be too cool for comfort towards others.

Sun Virgo, Moon Sagittarius ☉ ♍ ☽ ♐

Humanitarian and thoughtful, you are interested in education. Warm and friendly and sometimes impulsive, you can also attend to details. Could make a good teacher but an even better travel agent.

Sun Virgo, Moon Capricorn ☉ ♍ ☽ ♑

Good in business but possibly too self-disciplined and serious. You are capable, conscientious and clever but you need to cultivate a sense of fun and give some attention to the need of others. Very reliable family member.

Sun Virgo, Moon Aquarius ☉ ♍ ☽ ♒

You could be a wonderful teacher. Deep thinker, very helpful to those in need. Don't let your need for independence deprive you of family life or keep you separated from your feelings.

Sun Virgo, Moon Pisces ☉ ♍ ☽ ♓

You live to serve the needs of others and then wonder why your own needs are not being met. Your mind is good when projected outwardly towards intellectual pursuits. Intuitive, interested in medicine and nutrition.

Sun Libra, Moon Aries ☉ ♎ ☽ ♈

You are a good initiator but might find it difficult to finish what you start. Others may help you to do this. You are clever and intuitive but can be selfish and impatient. Good in a crisis.

Sun Libra, Moon Taurus ☉ ♎ ☽ ♉

You are attractive to look at and have excellent taste. You love music and art but may be too lazy to become skilled yourself. Good homemaker and family person with practical business mind.

Sun Libra, Moon Gemini ☉ ♎ ☽ ♊

A theorizer with a good mind, you can be superficial. Dextrous and clever you have the ability to put techniques into practice as long as you have help from others. Keep in touch with your feelings and those of others.

Sun Libra, Moon Cancer ☉ ♎ ☽ ♋

Kind and pleasant, you make a nice home and are a good caring family member. Good personnel manager or accountant. You need to close off from others from time to time to do your own thing.

Sun Libra, Moon Leo ☉ ♎ ☽ ♌

You are in love with love half the time with a romantic and dramatic attitude to life. Clever and creative but could become easily bored. Very clever in business or politics.

Sun Libra, Moon Virgo ☉ ♎ ☽ ♍

Pleasant, charming and sensible, you can do most things as long as they are not messy or dirty. Loyal to friends. Good at detailed work. Literate and musical.

Sun Libra, Moon Libra ☉ ♎ ☽ ♎

You are very attractive both in looks and as a personality but you may be in a bit of a dream half the time. You may need to be more decisive and more energetic.

Sun Libra, Moon Scorpio ☉ ♎ ☽ ♏

Strongly sexed and intense, you would be a handful for anyone who comes close to you. You are determined and businesslike but must watch a tendency to dominate others.

Sun Libra, Moon Sagittarius ☉ ♎ ☽ ♐

You will probably travel quite a bit on business and should be great at dealing with and negotiating with foreigners. The legal profession would draw you as you have a good sense of judgement.

Sun Libra, Moon Capricorn ☉ ♎ ☽ ♑

You are very purposeful and a harder worker than Librans usually are. You could be very successful as your judgement of people is pretty acute.

Sun Libra, Moon Aquarius ☉ ♎ ☽ ♒

Very independent and also quite clever. You have good judgement and are able to lead others strongly but calmly. Your imagination is strong and could be used to make your living.

Sun Libra, Moon Pisces ☉ ♎ ☽ ♓

Very artistic and musical, you can be a dreamy romantic. Both your appearance and your nature are attractive. You have a deep level of intuition but may be a bit slow to put things into action.

Sun Scorpio, Moon Aries ☉ ♏ ☽ ♈

You have a strong character but might be *too* ready to fight everything and everyone. Your feelings are intense and your temper rather short but you have deep reserves of courage and can achieve a great deal.

Sun Scorpio, Moon Taurus ☉ ♏ ☽ ♉

Sensual and musical you might have great talent for something attractive like horticulture. You may be too obstinate or too practical. A very reliable type.

Sun Scorpio, Moon Gemini ☉ ♏ ☽ ♊

This combination shows a difficult childhood and an early sense of loss. Don't continue to view the world with too much suspicion. Very clever and intuitive about people.

Sun Scorpio, Moon Cancer ☉ ♏ ☽ ♋

Attractive to look at and talk too, you are deeply intuitive but may be able to relate more easily to animals than to people. Your moodiness will be your weak point.

Sun Scorpio, Moon Leo ☉ ♏ ☽ ♌

Very fixed opinions it is hard for you to adapt. Loyal to your family especially your children. You can finish what you start. Guard against overdramatizing everything.

Sun Scorpio, Moon Virgo ☉ ♏ ☽ ♍

This shows a difficult childhood with feelings of alienation. Try to develop trust in others. Clever and dutiful you could be drawn to a career in the medical profession.

Sun Scorpio, Moon Libra ☉ ♏ ☽ ♎

You are attractive and clever, this combination gives diplomacy and determination, you would make a good politician. You may either swamp your family with your personality or ignore them while pursuing your career.

Sun Scorpio, Moon Scorpio ☉ ♏ ☽ ♏

You have a powerful personality and often feel passionate about everything. Try not to dominate others. You can achieve almost anything you set your mind to.

Sun Scorpio, Moon Sagittarius ☉ ♏ ☽ ♐
Clever and clairvoyant, you would make a good lawyer or businessman but also a good detective. Your sense of humour helps you to keep everything in perspective.

Sun Scorpio, Moon Capricorn ☉ ♏ ☽ ♑
You could be a rather serious and determined person. You would reach the top in any field you set your heart on but could miss out on the personal side of life until your later years.

Sun Scorpio, Moon Aquarius ☉ ♏ ☽ ♒
You are independent and clever with a strong intuitive streak. You are decisive and instinctive but might be something of an intolerant tough guy.

Sun Scorpio, Moon Pisces ☉ ♏ ☽ ♓
Intuitive and artistic, probably musical. You have a strong drive to help others, probably in the field of health. You can withdraw into injured silence or spitefulness if you feel threatened.

Sun Sagittarius, Moon Aries ☉ ♐ ☽ ♈
You are open and honest but may be too quick to jump into exciting new schemes. Your restlessness might take you around the world but also may make it difficult for you to hang on to relationships.

Sun Sagittarius, Moon Taurus ☉ ♐ ☽ ♉
You are kind and good-hearted with great enthusiasm for the good things of life. You could be an inspired cook or artist and have the ability to combine practicality with imagination.

Sun Sagittarius, Moon Gemini ☉ ♐ ☽ ♊
You are always busy and restless. You could be a very good sportsman or entertainer. Clever and articulate you could make a good writer.

Sun Sagittarius, Moon Cancer ☉ ♐ ☽ ♋
You are intuitive and creative and would make a good medium. There is a split between your need for home comforts and your need for freedom. Childish at times.

Sun Sagittarius, Moon Leo ☉ ♐ ☽ ♌

Dramatic and outgoing you would do well on the stage. Try to tune in a bit more to the needs of others. Youthful and active, you are great fun to be with.

Sun Sagittarius, Moon Virgo ☉ ♐ ☽ ♍

You have the ability to think both deeply and in an organized manner. You would make a wonderful teacher. Don't lay the law down to others.

Sun Sagittarius, Moon Libra ☉ ♐ ☽ ♎

You would make a fabulous barrister as you have a gift for all things legal. Don't be too hard on others who are not as bright or as successful as you.

Sun Sagittarius, Moon Scorpio ☉ ♐ ☽ ♏

You could make a good detective as you have both investigative ability and a legal mind. Don't be too hard on those who either don't share your interests or are not as capable as you.

Sun Sagittarius, Moon Sagittarius ☉ ♐ ☽ ♐

You would make a terrific explorer as you love travel and are too restless to sit still for long. Try to tune into ordinary people as not everyone will understand the breadth of your mind.

Sun Sagittarius, Moon Capricorn ☉ ♐ ☽ ♑

Clever and determined, honest and entertaining, you could go far in life. You should travel and be involved with business but you must have some patience with less capable people.

Sun Sagittarius, Moon Aquarius ☉ ♐ ☽ ♒

Your mind is broad and you can teach others. You tend to live in a world of your own which is out of step with most of the rest of the world. Could be an eccentric genius.

Sun Sagittarius, Moon Pisces ☉ ♐ ☽ ♓

You are intuitive, kind and spiritual and would make a good teacher. You are artistic and imaginative and have much to give others but you may be a bit vague and impractical at times.

Sun Capricorn, Moon Aries ☉ ♑ ☽ ♈

You have a great deal of determination and may be very clever as well. Once you have set your mind on something, you will get there for sure but you may tread on a few toes while doing it.

Sun Capricorn, Moon Taurus ☉ ♑ ☽ ♉

Practical and sensible you can achieve much both in the artistic and the business world. Guard against stubbornness and try to see the other person's point of view.

Sun Capricorn, Moon Gemini ☉ ♑ ☽ ♊

Clever but organized. Could make a good writer, salesman, business person with the ability to put good ideas into practice and finish what you start.

Sun Capricorn, Moon Cancer ☉ ♑ ☽ ♋

Home-loving family person, very loyal, decent, also extremely business-like. Can have a tendency to withdraw into your shell. You worry about everything. A good teacher or counsellor.

Sun Capricorn, Moon Leo ☉ ♑ ☽ ♌

Good in positions of authority. A caring boss. Decent, reliable, but also very determined, may be apt to ride over people who are weaker.

Sun Capricorn, Moon Virgo ☉ ♑ ☽ ♍

Very stable, reliable, family person. Probably a very good cook. Very good head for business. Could be a bit too lacking in humour or too pedantic.

Sun Capricorn, Moon Libra ☉ ♑ ☽ ♎

A good mixture of stability plus business ability. Can get on with people and also achieve a great deal, but maybe a bit over enthusiastic when it comes to money-making ideas.

Sun Capricorn, Moon Scorpio ☉ ♑ ☽ ♏

Great strength of character. Clear idea of where you are going and what you want out of life. Very dependable, loyal, kind, but you have no time for fools. You hate to show your feelings.

Sun Capricorn, Moon Sagittarius ☉ ♑ ☽ ♐

Great stability and ability plus a broad sweeping mind. Could work in the travel industry or teaching, legal or church work. Good in any sort of concentrated work where you deal with people in authority.

Sun Capricorn, Moon Capricorn ☉ ♑ ☽ ♑

Very shy and withdrawn. Very hard worker, good with the elderly. Could find life very difficult until later on. A creative hobby or outlet would be very beneficial to you.

Sun Capricorn, Moon Aquarius ☉ ♑ ☽ ♒

Good organizer. Able to do things on a big scale. Can be a bit hard on yourself and on other people, but very determined and capable.

Sun Capricorn, Moon Pisces ☉ ♑ ☽ ♓

Deep, kindly, intuitive, very good in a caring profession, particularly dealing with the old, but could be a bit too shy and too easily hurt. Rather serious.

Sun Aquarius, Moon Aries ☉ ♒ ☽ ♈

A very broad-ranging mind. Good teacher, engineer, very clever, but might be difficult to live with. Don't judge other people too harshly. Good sense of humour.

Sun Aquarius, Moon Taurus ☉ ♒ ☽ ♉

You can cope with a lot and achieve a lot. You are very steady, determined and reliable, but could be too stubborn. You may be interested in music, art or beauty products.

Sun Aquarius, Moon Gemini ☉ ♒ ☽ ♊

A natural student or teacher, very clever. A bit inclined to flip from one idea to another and also need to develop stability in relationships with other people.

Sun Aquarius, Moon Cancer ☉ ♒ ☽ ♋

A good family person, good with small children and animals. Can teach, a good companion but can be a bit inclined to withdraw into a shell.

Sun Aquarius, Moon Leo ☉ ≈ ☽ ♌

Very lively personality, always busy doing a lot of things at once. Loyal, a bit stubborn, determined, but can be independent and awkward.

Sun Aquarius, Moon Virgo ☉ ≈ ☽ ♍

Clever, studious, able to put ideas into practice in a very detailed way. Probably very good in research but could be a bit eccentric and nit-picking, difficult to live with.

Sun Aquarius, Moon Libra ☉ ≈ ☽ ♎

Great fun, easy-going, great friend to everybody, but a bit unreliable in close relationships. Good in almost any field that doesn't require too much steady effort.

Sun Aquarius, Moon Scorpio ☉ ≈ ☽ ♏

Full of self confidence. The ability to be a leader. Can be too inclined to ride roughshod over other people. A very original thinker. Easily irritated with fools.

Sun Aquarius, Moon Sagittarius ☉ ≈ ☽ ♐

Very independent, outspoken, a bit tactless, interested in any kind of novel idea. Intelligent, a good teacher. You have a tendency to rush into things without thinking.

Sun Aquarius, Moon Capricorn ☉ ≈ ☽ ♑

A mixture of seriousness and spontaneity. Responsible, capable, a good family person, a good business person. Original ideas and a lot of determination.

Sun Aquarius, Moon Aquarius ☉ ≈ ☽ ≈

Very eccentric, very freedom-loving, independent, great fun. Original ideas and an original lifestyle, but not really a family person. Don't judge others too harshly.

Sun Aquarius, Moon Pisces ☉ ≈ ☽ ♓

Very imaginative, intuitive, with the ability to blend common sense and mysticism. Kindly, intelligent, a bit apt to wander off on your own and go into flights of fancy.

Sun Pisces, Moon Aries ☉ ♓ ☽ ♈

Intuitive, quick and clever, quite determined, great fun and good friend, but not a very reliable family person. You may fluctuate between selfishness and consideration for others.

Sun Pisces, Moon Taurus ☉ ♓ ☽ ♉

Sociable and pleasant, artistic, kind and musical. It's difficult for you to start things but once started you will finish them. You are good looking and graceful. Inclined to be lazy.

Sun Pisces, Moon Gemini ☉ ♓ ☽ ♊

Nervous, talkative, clever, a worrier. You need a stable partner. You're good fun, good looking and interesting, but you never really grow up. Your nerves let you down from time to time.

Sun Pisces, Moon Cancer ☉ ♓ ☽ ♋

Sensitive, kind, thoughtful, very moody, but also kind and caring. You would make a good nurse, doctor or teacher. You may be interested in diets and cooking. Understanding but somewhat impractical.

Sun Pisces, Moon Leo ☉ ♓ ☽ ♌

Generous, imaginative, creative and kindly. You need to be out and about. You like stimulation of new people but your confidence goes very quickly and you can be susceptible to flattery.

Sun Pisces, Moon Virgo ☉ ♓ ☽ ♍

Nervous, thoughtful, deep, intuitive, could work very well on your own in a creative way. Can be too fussy, too worrying, would need a strong partner. Interested in food and diets.

Sun Pisces, Moon Libra ☉ ♓ ☽ ♎

You will need to keep in touch with reality. Your ideas are good. You could achieve a lot if allied to somebody with strength and practicality. You need other people to encourage you.

Sun Pisces, Moon Scorpio ☉ ♓ ☽ ♏

Perceptive, intuitive, deep, attracted to medicine, police and forensic work. Deep insight into people, can manipulate others.

Moody but also caring and kind. Can be self-absorbed and difficult to live with.

Sun Pisces, Moon Sagittarius ☉ ✕ ☽ ♐
Great traveller with a deep and thoughtful mind. Could work in the religious field or as a conservationist. Unreliable as a family person as your mind is elsewhere most of the time.

Sun Pisces, Moon Capricorn ☉ ✕ ☽ ♑
Creativity, intuition and practicality mixed together here, so you can make achievements on the work front and also be a good family person. The only problem is lack of confidence.

Sun Pisces, Moon Aquarius ☉ ✕ ☽ ♒
Friendly, could start projects and then lose interest. Mystical, a good teacher and a caring person but you need a stable and practical partner as you don't often have your feet on the ground.

Sun Pisces, Moon Pisces ☉ ✕ ☽ ✕
Very active imagination. You see omens and meanings in things. You prefer to work from home by yourself. You find people tend to wear you out, you soak up other people's problems and do find family life hard sometimes.

Conclusion

For those of you who have never delved deeper into astrology than to read about your Sun sign or to read the horoscopes in magazines and newspapers, I hope that this book will whet your appetite and encourage you to look deeper now. For those of you who are already interested in the subject, to the point of erecting charts and pursuing your own research, I hope that this book adds to your knowledge and understanding of how just *one* of the planets works through our lives.

I have learned a great deal about the Moon during the course of researching this book, I never realized that there was so much to be found in one tiny satellite. I dread to think of erecting charts for births on other planets such as Saturn which has around a dozen moons or more! I think I will leave the next generation of astrologers to grapple with that one.

Astrology is a living and growing subject, an intuitive science which will be taken more seriously as the age of Aquarius rolls in. I hope you now progress alongside your planets, learn and enjoy a totally fascinating subject.

APPENDIX 1

The Ephemeris

—————How to use the Ephemeris—————

The Ephemeris shows the position of the Moon at midnight on every other day. To find *your* Moon position:

1. Find the year of your birth.
2. Find the month of your birth.
3. Find the date of your birthday, or the date immediately preceding your birthday.
4. Unless you were born on or just after midnight on the date as shown you will have to make an adjustment by *counting forward half a degree per hour.*

   Midnight on birthday—position as shown in the Ephemeris

6 am	same day	add	3°
12 noon	same day	add	6°
6 pm	same day	add	9°
Midnight	next day	add	12°
6 am	next day	add	15°
12 noon	next day	add	18°
6 pm	next day	add	21°

If your counting takes you to more than 29° of any sign, the Moon will move to the *next sign.*

Remember, if you were born in New York—in addition to the above *add* a further five hours (or 2½°). If you were born in Bombay, subtract five hours (or 2½°). See page 21.

If you are now completely flummoxed, phone a friendly astrologer and ask for help.

1930

	Jan	Feb	Mar	Apr	May	Jun	Jul	Aug	Sep	Oct	Nov	Dec
1	20Cp	5Pi	14Pi	1Ta	7Ge	0Le	10Vi	1Sc	19Sg	22Cp	6Pi	8Ar
3	14Aq	29Pi	9Ar	27Ta	5Cn	29Le	8Li	27Sc	13Cp	16Aq	0Ar	2Ta
5	8Pi	24Ar	4Ta	25Ge	4Le	27Vi	4Sc	22Sg	7Aq	10Pi	24Ar	29Ta
7	2Ar	20Ta	0Ge	23Cn	2Vi	24Li	0Sg	16Cp	1Pi	4Ar	20Ta	26Ge
9	28Ar	18Ge	28Ge	22Le	0Li	20Sc	25Sg	10Aq	25Pi	28Ar	17Ge	25Cn
11	25Ta	18Cn	27Cn	20Vi	28Li	16Sg	19Cp	4Pi	19Ar	24Ta	14Cn	24Le
13	24Ge	18Le	26Le	19Li	24Sc	11Cp	13Aq	28Pi	14Ta	20Ge	13Le	22Vi
15	25Cn	18Vi	26Vi	16Sc	20Sg	5Aq	7Pi	22Ar	10Ge	18Cn	11Vi	20Li
17	25Le	17Li	24Li	12Sg	14Cp	28Aq	1Ar	17Ta	7Cn	16Le	9Li	17Sc
19	24Vi	13Sc	21Sc	7Cp	8Aq	22Pi	25Ar	14Ge	6Le	15Vi	7Sc	13Sg
21	22Li	8Sg	16Sg	1Aq	2Pi	17Ar	21Ta	12Cn	6Vi	14Li	5Sg	9Cp
23	17Sc	2Cp	11Cp	24Aq	26Pi	13Ta	19Ge	12Le	6Li	13Sc	1Cp	4Aq
25	12Sg	26Cp	4Aq	19Pi	22Ar	11Ge	19Cn	13Vi	5Sc	10Sg	26Cp	28Aq
27	6Cp	20Aq	28Aq	14Ar	18Ta	10Cn	19Le	12Li	2Sg	6Cp	20Aq	21Pi
29	29Cp		23Pi	10Ta	17Ge	10Le	19Vi	10Sc	28Sg	0Aq	14Pi	15Ar
31	23Aq		18Ar		16Cn		18Li	6Sg		24Aq		10Ta

1931

	Jan	Feb	Mar	Apr	May	Jun	Jul	Aug	Sep	Oct	Nov	Dec
1	23Ta	13Cn	21Cn	14Vi	23Li	14Sg	19Cp	5Pi	19Ar	22Ta	9Cn	16Le
3	20Ge	12Le	20Le	14Li	22Sc	11Cp	15Aq	29Pi	13Ta	16Ge	5Le	13Vi
5	19Cn	13Vi	21Vi	14Sc	20Sg	7Aq	9Pi	23Ar	7Ge	12Cn	3Vi	12Li
7	19Le	12Li	21Li	12Sg	16Cp	1Pi	3Ar	17Ta	3Cn	9Le	2Li	11Sc
9	18Vi	10Sc	20Sc	8Cp	11Aq	25Pi	26Ar	12Ge	1Le	8Vi	2Sc	10Sg
11	17Li	7Sg	16Sg	3Aq	5Pi	18Ar	21Ta	9Cn	0Vi	8Li	2Sg	8Cp
13	14Sc	2Cp	12Cp	27Aq	29Pi	13Ta	17Ge	7Le	0Li	9Sc	0Cp	5Aq
15	10Sg	27Cp	6Aq	20Pi	22Ar	9Ge	14Cn	7Vi	0Sc	8Sg	27Cp	0Pi
17	5Cp	21Aq	0Pi	14Ar	17Ta	5Cn	13Le	6Li	29Sc	5Cp	22Aq	24Pi
19	0Aq	15Pi	23Pi	8Ta	13Ge	3Le	12Vi	5Sc	26Sg	1Aq	16Pi	18Ar
21	24Aq	8Ar	17Ar	3Ge	9Cn	2Vi	11Li	3Sg	22Cp	26Aq	10Ar	12Ta
23	18Pi	2Ta	11Ta	29Ge	7Le	0Li	9Sc	0Cp	17Aq	20Pi	4Ta	6Ge
25	11Ar	27Ta	6Ge	26Cn	5Vi	28Li	6Sg	25Cp	11Pi	13Ar	28Ta	2Cn
27	6Ta	23Ge	2Cn	24Le	3Li	26Sc	3Cp	20Aq	4Ar	7Ta	23Ge	29Cn
29	1Ge		0Le	23Vi	2Sc	23Sg	28Cp	14Pi	28Ar	1Ge	19Cn	26Le
31	28Ge		29Le		0Sg		23Aq	7Ar		26Ge		24Vi

1932

	Jan	Feb	Mar	Apr	May	Jun	Jul	Aug	Sep	Oct	Nov	Dec
1	8Li	1Sg	26Sg	15Aq	18Pi	2Ta	5Ge	21Cn	10Vi	18Li	12Sg	20Cp
3	6Sc	29Sg	22Cp	9Pi	12Ar	26Ta	29Ge	17Le	9Li	18Sc	11Cp	17Aq
5	5Sg	25Cp	17Aq	3Ar	6Ta	21Ge	25Cn	15Vi	8Sc	17Sg	8Aq	13Pi
7	3Cp	21Aq	12Pi	27Ar	29Ta	16Cn	21Le	13Li	7Sg	15Cp	4Pi	8Ar
9	0Aq	16Pi	6Ar	20Ta	24Ge	11Le	18Vi	11Sc	5Cp	12Aq	29Pi	2Ta
11	25Aq	10Ar	0Ta	14Ge	18Cn	8Vi	16Li	10Sg	2Aq	7Pi	23Ar	25Ta
13	20Pi	3Ta	24Ta	9Cn	14Le	6Li	15Sc	8Cp	28Aq	2Ar	17Ta	19Ge
15	14Ar	27Ta	18Ge	5Le	11Vi	4Sc	14Sg	5Aq	23Pi	26Ar	10Ge	13Cn
17	7Ta	22Ge	13Cn	2Vi	10Li	4Sg	12Cp	2Pi	17Ar	20Ta	4Cn	8Le
19	2Ge	18Cn	10Le	1Li	10Sc	3Cp	10Aq	27Pi	11Ta	13Ge	29Cn	4Vi
21	27Ge	16Le	8Vi	2Sc	10Sg	2Aq	6Pi	21Ar	5Ge	7Cn	23Le	0Li
23	24Cn	15Vi	8Li	2Sg	10Cp	28Aq	1Ar	15Ta	29Ge	2Le	21Vi	28Li
25	22Le	15Li	9Sc	1Cp	7Aq	23Pi	25Ar	9Ge	24Cn	28Le	19Li	28Sc
27	20Vi	14Sc	8Sg	28Cp	3Pi	17Ar	19Ta	3Cn	20Le	26Vi	19Sc	28Sg
29	19Li	12Sg	6Cp	24Aq	27Pi	11Ta	13Ge	29Cn	18Vi	26Li	20Sg	27Cp
31	17Sc		2Aq		21Ar		8Cn	26Le		27Sc		25Aq

1933

	Jan	Feb	Mar	Apr	May	Jun	Jul	Aug	Sep	Oct	Nov	Dec
1	9Pi	24Ar	2Ta	16Ge	18Cn	4Vi	9Li	2Sg	25Cp	3Pi	22Ar	26Ta
3	4Ar	18Ta	26Ta	10Cn	12Le	0Li	7Sc	1Cp	24Aq	0Ar	17Ta	20Ge
5	28Ar	12Ge	20Ge	4Le	8Vi	28Li	7Sg	1Aq	22Pi	26Ar	12Ge	14Cn
7	22Ta	6Cn	14Cn	0Vi	5Li	28Sc	7Cp	29Aq	18Ar	21Ta	5Cn	7Le
9	16Ge	1Le	9Le	27Vi	4Sc	29Sg	7Aq	27Pi	13Ta	15Ge	29Cn	2Vi
11	10Cn	27Le	5Vi	26Li	5Sg	28Cp	5Pi	23Ar	8Ge	9Cn	23Le	27Vi
13	5Le	24Vi	3Li	26Sc	5Cp	27Aq	2Ar	18Ta	1Cn	3Le	18Vi	23Li
15	1Vi	21Li	2Sc	25Sg	4Aq	23Pi	27Ar	11Ge	25Cn	28Le	15Li	22Sc
17	27Vi	20Sc	1Sg	24Cp	1Pi	18Ar	21Ta	5Cn	20Le	24Vi	14Sc	22Sg
19	25Li	18Sg	29Sg	21Aq	27Pi	12Ta	15Ge	29Cn	16Vi	21Li	14Sg	23Cp
21	23Sc	16Cp	27Cp	17Pi	21Ar	6Ge	9Cn	24Le	13Li	20Sc	14Cp	22Aq
23	22Sg	14Aq	24Aq	12Ar	15Ta	0Cn	3Le	20Vi	11Sc	20Sg	13Aq	20Pi
25	21Cp	11Pi	20Pi	6Ta	9Ge	24Cn	28Le	17Li	9Sg	18Cp	10Pi	16Ar
27	19Aq	7Ar	15Ar	0Ge	3Cn	18Le	23Vi	14Sc	8Cp	16Aq	6Ar	11Ta
29	16Pi		10Ta	24Ge	27Cn	13Vi	20Li	12Sg	6Aq	13Pi	2Ta	5Ge
31	12Ar		4Ge		21Le		17Sc	11Cp		9Ar		29Ge

1934

	Jan	Feb	Mar	Apr	May	Jun	Jul	Aug	Sep	Oct	Nov	Dec
1	11Cn	25Le	4Vi	22Li	29Sc	22Cp	1Pi	22Ar	9Ge	12Cn	25Le	27Vi
3	4Le	20Vi	29Vi	19Sc	28Sg	21Aq	29Pi	18Ta	4Cn	6Le	19Vi	22Li
5	28Le	16Li	26Li	17Sg	26Cp	19Pi	26Ar	13Ge	27Cn	29Le	14Li	19Sc
7	23Vi	12Sc	23Sc	16Cp	25Aq	16Ar	21Ta	7Cn	21Le	24Vi	11Sc	17Sg
9	19Li	10Sg	20Sg	14Aq	22Pi	12Ta	16Ge	0Le	15Vi	19Li	8Sg	16Cp
11	16Sc	9Cp	19Cp	12Pi	19Ar	7Ge	10Cn	24Le	10Li	15Sc	7Cp	15Aq
13	15Sg	9Aq	18Aq	9Ar	15Ta	1Cn	3Le	18Vi	5Sc	12Sg	5Aq	14Pi
15	16Cp	8Pi	17Pi	6Ta	10Ge	25Cn	27Le	13Li	2Sg	10Cp	3Pi	12Ar
17	16Aq	7Ar	14Ar	2Ge	4Cn	18Le	21Vi	8Sc	29Sg	8Aq	1Ar	8Ta
19	15Pi	3Ta	11Ta	26Ge	28Cn	12Vi	16Li	5Sg	28Cp	7Pi	29Ar	4Ge
21	12Ar	28Ta	6Ge	20Cn	22Le	7Li	12Sc	3Cp	27Aq	5Ar	25Ta	29Ge
23	8Ta	22Ge	0Cn	14Le	16Vi	3Sc	10Sg	3Aq	26Pi	3Ta	21Ge	24Cn
25	2Ge	16Cn	24Cn	8Vi	12Li	1Sg	9Cp	3Pi	25Ar	0Ge	16Cn	17Le
27	26Ge	10Le	18Le	4Li	9Sc	1Cp	10Aq	3Ar	22Ta	26Ge	9Le	11Vi
29	20Cn		13Vi	1Sc	8Sg	1Aq	10Pi	1Ta	18Ge	20Cn	3Vi	5Li
31	13Le		8Li		7Cp		8Ar	27Ta		13Le		0Sc

1935

	Jan	Feb	Mar	Apr	May	Jun	Jul	Aug	Sep	Oct	Nov	Dec
1	13Sc	3Cp	12Cp	5Pi	14Ar	5Ge	10Cn	25Le	9Li	13Sc	0Cp	7Aq
3	11Sg	3Aq	11Aq	5Ar	12Ta	1Cn	4Le	19Vi	3Sc	8Sg	27Cp	5Pi
5	10Cp	3Pi	11Pi	4Ta	10Ge	26Cn	28Le	12Li	28Sc	3Cp	25Aq	4Ar
7	10Aq	3Ar	12Ar	2Ge	6Cn	20Le	22Vi	7Sc	24Sg	0Aq	23Pi	2Ta
9	10Pi	2Ta	10Ta	28Ge	1Le	14Vi	16Li	2Sg	21Cp	29Aq	23Ar	1Ge
11	8Ar	28Ta	7Ge	23Cn	24Le	8Li	11Sc	29Sg	21Aq	29Pi	22Ta	28Ge
13	5Ta	23Ge	2Cn	16Le	18Vi	3Sc	7Sg	27Cp	21Pi	0Ta	21Ge	25Cn
15	1Ge	17Cn	26Cn	10Vi	12Li	29Sc	5Cp	27Aq	21Ar	29Ta	17Cn	20Le
17	26Ge	11Le	20Le	4Li	8Sc	26Sg	4Aq	28Pi	20Ta	26Ge	12Le	14Vi
19	20Cn	5Vi	13Vi	29Li	4Sg	25Cp	4Pi	27Ar	17Ge	22Cn	6Vi	7Li
21	14Le	28Vi	8Li	25Sc	1Cp	24Aq	3Ar	25Ta	13Cn	16Le	0Li	2Sc
23	8Vi	23Li	2Sc	21Sg	29Cp	22Pi	1Ta	21Ge	7Le	9Vi	24Li	26Sc
25	2Li	18Sc	28Sc	18Cp	27Aq	20Ar	28Ta	16Cn	1Vi	3Li	18Sc	23Sg
27	26Li	14Sg	24Sg	16Aq	25Pi	18Ta	24Ge	10Le	25Vi	27Li	14Sg	20Cp
29	22Sc		21Cp	15Pi	24Ar	14Ge	19Cn	4Vi	18Li	22Sc	10Cp	18Aq
31	19Sg		20Aq		21Ta		13Le	27Vi		17Sg		16Pi

1936

	Jan	Feb	Mar	Apr	May	Jun	Jul	Aug	Sep	Oct	Nov	Dec
1	1Ar	23Ta	17Ge	5Le	8Vi	22Li	25Sc	11Cp	1Pi	9Ar	3Ge	10Cn
3	29Ar	20Ge	13Cn	29Le	2Li	16Sc	20Sg	8Aq	0Ar	9Ta	2Cn	8Le
5	27Ta	16Cn	8Le	23Vi	26Li	11Sg	16Cp	6Pi	0Ta	9Ge	29Cn	3Vi
7	24Ge	11Le	2Vi	17Li	20Sc	6Cp	13Aq	5Ar	29Ta	7Cn	25Le	28Vi
9	20Cn	6Vi	26Vi	11Sc	14Sg	3Aq	11Pi	4Ta	27Ge	3Le	19Vi	22Li
11	15Le	0Li	20Li	5Sg	10Cp	0Pi	9Ar	2Ge	23Cn	28Le	13Li	16Sc
13	10Vi	23Li	14Sc	0Cp	6Aq	28Pi	7Ta	0Cn	18Le	22Vi	7Sc	9Sg
15	3Li	17Sc	8Sg	26Cp	3Pi	27Ar	6Ge	26Cn	13Vi	16Li	1Sg	4Cp
17	27Li	12Sg	3Cp	23Aq	2Ar	26Ta	3Cn	22Le	7Li	10Sc	25Sg	29Cp
19	22Sc	8Cp	0Aq	22Pi	2Ta	24Ge	0Le	17Vi	1Sc	4Sg	19Cp	25Aq
21	17Sg	6Aq	29Aq	23Ar	1Ge	22Cn	26Le	11Li	25Sc	28Sg	15Aq	22Pi
23	14Cp	6Pi	29Pi	23Ta	0Cn	18Le	21Vi	5Sc	19Sg	23Cp	12Pi	20Ar
25	13Aq	6Ar	0Ta	22Ge	27Cn	13Vi	15Li	28Sc	14Cp	19Aq	11Ar	19Ta
27	12Pi	6Ta	29Ta	19Cn	22Le	7Li	8Sc	23Sg	10Aq	17Pi	10Ta	19Ge
29	11Ar	4Ge	27Ge	14Le	17Vi	1Sc	3Sg	19Cp	9Pi	17Ar	11Ge	18Cn
31	10Ta		23Cn		11Li		28Sg	16Aq		18Ta		15Le

1937

	Jan	Feb	Mar	Apr	May	Jun	Jul	Aug	Sep	Oct	Nov	Dec
1	29Le	14Li	22Li	6Sg	8Cp	25Aq	1Ar	24Ta	17Cn	25Le	13Li	17Sc
3	24Vi	8Sc	16Sc	29Sg	3Aq	21Pi	29Ar	23Ge	15Le	21Vi	8Sc	10Sg
5	18Li	1Sg	9Sg	24Cp	28Aq	19Ar	28Ta	21Cn	12Vi	17Li	2Sg	4Cp
7	12Sc	26Sg	3Cp	20Aq	26Pi	19Ta	28Ge	20Le	8Li	11Sc	25Sg	28Cp
9	6Sg	21Cp	29Cp	18Pi	25Ar	19Ge	27Cn	17Vi	3Sc	5Sg	19Cp	22Aq
11	0Cp	17Aq	26Aq	17Ar	26Ta	19Cn	25Le	13Li	27Sc	29Sg	13Aq	17Pi
13	25Cp	15Pi	24Pi	17Ta	26Ge	17Le	22Vi	7Sc	21Sg	23Cp	9Pi	14Ar
15	22Aq	14Ar	23Ar	17Ge	25Cn	14Vi	17Li	1Sg	15Cp	18Aq	6Ar	13Ta
17	19Pi	12Ta	23Ta	15Cn	22Le	9Li	11Sc	25Sg	10Aq	14Pi	5Ta	13Ge
19	17Ar	10Ge	21Ge	12Le	17Vi	3Sc	5Sg	19Cp	6Pi	12Ar	5Ge	13Cn
21	15Ta	8Cn	19Cn	8Vi	12Li	26Sc	29Sg	14Aq	4Ar	12Ta	5Cn	13Le
23	14Ge	5Le	15Le	3Li	6Sc	20Sg	23Cp	11Pi	3Ta	11Ge	4Le	11Vi
25	12Cn	2Vi	11Vi	27Li	29Sc	14Cp	18Aq	9Ar	1Ge	10Cn	2Vi	7Li
27	10Le	27Vi	6Li	21Sc	23Sg	9Aq	15Pi	7Ta	0Cn	8Le	28Vi	2Sc
29	6Vi		0Sc	14Sg	17Cp	5Pi	12Ar	5Ge	28Cn	5Vi	23Li	25Sc
31	2Li		24Sc		12Aq		10Ta	3Cn		1Li		19Sg

1938

	Jan	Feb	Mar	Apr	May	Jun	Jul	Aug	Sep	Oct	Nov	Dec
1	1Cp	16Aq	25Aq	13Ar	20Ta	13Cn	22Le	13Li	29Sc	1Cp	15Aq	17Pi
3	25Cp	11Pi	21Pi	11Ta	19Ge	13Le	20Vi	9Sc	23Sg	25Cp	9Pi	12Ar
5	19Aq	7Ar	17Ar	9Ge	18Cn	11Vi	17Li	3Sg	17Cp	19Aq	5Ar	9Ta
7	14Pi	4Ta	15Ta	8Cn	17Le	7Li	12Sc	27Sg	11Aq	14Pi	1Ta	8Ge
9	10Ar	2Ge	13Ge	6Le	14Vi	3Sc	6Sg	20Cp	5Pi	10Ar	29Ta	8Cn
11	8Ta	0Cn	11Cn	4Vi	10Li	27Sc	0Cp	14Aq	1Ar	6Ta	28Ge	7Le
13	6Ge	0Le	9Le	1Li	6Sc	21Sg	24Cp	9Pi	27Ar	4Ge	27Cn	6Vi
15	6Cn	29Le	8Vi	27Li	0Sg	15Cp	17Aq	4Ar	24Ta	2Cn	26Le	4Li
17	6Le	27Vi	5Li	22Sc	24Sg	8Aq	12Pi	0Ta	21Ge	0Le	23Vi	0Sc
19	5Vi	23Li	1Sc	16Sg	18Cp	3Pi	7Ar	27Ta	20Cn	29Le	20Li	25Sc
21	3Li	18Sc	26Sc	10Cp	12Aq	28Pi	3Ta	25Ge	19Le	27Vi	16Sc	20Sg
23	28Li	12Sg	20Sg	3Aq	6Pi	24Ar	1Ge	24Cn	18Vi	24Li	11Sg	14Cp
25	22Sc	6Cp	14Cp	28Aq	2Ar	22Ta	0Cn	24Le	16Li	20Sc	5Cp	7Aq
27	16Sg	0Aq	8Aq	24Pi	29Ar	22Ge	1Le	23Vi	12Sc	15Sg	29Cp	1Pi
29	9Cp		3Pi	21Ar	28Ta	22Cn	1Vi	21Li	7Sg	9Cp	23Aq	25Pi
31	4Aq		29Pi		28Ge		29Vi	17Sc		3Aq		20Ar

1939

	Jan	Feb	Mar	Apr	May	Jun	Jul	Aug	Sep	Oct	Nov	Dec
1	3Ta	24Ge	3Cn	27Le	5Li	26Sc	0Cp	15Aq	0Ar	3Ta	22Ge	0Le
3	1Ge	24Cn	2Le	26Vi	3Sc	21Sg	25Cp	9Pi	24Ar	29Ta	19Cn	28Le
5	1Cn	24Le	2Vi	25Li	0Sg	16Cp	18Aq	3Ar	19Ta	25Ge	17Le	26Vi
7	1Le	24Vi	2Li	22Sc	26Sg	10Aq	12Pi	27Ar	15Ge	22Cn	16Vi	24Li
9	1Vi	23Li	1Sc	18Sg	20Cp	4Pi	6Ar	22Ta	12Cn	21Le	14Li	22Sc
11	0Li	19Sc	27Sc	12Cp	14Aq	28Pi	1Ta	19Ge	12Le	21Vi	13Sc	19Sg
13	27Li	14Sg	22Sg	6Aq	8Pi	23Ar	27Ta	18Cn	12Vi	20Li	10Sg	15Cp
15	22Sc	8Cp	16Cp	0Pi	2Ar	19Ta	25Ge	18Le	12Li	19Sc	7Cp	9Aq
17	17Sg	1Aq	10Aq	24Pi	28Ar	17Ge	25Cn	19Vi	11Sc	16Sg	2Aq	3Pi
19	11Cp	25Aq	4Pi	19Ar	24Ta	16Cn	25Le	18Li	8Sg	11Cp	26Aq	27Pi
21	4Aq	19Pi	28Pi	15Ta	22Ge	16Le	25Vi	16Sc	3Cp	6Aq	19Pi	21Ar
23	28Aq	14Ar	23Ar	12Ge	21Cn	15Vi	23Li	12Sg	27Cp	29Aq	13Ar	16Ta
25	22Pi	9Ta	19Ta	10Cn	20Le	12Li	19Sc	6Cp	21Aq	23Pi	8Ta	13Ge
27	17Ar	5Ge	16Ge	8Le	18Vi	9Sc	15Sg	0Aq	15Pi	18Ar	4Ge	11Cn
29	12Ta		13Cn	7Vi	16Li	5Sg	9Cp	24Aq	9Ar	13Ta	2Cn	10Le
31	9Ge		12Le		12Sc		3Aq	18Pi		9Ge		9Vi

1940

	Jan	Feb	Mar	Apr	May	Jun	Jul	Aug	Sep	Oct	Nov	Dec
1	23Vi	15Sc	8Sg	26Cp	29Aq	12Ar	14Ta	1Cn	22Le	0Li	23Sc	0Cp
3	21Li	12Sg	4Cp	20Aq	22Pi	6Ta	10Ge	29Cn	21Vi	0Sc	22Sg	28Cp
5	18Sc	7Cp	29Cp	14Pi	16Ar	1Ge	6Cn	28Le	21Li	0Sg	20Cp	24Aq
7	15Sg	2Aq	23Aq	7Ar	10Ta	27Ge	4Le	27Vi	20Sc	28Sg	15Aq	18Pi
9	10Cp	26Aq	17Pi	1Ta	5Ge	24Cn	3Vi	26Li	18Sg	24Cp	10Pi	12Ar
11	5Aq	20Pi	10Ar	26Ta	1Cn	22Le	1Li	24Sc	14Cp	19Aq	3Ar	5Ta
13	29Aq	13Ar	4Ta	21Ge	28Cn	20Vi	29Li	21Sg	9Aq	13Pi	27Ar	29Ta
15	23Pi	7Ta	29Ta	17Cn	25Le	19Li	27Sc	17Cp	4Pi	6Ar	21Ta	25Ge
17	17Ar	2Ge	24Ge	15Le	24Vi	17Sc	24Sg	13Aq	28Pi	0Ta	15Ge	21Cn
19	11Ta	28Ge	21Cn	14Vi	23Li	15Sg	21Cp	7Pi	21Ar	24Ta	11Cn	17Le
21	7Ge	27Cn	20Le	14Li	22Sc	12Cp	16Aq	1Ar	15Ta	18Ge	7Le	15Vi
23	4Cn	27Le	20Vi	13Sc	20Sg	8Aq	11Pi	24Ar	9Ge	14Cn	4Vi	13Li
25	4Le	27Vi	20Li	12Sg	17Cp	3Pi	4Ar	18Ta	4Cn	10Le	2Li	11Sc
27	4Vi	27Li	20Sc	9Cp	12Aq	26Pi	28Ar	13Ge	1Le	8Vi	2Sc	10Sg
29	3Li	25Sc	17Sg	4Aq	7Pi	20Ar	22Ta	9Cn	0Vi	8Li	1Sg	8Cp
31	2Sc		13Cp		0Ar		18Ge	7Le		8Sc		6Aq

1941

	Jan	Feb	Mar	Apr	May	Jun	Jul	Aug	Sep	Oct	Nov	Dec
1	19Aq	3Ar	12Ar	25Ta	29Ge	16Le	23Vi	16Sc	9Cp	16Aq	4Ar	7Ta
3	14Pi	27Ar	5Ta	19Ge	23Cn	13Vi	21Li	14Sg	6Aq	12Pi	28Ar	0Ge
5	8Ar	21Ta	29Ta	14Cn	19Le	11Li	20Sc	13Cp	3Pi	7Ar	22Ta	24Ge
7	1Ta	15Ge	23Ge	10Le	17Vi	10Sc	19Sg	11Aq	28Pi	1Ta	15Ge	18Cn
9	25Ta	11Cn	19Cn	8Vi	16Li	10Sg	18Cp	7Pi	23Ar	25Ta	9Cn	13Le
11	20Ge	8Le	16Le	8Li	16Sc	10Cp	16Aq	2Ar	17Ta	19Ge	4Le	9Vi
13	16Cn	6Vi	15Vi	8Sc	17Sg	8Aq	12Pi	27Ar	10Ge	13Cn	29Le	5Li
15	13Le	5Li	15Li	8Sg	16Cp	4Pi	7Ar	21Ta	5Cn	8Le	26Vi	4Sc
17	11Vi	4Sc	14Sc	7Cp	13Aq	29Pi	1Ta	14Ge	0Le	4Vi	25Li	4Sg
19	9Li	3Sg	13Sg	4Aq	8Pi	23Ar	24Ta	9Cn	26Le	3Li	26Sc	4Cp
21	8Sc	0Cp	11Cp	29Aq	2Ar	16Ta	19Ge	5Le	25Vi	2Sc	26Sg	4Aq
23	6Sg	27Cp	7Aq	23Pi	26Ar	10Ge	14Cn	2Vi	24Li	3Sg	26Cp	1Pi
25	4Cp	23Aq	2Pi	17Ar	19Ta	5Cn	9Le	0Li	23Sc	2Cp	23Aq	27Pi
27	1Aq	17Pi	26Pi	11Ta	13Ge	0Le	6Vi	28Li	22Sg	0Aq	18Pi	22Ar
29	27Aq		20Ar	4Ge	8Cn	26Le	4Li	27Sc	20Cp	26Aq	13Ar	15Ta
31	21Pi		14Ta		3Le		2Sc	25Sg		22Pi		9Ge

1942

	Jan	Feb	Mar	Apr	May	Jun	Jul	Aug	Sep	Oct	Nov	Dec
1	21Ge	7Le	'15Le	3Li	11Sc	5Cp	13Aq	3Ar	19Ta	21Ge	5Le	7Vi
3	15Cn	2Vi	11Vi	2Sc	11Sg	4Aq	11Pi	29Ar	13Ge	15Cn	29Le	2Li
5	10Le	29Vi	9Li	1Sg	10Cp	2Pi	7Ar	23Ta	7Cn	9Le	24Vi	29Li
7	6Vi	26Li	7Sc	0Cp	9Aq	28Pi	2Ta	17Ge	1Le	4Vi	22Li	29Sc
9	2Li	24Sc	5Sg	28Cp	6Pi	23Ar	26Ta	11Cn	26Le	0Li	20Sc	29Sg
11	29Li	23Sg	4Cp	25Aq	1Ar	17Ta	20Ge	5Le	21Vi	27Li	20Sg	29Cp
13	28Sc	21Cp	2Aq	22Pi	26Ar	11Ge	14Cn	29Le	18Li	26Sc	19Cp	28Aq
15	28Sg	20Aq	29Aq	17Ar	20Ta	5Cn	8Le	25Vi	16Sc	25Sg	18Aq	25Pi
17	27Cp	17Pi	25Pi	12Ta	14Ge	29Cn	3Vi	21Li	14Sg	23Cp	15Pi	21Ar
19	26Aq	13Ar	21Ar	6Ge	8Cn	23Le	28Vi	19Sc	12Cp	21Aq	11Ar	16Ta
21	22Pi	8Ta	15Ta	29Ge	2Le	18Vi	24Li	17Sg	10Aq	18Pi	7Ta	10Ge
23	18Ar	2Ge	9Ge	23Cn	26Le	15Li	22Sc	16Cp	8Pi	15Ar	1Ge	4Cn
25	12Ta	25Ge	3Cn	18Le	22Vi	13Sc	22Sg	15Aq	6Ar	10Ta	25Ge	28Cn
27	6Ge	20Cn	27Cn	14Vi	20Li	13Sg	22Cp	14Pi	2Ta	5Ge	19Cn	21Le
29	29Ge		23Le	11Li	19Sc	13Cp	21Aq	11Ar	27Ta	29Ge	13Le	16Vi
31	24Cn		19Vi		20Sg		19Pi	7Ta		23Cn		11Li

1943

	Jan	Feb	Mar	Apr	May	Jun	Jul	Aug	Sep	Oct	Nov	Dec
1	24Li	15Sg	25Sg	19Aq	27Pi	17Ta	21Ge	6Le	20Vi	24Li	14Sg	22Cp
3	22Sc	15Cp	24Cp	17Pi	24Ar	12Ge	15Cn	29Le	15Li	20Sc	11Cp	20Aq
5	22Sg	15Aq	23Aq	15Ar	20Ta	6Cn	9Le	23Vi	10Sc	17Sg	9Aq	18Pi
7	22Cp	15Pi	23Pi	12Ta	16Ge	0Le	2Vi	18Li	6Sg	14Cp	8Pi	16Ar
9	22Aq	13Ar	21Ar	8Ge	10Cn	24Le	26Vi	13Sc	4Cp	13Aq	6Ar	13Ta
11	21Pi	9Ta	17Ta	2Cn	4Le	18Vi	21Li	10Sg	3Aq	12Pi	4Ta	10Ge
13	18Ar	4Ge	12Ge	26Cn	27Le	13Li	18Sc	9Cp	3Pi	11Ar	1Ge	5Cn
15	13Ta	28Ge	6Cn	19Le	22Vi	9Sc	16Sg	9Aq	2Ar	9Ta	27Ge	29Cn
17	7Ge	21Cn	0Le	14Vi	18Li	8Sg	16Cp	9Pi	1Ta	6Ge	21Cn	23Le
19	1Cn	15Le	24Le	9Li	15Sc	7Cp	16Aq	9Ar	28Ta	1Cn	15Le	17Vi
21	25Cn	10Vi	18Vi	6Sc	14Sg	7Aq	16Pi	6Ta	23Ge	25Cn	9Vi	11Li
23	18Le	5Li	14Li	4Sg	13Cp	6Pi	14Ar	2Ge	17Cn	19Le	3Li	6Sc
25	13Vi	0Sc	11Sc	3Cp	12Aq	4Ar	10Ta	27Ge	11Le	13Vi	28Li	3Sg
27	7Li	27Sc	8Sg	1Aq	10Pi	1Ta	6Ge	21Cn	5Vi	8Li	25Sc	2Cp
29	3Sc		6Cp	29Aq	7Ar	26Ta	0Cn	14Le	29Vi	3Sc	23Sg	1Aq
31	1Sg		4Aq		4Ta		24Cn	8Vi		0Sg		1Pi

1944

	Jan	Feb	Mar	Apr	May	Jun	Jul	Aug	Sep	Oct	Nov	Dec
1	15Pi	7Ta	29Ta	16Cn	18Le	2Li	4Sc	21Sg	12Aq	20Pi	14Ta	21Ge
3	13Ar	3Ge	25Ge	10Le	12Vi	26Li	0Sg	19Cp	12Pi	21Ar	13Ge	18Cn
5	10Ta	28Ge	19Cn	4Vi	6Li	22Sc	27Sg	19Aq	12Ar	21Ta	10Cn	13Le
7	6Ge	22Cn	13Le	27Vi	0Sc	18Sg	25Cp	19Pi	12Ta	18Ge	5Le	7Vi
9	1Cn	16Le	7Vi	22Li	26Sc	16Cp	24Aq	18Ar	10Ge	15Cn	0Vi	1Li
11	26Cn	10Vi	1Li	17Sc	22Sg	14Aq	23Pi	16Ta	5Cn	9Le	23Vi	25Li
13	19Le	4Li	25Li	12Sg	20Cp	13Pi	22Ar	13Ge	0Le	3Vi	17Li	20Sc
15	13Vi	28Li	20Sc	9Cp	17Aq	11Ar	19Ta	8Cn	24Le	27Vi	11Sc	15Sg
17	7Li	23Sc	15Sg	7Aq	16Pi	9Ta	16Ge	3Le	18Vi	20Li	6Sg	12Cp
19	1Sc	19Sg	13Cp	5Pi	14Ar	6Ge	11Cn	27Le	11Li	15Sc	2Cp	9Aq
21	27Sc	18Cp	11Aq	5Ar	13Ta	2Cn	6Le	21Vi	5Sc	9Sg	29Cp	7Pi
23	25Sg	17Aq	11Pi	4Ta	11Ge	28Cn	0Vi	14Li	0Sg	5Cp	26Aq	5Ar
25	24Cp	18Pi	11Ar	2Ge	7Cn	22Le	24Vi	8Sc	25Sg	2Aq	24Pi	3Ta
27	25Aq	18Ar	10Ta	29Ge	2Le	16Vi	18Li	3Sg	22Cp	0Pi	23Ar	2Ge
29	24Pi	16Ta	8Ge	24Cn	26Le	10Li	12Sc	29Sg	20Aq	29Pi	22Ta	29Ge
31	23Ar		4Cn		20Vi		8Sg	27Cp		29Ar		26Cn

1945

	Jan	Feb	Mar	Apr	May	Jun	Jul	Aug	Sep	Oct	Nov	Dec
1	8Le	23Vi	2Li	16Sc	19Sg	7Aq	15Pi	9Ta	1Cn	8Le	24Vi	27Li
3	3Vi	17Li	25Li	10Sg	14Cp	4Pi	13Ar	7Ge	28Cn	3Vi	18Li	21Sc
5	27Vi	11Sc	19Sc	5Cp	10Aq	3Ar	12Ta	4Cn	23Le	27Vi	12Sc	15Sg
7	21Li	5Sg	13Sg	1Aq	8Pi	2Ta	11Ge	1Le	18Vi	21Li	6Sg	9Cp
9	15Sc	1Cp	9Cp	29Aq	7Ar	1Ge	9Cn	27Le	13Li	15Sc	0Cp	4Aq
11	10Sg	28Cp	6Aq	28Pi	7Ta	0Cn	6Le	22Vi	7Sc	9Sg	24Cp	0Pi
13	7Cp	27Aq	5Pi	29Ar	7Ge	28Cn	2Vi	16Li	0Sg	3Cp	20Aq	27Pi
15	4Aq	27Pi	6Ar	29Ta	6Cn	24Le	26Vi	10Sc	24Sg	28Cp	17Pi	26Ar
17	3Pi	26Ar	6Ta	28Ge	3Le	18Vi	20Li	4Sg	19Cp	25Aq	16Ar	25Ta
19	2Ar	25Ta	5Ge	24Cn	28Le	12Li	14Sc	29Sg	16Aq	23Pi	17Ta	25Ge
21	0Ta	22Ge	2Cn	19Le	22Vi	6Sc	8Sg	25Cp	15Pi	23Ar	17Ge	24Cn
23	28Ta	18Cn	28Cn	14Vi	16Li	0Sg	4Cp	22Aq	15Ar	24Ta	16Cn	21Le
25	25Ge	13Le	22Le	7Li	10Sc	25Sg	0Aq	21Pi	15Ta	23Ge	13Le	17Vi
27	21Cn	7Vi	16Vi	1Sc	4Sg	21Cp	27Aq	21Ar	14Ge	21Cn	9Vi	12Li
29	17Le		10Li	25Sc	29Sg	18Aq	26Pi	20Ta	12Cn	17Le	3Li	6Sc
31	11Vi		4Sc		24Cp		24Ar	18Ge		12Vi		29Sc

1946

	Jan	Feb	Mar	Apr	May	Jun	Jul	Aug	Sep	Oct	Nov	Dec
1	11Sg	27Cp	5Aq	24Pi	2Ta	25Ge	3Le	23Vi	9Sc	11Sg	24Cp	27Aq
3	6Cp	23Aq	2Pi	23Ar	2Ge	25Cn	1Vi	19Li	3Sg	4Cp	19Aq	23Pi
5	1Aq	20Pi	0Ar	23Ta	2Cn	23Le	28Vi	13Sc	26Sg	28Cp	15Pi	20Ar
7	27Aq	18Ar	29Ar	22Ge	0Le	19Vi	23Li	7Sg	20Cp	23Aq	12Ar	19Ta
9	24Pi	17Ta	28Ta	20Cn	27Le	14Li	17Sc	0Cp	15Aq	20Pi	11Ta	19Ge
11	22Ar	15Ge	26Ge	17Le	22Vi	8Sc	10Sg	25Cp	12Pi	18Ar	11Ge	20Cn
13	20Ta	13Cn	23Cn	13Vi	17Li	2Sg	4Cp	20Aq	9Ar	18Ta	11Cn	19Le
15	19Ge	10Le	20Le	8Li	11Sc	25Sg	28Cp	16Pi	8Ta	17Ge	10Le	16Vi
17	18Cn	7Vi	16Vi	2Sc	5Sg	19Cp	23Aq	13Ar	6Ge	15Cn	7Vi	12Li
19	16Le	3Li	11Li	26Sc	28Sg	14Aq	20Pi	11Ta	4Cn	13Le	3Li	7Sc
21	12Vi	27Li	5Sc	19Sg	22Cp	9Pi	16Ar	9Ge	2Le	10Vi	27Li	1Sg
23	8Li	21Sc	29Sc	13Cp	17Aq	6Ar	14Ta	8Cn	0Vi	6Li	22Sc	24Sg
25	2Sc	15Sg	23Sg	8Aq	13Pi	4Ta	13Ge	6Le	26Vi	1Sc	15Sg	18Cp
27	25Sc	9Cp	17Cp	4Pi	11Ar	4Ge	13Cn	4Vi	22Li	25Sc	9Cp	12Aq
29	19Sg		12Aq	2Ar	10Ta	4Cn	12Le	1Li	17Sc	19Sg	3Aq	6Pi
31	14Cp		10Pi		10Ge		10Vi	27Li		12Cp		2Ar

1947

	Jan	Feb	Mar	Apr	May	Jun	Jul	Aug	Sep	Oct	Nov	Dec
1	15Ar	7Ge	17Ge	10Le	19Vi	8Sc	11Sg	26Cp	11Pi	15Ar	5Ge	13Cn
3	13Ta	6Cn	16Cn	9Vi	15Li	2Sg	5Cp	20Aq	6Ar	12Ta	3Cn	13Le
5	12Ge	6Le	15Le	6Li	11Sc	26Sg	29Cp	14Pi	2Ta	9Ge	2Le	11Vi
7	13Cn	5Vi	13Vi	2Sc	6Sg	20Cp	22Aq	9Ar	28Ta	7Cn	0Vi	8Li
9	13Le	3Li	11Li	27Sc	0Cp	14Aq	17Pi	5Ta	26Ge	5Le	28Vi	5Sc
11	11Vi	29Li	7Sc	22Sg	23Cp	8Pi	12Ar	2Ge	25Cn	4Vi	25Li	0Sg
13	8Li	24Sc	2Sg	15Cp	17Aq	3Ar	8Ta	0Cn	24Le	2Li	21Sc	25Sg
15	3Sc	18Sg	26Sg	9Aq	12Pi	0Ta	7Ge	0Le	23Vi	0Sc	16Sg	19Cp
17	28Sc	11Cp	19Cp	4Pi	8Ar	28Ta	6Cn	0Vi	22Li	26Sc	11Cp	13Aq
19	21Sg	5Aq	13Aq	0Ar	5Ta	28Ge	7Le	29Vi	18Sc	21Sg	5Aq	6Pi
21	15Cp	0Pi	9Pi	27Ar	5Ge	28Cn	7Vi	27Li	13Sg	15Cp	28Aq	1Ar
23	9Aq	26Pi	5Ar	26Ta	4Cn	28Le	5Li	23Sc	7Cp	9Aq	23Pi	26Ar
25	3Pi	22Ar	2Ta	24Ge	4Le	26Vi	1Sc	17Sg	1Aq	3Pi	18Ar	23Ta
27	29Pi	19Ta	0Ge	23Cn	2Vi	22Li	26Sc	11Cp	25Aq	28Pi	15Ta	22Ge
29	25Ar		28Ge	21Le	29Vi	17Sc	20Sg	4Aq	19Pi	24Ar	14Ge	22Cn
31	23Ta		26Cn		25Li		14Cp	28Aq		21Ta		22Le

1948

	Jan	Feb	Mar	Apr	May	Jun	Jul	Aug	Sep	Oct	Nov	Dec
1	7Vi	28Li	20Sc	6Cp	8Aq	21Pi	24Ar	11Ge	3Le	12Vi	5Sc	11Sg
3	5Li	24Sc	15Sg	0Aq	2Pi	16Ar	20Ta	10Cn	3Vi	12Li	3Sg	8Cp
5	2Sc	19Sg	10Cp	24Aq	26Pi	12Ta	17Ge	9Le	4Li	11Sc	0Cp	3Aq
7	27Sc	13Cp	3Aq	18Pi	21Ar	9Ge	16Cn	10Vi	3Sc	9Sg	25Cp	27Aq
9	22Sg	6Aq	27Aq	12Ar	16Ta	7Cn	16Le	10Li	0Sg	5Cp	19Aq	21Pi
11	16Cp	0Pi	21Pi	8Ta	14Ge	6Le	15Vi	8Sc	26Sg	29Cp	13Pi	15Ar
13	9Aq	24Pi	16Ar	4Ge	11Cn	5Vi	14Li	4Sg	20Cp	23Aq	7Ar	9Ta
15	3Pi	19Ar	11Ta	1Cn	10Le	3Li	11Sc	29Sg	14Aq	17Pi	1Ta	5Ge
17	27Pi	14Ta	7Ge	29Cn	8Vi	1Sc	7Sg	23Cp	8Pi	11Ar	27Ta	2Cn
19	22Ar	10Ge	4Cn	27Le	6Li	27Sc	2Cp	17Aq	2Ar	5Ta	23Ge	1Le
21	18Ta	8Cn	3Le	26Vi	4Sc	23Sg	26Cp	11Pi	26Ar	0Ge	21Cn	29Le
23	15Ge	8Le	2Vi	25Li	1Sg	18Cp	20Aq	5Ar	21Ta	27Ge	18Le	28Vi
25	15Cn	9Vi	2Li	23Sc	27Sg	12Aq	14Pi	29Ar	16Ge	24Cn	17Vi	26Li
27	16Le	9Li	1Sc	19Sg	22Cp	6Pi	8Ar	24Ta	13Cn	22Le	15Li	23Sc
29	16Vi	7Sc	28Sc	14Cp	16Aq	0Ar	2Ta	20Ge	12Le	21Vi	13Sc	20Sg
31	15Li		24Sg		10Pi		28Ta	18Cn		20Li		16Cp

1949

	Jan	Feb	Mar	Apr	May	Jun	Jul	Aug	Sep	Oct	Nov	Dec
1	28Cp	13Pi	22Pi	6Ta	10Ge	29Cn	7Vi	1Sc	23Sg	29Cp	15Pi	17Ar
3	23Aq	7Ar	15Ar	1Ge	6Cn	27Le	6Li	29Sc	19Cp	24Aq	9Ar	11Ta
5	17Pi	1Ta	9Ta	26Ge	2Le	25Vi	4Sc	26Sg	14Aq	18Pi	2Ta	5Ge
7	11Ar	25Ta	4Ge	22Cn	0Vi	23Li	2Sg	22Cp	9Pi	12Ar	26Ta	0Cn
9	5Ta	21Ge	29Ge	20Le	29Vi	22Sc	29Sg	18Aq	3Ar	5Ta	20Ge	25Cn
11	0Ge	19Cn	27Cn	20Vi	28Li	20Sg	26Cp	12Pi	26Ar	29Ta	16Cn	22Le
13	27Ge	18Le	26Le	20Li	28Sc	18Cp	22Aq	6Ar	20Ta	23Ge	12Le	19Vi
15	25Cn	18Vi	27Vi	20Sc	26Sg	14Aq	16Pi	0Ta	14Ge	19Cn	9Vi	17Li
17	25Le	18Li	27Li	18Sg	23Cp	8Pi	10Ar	24Ta	10Cn	16Le	8Li	16Sc
19	24Vi	17Sc	26Sc	15Cp	18Aq	2Ar	4Ta	19Ge	7Le	14Vi	7Sc	16Sg
21	23Li	13Sg	23Sg	10Aq	12Pi	26Ar	28Ta	15Cn	6Vi	14Li	7Sg	14Cp
23	20Sc	9Cp	19Cp	4Pi	6Ar	20Ta	24Ge	13Le	6Li	14Sc	6Cp	12Aq
25	16Sg	4Aq	13Aq	28Pi	0Ta	15Ge	21Cn	13Vi	6Sc	14Sg	4Aq	7Pi
27	12Cp	28Aq	7Pi	21Ar	24Ta	12Cn	19Le	12Li	5Sg	12Cp	29Aq	1Ar
29	7Aq		1Ar	15Ta	19Ge	9Le	18Vi	11Sc	3Cp	8Aq	23Pi	25Ar
31	1Pi		24Ar		16Cn		17Li	9Sg		3Pi		19Ta

1950

	Jan	Feb	Mar	Apr	May	Jun	Jul	Aug	Sep	Oct	Nov	Dec
1	1Ge	17Cn	25Cn	14Vi	22Li	16Sg	24Cp	13Pi	28Ar	0Ge	14Cn	18Le
3	26Ge	14Le	22Le	14Li	23Sc	16Cp	22Aq	8Ar	22Ta	24Ge	9Le	14Vi
5	22Cn	12Vi	21Vi	14Sc	23Sg	14Aq	18Pi	2Ta	16Ge	18Cn	5Vi	11Li
7	19Le	11Li	20Li	14Sg	21Cp	10Pi	12Ar	26Ta	10Cn	14Le	2Li	10Sc
9	16Vi	9Sc	20Sc	12Cp	18Aq	4Ar	6Ta	20Ge	6Le	10Vi	2Sc	10Sg
11	14Li	7Sg	18Sg	9Aq	13Pi	28Ar	0Ge	15Cn	2Vi	9Li	2Sg	11Cp
13	12Sc	5Cp	15Cp	4Pi	7Ar	22Ta	24Ge	11Le	0Li	9Sc	2Cp	10Aq
15	11Sg	2Aq	11Aq	28Pi	1Ta	15Ge	19Cn	7Vi	29Li	8Sg	1Aq	7Pi
17	9Cp	28Aq	7Pi	22Ar	25Ta	10Cn	15Le	5Li	28Sc	7Cp	28Aq	3Ar
19	6Aq	23Pi	1Ar	16Ta	19Ge	5Le	11Vi	3Sc	27Sg	5Aq	24Pi	27Ar
21	2Pi	17Ar	25Ar	9Ge	13Cn	1Vi	8Li	2Sg	24Cp	1Pi	18Ar	21Ta
23	27Pi	11Ta	19Ta	4Cn	8Le	28Vi	6Sc	0Cp	21Aq	26Pi	12Ta	14Ge
25	21Ar	4Ge	13Ge	28Cn	4Vi	26Li	5Sg	28Cp	17Pi	21Ar	6Ge	8Cn
27	15Ta	29Ge	7Cn	25Le	2Li	25Sc	4Cp	25Aq	12Ar	15Ta	29Ge	3Le
29	9Ge		3Le	23Vi	1Sc	25Sg	2Aq	21Pi	6Ta	9Ge	23Cn	28Le
31	4Cn		0Vi		1Sg		0Pi	16Ar		2Cn		23Vi

1951

	Jan	Feb	Mar	Apr	May	Jun	Jul	Aug	Sep	Oct	Nov	Dec
1	7Li	29Sc	10Sg	3Aq	10Pi	28Ar	2Ge	16Cn	1Vi	6Li	26Sc	5Cp
3	4Sc	28Sg	8Cp	0Pi	6Ar	22Ta	25Ge	10Le	27Vi	3Sc	25Sg	5Aq
5	3Sg	27Cp	6Aq	27Pi	1Ta	16Ge	19Cn	5Vi	23Li	1Sg	24Cp	3Pi
7	4Cp	26Aq	4Pi	22Ar	26Ta	10Cn	13Le	0Li	20Sc	29Sg	22Aq	0Ar
9	3Aq	23Pi	1Ar	17Ta	20Ge	4Le	7Vi	26Li	18Sg	28Cp	20Pi	26Ar
11	2Pi	19Ar	27Ar	11Ge	13Cn	28Le	3Li	23Sc	17Cp	26Aq	16Ar	21Ta
13	28Pi	13Ta	21Ta	5Cn	7Le	23Vi	29Li	22Sg	16Aq	23Pi	12Ta	15Ge
15	23Ar	7Ge	15Ge	29Cn	2Vi	20Li	28Sc	22Cp	14Pi	20Ar	7Ge	9Cn
17	17Ta	1Cn	9Cn	24Le	28Vi	19Sc	27Sg	21Aq	12Ar	16Ta	1Cn	3Le
19	11Ge	25Cn	3Le	20Vi	26Li	19Sg	28Cp	20Pi	8Ta	11Ge	24Cn	27Le
21	5Cn	21Le	29Le	18Li	25Sc	19Cp	27Aq	17Ar	3Ge	5Cn	18Le	21Vi
23	29Cn	17Vi	25Vi	17Sc	26Sg	19Aq	25Pi	12Ta	27Ge	28Cn	13Vi	16Li
25	24Le	14Li	23Li	16Sg	25Cp	17Pi	22Ar	7Ge	20Cn	22Le	8Li	14Sc
27	20Vi	11Sc	22Sc	16Cp	24Aq	13Ar	16Ta	1Cn	15Le	17Vi	6Sc	13Sg
29	17Li		21Sg	14Aq	20Pi	8Ta	10Ge	24Cn	9Vi	14Li	5Sg	13Cp
31	15Sc		19Cp		16Ar		4Cn	19Le		12Sc		14Aq

1952

	Jan	Feb	Mar	Apr	May	Jun	Jul	Aug	Sep	Oct	Nov	Dec
1	28Aq	19Ar	10Ta	26Ge	27Cn	11Vi	14Li	2Sg	24Cp	3Pi	25Ar	2Ge
3	26Pi	15Ta	5Ge	20Cn	21Le	6Li	10Sc	0Cp	24Aq	2Ar	23Ta	28Ge
5	23Ar	9Ge	0Cn	13Le	15Vi	2Sc	8Sg	0Aq	24Pi	1Ta	20Ge	23Cn
7	18Ta	3Cn	23Cn	7Vi	10Li	29Sc	7Cp	1Pi	23Ar	29Ta	15Cn	17Le
9	12Ge	27Cn	17Le	2Li	7Sc	28Sg	7Aq	0Ar	21Ta	25Ge	9Le	10Vi
11	6Cn	21Le	11Vi	28Li	5Sg	28Cp	7Pi	29Ar	16Ge	19Cn	3Vi	4Li
13	0Le	15Vi	6Li	25Sc	4Cp	27Aq	5Ar	25Ta	11Cn	13Le	26Vi	29Li
15	24Le	9Li	2Sc	23Sg	2Aq	25Pi	2Ta	20Ge	5Le	7Vi	21Li	26Sc
17	18Vi	5Sc	29Sc	21Cp	1Pi	22Ar	28Ta	14Cn	28Le	1Li	17Sc	23Sg
19	12Li	2Sg	26Sg	20Aq	28Pi	18Ta	23Ge	8Le	22Vi	26Li	15Sg	22Cp
21	9Sc	0Cp	25Cp	18Pi	25Ar	14Ge	17Cn	1Vi	17Li	22Sc	13Cp	21Aq
23	6Sg	0Aq	24Aq	16Ar	22Ta	8Cn	11Le	25Vi	12Sc	18Sg	11Aq	20Pi
25	6Cp	29Aq	23Pi	13Ta	17Ge	2Le	4Vi	20Li	8Sg	16Cp	9Pi	18Ar
27	6Aq	29Pi	21Ar	9Ge	12Cn	26Le	28Vi	15Sc	5Cp	14Aq	7Ar	15Ta
29	6Pi	27Ar	18Ta	4Cn	5Le	19Vi	23Li	11Sg	3Aq	12Pi	5Ta	11Ge
31	5Ar		13Ge		29Le		18Sc	9Cp		11Ar		6Cn

1953

	Jan	Feb	Mar	Apr	May	Jun	Jul	Aug	Sep	Oct	Nov	Dec
1	19Cn	3Vi	12Vi	27Li	1Sg	21Cp	29Aq	23Ar	15Ge	20Cn	5Vi	7Li
3	13Le	27Vi	6Li	22Sc	27Sg	19Aq	28Pi	21Ta	10Cn	14Le	29Vi	1Sc
5	7Vi	21Li	0Sc	17Sg	24Cp	17Pi	26Ar	18Ge	5Le	8Vi	22Li	25Sc
7	0Li	15Sc	25Sc	14Cp	22Aq	15Ar	24Ta	13Cn	29Le	2Li	17Sc	21Sg
9	24Li	11Sg	20Sg	12Aq	21Pi	14Ta	21Ge	8Le	23Vi	26Li	11Sg	17Cp
11	20Sc	9Cp	18Cp	11Pi	20Ar	11Ge	17Cn	2Vi	17Li	20Sc	7Cp	14Aq
13	17Sg	9Aq	17Aq	11Ar	19Ta	8Cn	12Le	26Vi	10Sc	14Sg	3Aq	11Pi
15	16Cp	9Pi	17Pi	10Ta	17Ge	3Le	6Vi	20Li	5Sg	10Cp	1Pi	10Ar
17	16Aq	9Ar	17Ar	8Ge	13Cn	28Le	29Vi	14Sc	0Cp	7Aq	29Pi	8Ta
19	15Pi	8Ta	16Ta	5Cn	8Le	21Vi	23Li	9Sg	27Cp	5Pi	29Ar	7Ge
21	14Ar	5Ge	14Ge	0Le	2Vi	15Li	18Sc	5Cp	26Aq	5Ar	28Ta	5Cn
23	12Ta	0Cn	9Cn	24Le	25Vi	10Sc	14Sg	3Aq	27Pi	5Ta	27Ge	1Le
25	8Ge	24Cn	3Le	17Vi	19Li	6Sg	11Cp	3Pi	27Ar	5Ge	24Cn	27Le
27	3Cn	18Le	27Le	11Li	14Sc	3Cp	10Aq	3Ar	27Ta	3Cn	19Le	21Vi
29	27Cn		21Vi	6Sc	10Sg	1Aq	9Pi	3Ta	24Ge	29Cn	13Vi	15Li
31	21Le		15Li		7Cp		9Ar	1Ge		23Le		9Sc

1954

	Jan	Feb	Mar	Apr	May	Jun	Jul	Aug	Sep	Oct	Nov	Dec
1	21Sc	7Cp	15Cp	5Pi	13Ar	7Ge	14Cn	3Vi	18Li	20Sc	5Cp	9Aq
3	16Sg	4Aq	12Aq	5Ar	14Ta	6Cn	12Le	28Vi	12Sc	14Sg	29Cp	5Pi
5	12Cp	3Pi	12Pi	5Ta	14Ge	4Le	7Vi	22Li	6Sg	8Cp	25Aq	2Ar
7	10Aq	2Ar	12Ar	5Ge	12Cn	29Le	2Li	16Sc	0Cp	3Aq	23Pi	1Ta
9	8Pi	1Ta	11Ta	3Cn	8Le	24Vi	26Li	10Sg	25Cp	1Pi	23Ar	1Ge
11	6Ar	0Ge	10Ge	29Cn	3Vi	18Li	20Sc	5Cp	22Aq	0Ar	23Ta	1Cn
13	5Ta	27Ge	7Cn	24Le	27Vi	12Sc	14Sg	1Aq	21Pi	0Ta	23Ge	0Le
15	3Ge	23Cn	3Le	19Vi	21Li	6Sg	9Cp	28Aq	21Ar	0Ge	22Cn	27Le
17	0Cn	18Le	27Le	12Li	15Sc	1Cp	5Aq	27Pi	21Ta	29Ge	19Le	23Vi
19	27Cn	13Vi	22Vi	6Sc	9Sg	26Cp	3Pi	26Ar	19Ge	26Cn	14Vi	17Li
21	22Le	7Li	15Li	0Sg	4Cp	22Aq	1Ar	24Ta	16Cn	22Le	9Li	11Sc
23	17Vi	1Sc	9Sc	24Sg	29Cp	20Pi	29Ar	22Ge	12Le	17Vi	2Sc	5Sg
25	11Li	24Sc	3Sg	19Cp	25Aq	18Ar	27Ta	19Cn	8Vi	11Li	26Sc	29Sg
27	4Sc	19Sg	27Sg	16Aq	23Pi	17Ta	26Ge	16Le	2Li	5Sc	20Sg	23Cp
29	29Sc		23Cp	14Pi	22Ar	16Ge	23Cn	11Vi	27Li	29Sc	14Cp	19Aq
31	24Sg		20Aq		22Ta		20Le	6Li		23Sg		15Pi

1955

	Jan	Feb	Mar	Apr	May	Jun	Jul	Aug	Sep	Oct	Nov	Dec
1	28Pi	21Ta	2Ge	25Cn	2Vi	19Li	22Sc	6Cp	21Aq	26Pi	18Ta	26Ge
3	26Ar	20Ge	0Cn	22Le	27Vi	13Sc	15Sg	0Aq	17Pi	24Ar	17Ge	26Cn
5	25Ta	18Cn	28Cn	18Vi	22Li	7Sg	9Cp	25Aq	15Ar	23Ta	16Cn	24Le
7	25Ge	16Le	25Le	13Li	16Sc	0Cp	3Aq	21Pi	13Ta	22Ge	14Le	21Vi
9	24Cn	13Vi	21Vi	7Sc	10Sg	24Cp	28Aq	18Ar	11Ge	20Cn	11Vi	17Li
11	22Le	9Li	17Li	1Sg	3Cp	19Aq	24Pi	16Ta	9Cn	17Le	7Li	12Sc
13	18Vi	3Sc	11Sc	25Sg	27Cp	14Pi	21Ar	14Ge	7Le	15Vi	2Sc	6Sg
15	13Li	27Sc	5Sg	19Cp	22Aq	11Ar	19Ta	13Cn	5Vi	11Li	27Sc	29Sg
17	7Sc	21Sg	28Sg	13Aq	18Pi	10Ta	19Ge	12Le	2Li	6Sc	21Sg	23Cp
19	1Sg	15Cp	23Cp	10Pi	17Ar	10Ge	18Cn	10Vi	28Li	0Sg	14Cp	17Aq
21	25Sg	11Aq	18Aq	8Ar	16Ta	10Cn	18Le	7Li	22Sc	24Sg	8Aq	11Pi
23	20Cp	7Pi	16Pi	8Ta	17Ge	9Le	16Vi	2Sc	16Sg	18Cp	3Pi	7Ar
25	15Aq	5Ar	15Ar	8Ge	16Cn	7Vi	12Li	27Sc	10Cp	12Aq	29Pi	4Ta
27	12Pi	4Ta	14Ta	7Cn	15Le	3Li	6Sc	20Sg	4Aq	7Pi	26Ar	3Ge
29	9Ar		13Ge	5Le	11Vi	28Li	0Sg	14Cp	29Aq	4Ar	26Ta	4Cn
31	7Ta		11Cn		7Li		24Sg	9Aq		3Ta		4Le

1956

	Jan	Feb	Mar	Apr	May	Jun	Jul	Aug	Sep	Oct	Nov	Dec
1	19Le	9Li	0Sc	15Sg	17Cp	1Pi	4Ar	23Ta	15Cn	24Le	17Li	23Sc
3	17Vi	5Sc	25Sc	9Cp	11Aq	26Pi	0Ta	21Ge	15Le	23Vi	14Sc	18Sg
5	14Li	29Sc	19Sg	3Aq	5Pi	22Ar	28Ta	21Cn	15Vi	22Li	10Sg	12Cp
7	9Sc	23Sg	13Cp	27Aq	1Ar	20Ta	27Ge	21Le	14Li	19Sc	4Cp	6Aq
9	3Sg	17Cp	7Aq	23Pi	28Ar	19Ge	28Cn	21Vi	11Sc	14Sg	28Cp	0Pi
11	26Sg	11Aq	1Pi	19Ar	26Ta	19Cn	28Le	19Li	6Sg	9Cp	22Aq	24Pi
13	20Cp	5Pi	27Pi	17Ta	25Ge	19Le	27Vi	15Sc	1Cp	2Aq	16Pi	19Ar
15	14Aq	1Ar	24Ar	15Ge	24Cn	17Vi	24Li	10Sg	24Cp	26Aq	11Ar	16Ta
17	8Pi	27Ar	21Ta	14Cn	23Le	14Li	19Sc	4Cp	18Aq	21Pi	8Ta	14Ge
19	4Ar	24Ta	19Ge	12Le	20Vi	9Sc	13Sg	28Cp	12Pi	16Ar	6Ge	13Cn
21	0Ta	22Ge	17Cn	10Vi	17Li	4Sg	7Cp	22Aq	8Ar	13Ta	4Cn	13Le
23	28Ta	21Cn	15Le	7Li	13Sc	28Sg	1Aq	16Pi	3Ta	10Ge	3Le	12Vi
25	27Ge	20Le	14Vi	3Sc	7Sg	22Cp	25Aq	11Ar	0Ge	8Cn	2Vi	10Li
27	27Cn	19Vi	12Li	29Sc	1Cp	16Aq	19Pi	6Ta	27Ge	6Le	29Vi	6Sc
29	27Le	17Li	8Sc	23Sg	25Cp	10Pi	14Ar	3Ge	25Cn	5Vi	26Li	2Sg
31	26Vi		3Sg		19Aq		10Ta	1Cn		3Li		27Sg

1957

	Jan	Feb	Mar	Apr	May	Jun	Jul	Aug	Sep	Oct	Nov	Dec
1	9Cp	23Aq	2Pi	17Ar	22Ta	12Cn	21Le	15Li	5Sg	10Cp	25Aq	27Pi
3	3Aq	17Pi	26Pi	13Ta	19Ge	11Le	20Vi	13Sc	1Cp	5Aq	19Pi	20Ar
5	27Aq	11Ar	21Ar	9Ge	16Cn	10Vi	19Li	9Sg	26Cp	28Aq	12Ar	15Ta
7	20Pi	6Ta	16Ta	5Cn	14Le	8Li	16Sc	4Cp	20Aq	22Pi	7Ta	11Ge
9	15Ar	2Ge	12Ge	3Le	13Vi	5Sc	12Sg	28Cp	13Pi	16Ar	2Ge	8Cn
11	10Ta	0Cn	9Cn	2Vi	11Li	2Sg	7Cp	23Aq	7Ar	10Ta	28Ge	6Le
13	7Ge	29Cn	8Le	2Li	9Sc	28Sg	2Aq	16Pi	1Ta	5Ge	25Cn	4Vi
15	6Cn	0Vi	8Vi	1Sc	7Sg	23Cp	26Aq	10Ar	26Ta	1Cn	23Le	2Li
17	7Le	0Li	8Li	29Sc	3Cp	17Aq	20Pi	4Ta	21Ge	28Cn	21Vi	0Sc
19	7Vi	29Li	7Sc	25Sg	27Cp	11Pi	13Ar	29Ta	19Cn	27Le	20Li	28Sc
21	6Li	26Sc	4Sg	20Cp	21Aq	5Ar	8Ta	26Ge	18Le	26Vi	19Sc	25Sg
23	3Sc	21Sg	29Sg	13Aq	15Pi	0Ta	4Ge	24Cn	18Vi	26Li	17Sg	21Cp
25	29Sc	15Cp	23Cp	7Pi	9Ar	26Ta	1Cn	24Le	18Li	25Sc	13Cp	16Aq
27	24Sg	9Aq	17Aq	1Ar	4Ta	23Ge	1Le	25Vi	17Sc	23Sg	9Aq	11Pi
29	18Cp		11Pi	26Ar	1Ge	22Cn	1Vi	24Li	14Sg	18Cp	3Pi	4Ar
31	12Aq		5Ar		28Ge		1Li	22Sc		13Aq		28Ar

1958

	Jan	Feb	Mar	Apr	May	Jun	Jul	Aug	Sep	Oct	Nov	Dec
1	10Ta	27Ge	5Cn	26Le	4Li	28Sc	5Cp	23Aq	8Ar	10Ta	25Ge	0Le
3	6Ge	25Cn	3Le	26Vi	4Sc	26Sg	2Aq	18Pi	2Ta	4Ge	20Cn	27Le
5	3Cn	24Le	2Vi	26Li	4Sg	24Cp	27Aq	12Ar	25Ta	28Ge	17Le	24Vi
7	1Le	24Vi	3Li	26Sc	2Cp	19Aq	22Pi	5Ta	20Ge	24Cn	14Vi	23Li
9	0Vi	24Li	3Sc	24Sg	29Cp	14Pi	16Ar	29Ta	16Cn	21Le	14Li	22Sc
11	29Vi	21Sc	1Sg	20Cp	24Aq	8Ar	9Ta	24Ge	13Le	20Vi	14Sc	22Sg
13	27Li	18Sg	28Sg	15Aq	18Pi	1Ta	4Ge	21Cn	12Vi	21Li	14Sg	20Cp
15	25Sc	14Cp	24Cp	9Pi	11Ar	26Ta	29Ge	19Le	12Li	21Sc	13Cp	18Aq
17	21Sg	9Aq	18Aq	3Ar	5Ta	21Ge	26Cn	18Vi	12Sc	20Sg	9Aq	13Pi
19	17Cp	3Pi	12Pi	26Ar	29Ta	17Cn	24Le	18Li	11Sg	17Cp	5Pi	7Ar
21	12Aq	27Pi	6Ar	20Ta	24Ge	14Le	23Vi	16Sc	8Cp	13Aq	29Pi	1Ta
23	7Pi	21Ar	29Ar	15Ge	20Cn	12Vi	21Li	14Sg	4Aq	8Pi	22Ar	24Ta
25	0Ar	14Ta	23Ta	10Cn	17Le	10Li	19Sc	11Cp	29Aq	2Ar	16Ta	19Ge
27	24Ar	9Ge	18Ge	7Le	15Vi	9Sc	17Sg	7Aq	23Pi	26Ar	10Ge	14Cn
29	18Ta		14Cn	5Vi	14Li	7Sg	14Cp	2Pi	17Ar	19Ta	5Cn	10Le
31	14Ge		11Le		13Sc		10Aq	26Pi		13Ge		7Vi

1959

	Jan	Feb	Mar	Apr	May	Jun	Jul	Aug	Sep	Oct	Nov	Dec
1	21Vi	14Sc	24Sc	17Cp	23Aq	9Ar	12Ta	26Ge	12Le	17Vi	8Sc	17Sg
3	18Li	12Sg	23Sg	13Aq	18Pi	3Ta	5Ge	20Cn	8Vi	15Li	8Sg	17Cp
5	17Sc	10Cp	20Cp	9Pi	12Ar	27Ta	29Ge	16Le	6Li	14Sc	8Cp	16Aq
7	16Sg	7Aq	16Aq	3Ar	6Ta	21Ge	24Cn	13Vi	4Sc	14Sg	6Aq	13Pi
9	14Cp	3Pi	12Pi	27Ar	0Ge	15Cn	20Le	10Li	3Sg	12Cp	3Pi	8Ar
11	12Aq	29Pi	7Ar	21Ta	24Ge	10Le	16Vi	8Sc	1Cp	10Aq	28Pi	2Ta
13	8Pi	23Ar	1Ta	15Ge	18Cn	6Vi	13Li	6Sg	29Cp	6Pi	23Ar	26Ta
15	3Ar	16Ta	24Ta	9Cn	13Le	3Li	11Sc	5Cp	26Aq	1Ar	17Ta	20Ge
17	27Ar	10Ge	18Ge	4Le	9Vi	1Sc	10Sg	3Aq	22Pi	26Ar	11Ge	13Cn
19	20Ta	5Cn	13Cn	0Vi	7Li	1Sg	9Cp	1Pi	18Ar	20Ta	4Cn	8Le
21	15Ge	1Le	9Le	29Vi	7Sc	1Cp	8Aq	27Pi	12Ta	14Ge	28Cn	2Vi
23	10Cn	28Le	6Vi	29Li	7Sg	0Aq	6Pi	22Ar	6Ge	8Cn	23Le	28Vi
25	6Le	27Vi	5Li	29Sc	7Cp	28Aq	2Ar	16Ta	0Cn	2Le	19Vi	25Li
27	3Vi	26Li	5Sc	29Sg	6Aq	24Pi	26Ar	10Ge	24Cn	27Le	17Li	24Sc
29	1Li		5Sg	27Cp	2Pi	18Ar	20Ta	4Cn	20Le	24Vi	16Sc	25Sg
31	29Li		3Cp		27Pi		14Ge	29Cn		23Li		25Cp

1960

	Jan	Feb	Mar	Apr	May	Jun	Jul	Aug	Sep	Oct	Nov	Dec
1	10Aq	29Pi	20Ar	5Ge	7Cn	21Le	25Vi	14Sc	7Cp	16Aq	8Ar	13Ta
3	8Pi	25Ar	15Ta	29Ge	1Le	16Vi	21Li	13Sg	6Aq	15Pi	4Ta	8Ge
5	4Ar	19Ta	9Ge	22Cn	25Le	12Li	19Sc	12Cp	6Pi	12Ar	0Ge	3Cn
7	29Ar	13Ge	3Cn	17Le	20Vi	10Sc	18Sg	12Aq	4Ar	9Ta	24Ge	26Cn
9	23Ta	7Cn	27Cn	12Vi	18Li	10Sg	19Cp	12Pi	1Ta	4Ge	18Cn	20Le
11	16Ge	1Le	22Le	9Li	17Sc	10Cp	19Aq	10Ar	26Ta	28Ge	12Le	14Vi
13	10Cn	26Le	18Vi	8Sc	16Sg	10Aq	18Pi	6Ta	20Ge	22Cn	6Vi	9Li
15	5Le	22Vi	15Li	7Sg	16Cp	9Pi	14Ar	0Ge	14Cn	16Le	1Li	6Sc
17	29Le	19Li	13Sc	6Cp	15Aq	5Ar	9Ta	24Ge	8Le	11Vi	28Li	4Sg
19	25Vi	16Sc	11Sg	4Aq	12Pi	0Ta	4Ge	18Cn	3Vi	6Li	26Sc	4Cp
21	22Li	14Sg	9Cp	2Pi	8Ar	25Ta	27Ge	12Le	28Vi	3Sc	26Sg	5Aq
23	19Sc	13Cp	8Aq	28Pi	3Ta	19Ge	21Cn	6Vi	24Li	2Sg	25Cp	4Pi
25	18Sg	12Aq	5Pi	24Ar	28Ta	12Cn	15Le	2Li	22Sc	0Cp	24Aq	1Ar
27	18Cp	10Pi	2Ar	19Ta	22Ge	6Le	9Vi	28Li	20Sg	29Cp	21Pi	28Ar
29	18Aq	7Ar	28Ar	13Ge	15Cn	0Vi	5Li	25Sc	18Cp	27Aq	18Ar	23Ta
31	16Pi		23Ta		9Le		1Sc	23Sg		24Pi		17Ge

271

1961

	Jan	Feb	Mar	Apr	May	Jun	Jul	Aug	Sep	Oct	Nov	Dec
1	29Ge	14Le	22Le	8Li	13Sc	4Cp	13Aq	6Ar	26Ta	0Cn	15Le	16Vi
3	23Cn	8Vi	17Vi	4Sc	10Sg	3Aq	12Pi	4Ta	22Ge	25Cn	8Vi	10Li
5	17Le	2Li	11Li	0Sg	9Cp	2Pi	10Ar	0Ge	16Cn	18Le	2Li	5Sc
7	11Vi	27Li	7Sc	28Sg	7Aq	0Ar	7Ta	25Ge	10Le	12Vi	27Li	2Sg
9	5Li	23Sc	3Sg	26Cp	5Pi	27Ar	3Ge	19Cn	3Vi	6Li	23Sc	29Sg
11	1Sc	21Sg	1Cp	24Aq	3Ar	23Ta	28Ge	13Le	27Vi	1Sc	20Sg	28Cp
13	28Sc	21Cp	0Aq	23Pi	0Ta	19Ge	22Cn	6Vi	22Li	27Sc	17Cp	26Aq
15	27Sg	21Aq	29Aq	21Ar	27Ta	13Cn	16Le	0Li	17Sc	23Sg	15Aq	24Pi
17	28Cp	21Pi	29Pi	19Ta	23Ge	7Le	9Vi	24Li	13Sg	20Cp	13Pi	22Ar
19	28Aq	19Ar	27Ar	15Ge	17Cn	1Vi	3Li	20Sc	10Cp	19Aq	12Ar	20Ta
21	27Pi	16Ta	24Ta	9Cn	11Le	25Vi	28Li	17Sg	9Aq	18Pi	10Ta	16Ge
23	24Ar	11Ge	19Ge	3Le	5Vi	19Li	24Sc	15Cp	8Pi	17Ar	7Ge	12Cn
25	20Ta	5Cn	13Cn	27Le	29Vi	16Sc	22Sg	15Aq	8Ar	15Ta	4Cn	6Le
27	14Ge	29Cn	7Le	21Vi	24Li	14Sg	22Cp	15Pi	7Ta	13Ge	28Cn	0Vi
29	8Cn		1Vi	16Li	21Sc	13Cp	22Aq	15Ar	5Ge	8Cn	22Le	24Vi
31	2Le		25Vi		20Sg		22Pi	13Ta		3Le		18Li

1962

	Jan	Feb	Mar	Apr	May	Jun	Jul	Aug	Sep	Oct	Nov	Dec
1	0Sc	17Sg	26Sg	17Aq	26Pi	19Ta	26Ge	13Le	28Vi	1Sc	16Sg	22Cp
3	26Sc	15Cp	24Cp	16Pi	25Ar	17Ge	22Cn	8Vi	22Li	25Sc	12Cp	18Aq
5	23Sg	15Aq	23Aq	17Ar	25Ta	14Cn	17Le	1Li	16Sc	19Sg	8Aq	16Pi
7	22Cp	15Pi	23Pi	16Ta	23Ge	9Le	11Vi	25Li	10Sg	15Cp	5Pi	14Ar
9	22Aq	15Ar	24Ar	14Ge	19Cn	3Vi	5Li	19Sc	6Cp	12Aq	5Ar	14Ta
11	21Pi	13Ta	22Ta	11Cn	13Le	27Vi	29Li	14Sg	3Aq	11Pi	5Ta	13Ge
13	19Ar	10Ge	19Ge	5Le	7Vi	21Li	24Sc	11Cp	3Pi	11Ar	5Ge	11Cn
15	16Ta	5Cn	14Cn	29Le	1Li	16Sc	20Sg	10Aq	3Ar	12Ta	3Cn	7Le
17	13Ge	29Cn	9Le	23Vi	25Li	11Sg	17Cp	9Pi	3Ta	11Ge	0Le	3Vi
19	8Cn	23Le	2Vi	17Li	20Sc	8Cp	16Aq	9Ar	2Ge	8Cn	25Le	27Vi
21	3Le	17Vi	26Vi	11Sc	16Sg	6Aq	15Pi	8Ta	29Ge	4Le	19Vi	20Li
23	27Le	11Li	20Li	6Sg	12Cp	4Pi	14Ar	6Ge	25Cn	28Le	12Li	14Sc
25	20Vi	5Sc	14Sc	2Cp	10Aq	3Ar	12Ta	2Cn	19Le	22Vi	6Sc	9Sg
27	14Li	0Sg	9Sg	29Cp	7Pi	1Ta	9Ge	28Cn	13Vi	16Li	1Sg	5Cp
29	8Sc		5Cp	27Aq	6Ar	29Ta	5Cn	22Le	7Li	10Sc	26Sg	1Aq
31	4Sg		3Aq		5Ta		1Le	16Vi		4Sg		29Aq

1963

	Jan	Feb	Mar	Apr	May	Jun	Jul	Aug	Sep	Oct	Nov	Dec
1	13Pi	6Ta	17Ta	8Cn	14Le	29Vi	2Sc	16Sg	1Aq	7Pi	29Ar	8Ge
3	11Ar	4Ge	15Ge	4Le	9Vi	23Li	25Sc	10Cp	29Aq	6Ar	0Ge	8Cn
5	9Ta	1Cn	12Cn	29Le	3Li	17Sc	20Sg	6Aq	27Pi	6Ta	29Ge	6Le
7	8Ge	28Cn	7Le	24Vi	26Li	11Sg	15Cp	4Pi	26Ar	6Ge	28Cn	3Vi
9	5Cn	23Le	2Vi	18Li	20Sc	6Cp	11Aq	2Ar	25Ta	4Cn	24Le	28Vi
11	2Le	18Vi	27Vi	11Sc	14Sg	1Aq	7Pi	0Ta	24Ge	1Le	19Vi	23Li
13	28Le	12Li	21Li	5Sg	9Cp	27Aq	5Ar	29Ta	21Cn	27Le	14Li	16Sc
15	22Vi	6Sc	14Sc	29Sg	4Aq	24Pi	4Ta	27Ge	17Le	22Vi	7Sc	10Sg
17	16Li	0Sg	8Sg	24Cp	0Pi	23Ar	2Ge	24Cn	13Vi	17Li	1Sg	4Cp
19	10Sc	25Sg	3Cp	21Aq	28Pi	22Ta	1Cn	21Le	8Li	11Sc	25Sg	28Cp
21	4Sg	21Cp	29Cp	19Pi	28Ar	22Ge	29Cn	17Vi	2Sc	4Sg	19Cp	23Aq
23	0Cp	19Aq	26Aq	19Ar	28Ta	20Cn	26Le	12Li	26Sc	28Sg	14Aq	20Pi
25	27Cp	18Pi	26Pi	20Ta	28Ge	18Le	21Vi	6Sc	19Sg	22Cp	10Pi	17Ar
27	24Aq	17Ar	26Ar	20Ge	26Cn	13Vi	16Li	29Sc	14Cp	18Aq	8Ar	16Ta
29	23Pi		26Ta	18Cn	22Le	8Li	10Sc	23Sg	9Aq	15Pi	7Ta	16Ge
31	22Ar		25Ge		17Vi		3Sg	18Cp		14Ar		15Cn

1964

	Jan	Feb	Mar	Apr	May	Jun	Jul	Aug	Sep	Oct	Nov	Dec
1	0Le	19Vi	10Li	25Sc	27Sg	11Aq	16Pi	6Ta	29Ge	8Le	29Vi	4Sc
3	28Le	15Li	5Sc	18Sg	20Cp	6Pi	12Ar	5Ge	28Cn	6Vi	25Li	29Sc
5	24Vi	9Sc	29Sc	12Cp	15Aq	3Ar	10Ta	4Cn	26Le	3Li	20Sc	23Sg
7	19Li	3Sg	22Sg	7Aq	11Pi	1Ta	10Ge	3Le	24Vi	29Li	14Sg	16Cp
9	13Sc	26Sg	16Cp	2Pi	8Ar	1Ge	10Cn	2Vi	21Li	24Sc	8Cp	10Aq
11	7Sg	21Cp	11Aq	0Ar	7Ta	1Cn	9Le	0Li	16Sc	18Sg	1Aq	4Pi
13	0Cp	16Aq	8Pi	29Ar	8Ge	1Le	8Vi	26Li	10Sg	12Cp	26Aq	29Pi
15	25Cp	13Pi	6Ar	29Ta	8Cn	29Le	5Li	20Sc	4Cp	5Aq	21Pi	26Ar
17	20Aq	10Ar	5Ta	28Ge	6Le	26Vi	0Sc	14Sg	28Cp	0Pi	18Ar	25Ta
19	17Pi	8Ta	3Ge	26Cn	3Vi	21Li	24Sc	8Cp	22Aq	27Pi	17Ta	25Ge
21	14Ar	7Ge	2Cn	23Le	29Vi	15Sc	17Sg	2Aq	18Pi	25Ar	17Ge	25Cn
23	12Ta	5Cn	29Cn	19Vi	24Li	9Sg	11Cp	27Aq	16Ar	23Ta	17Cn	25Le
25	10Ge	3Le	26Le	15Li	18Sc	2Cp	5Aq	23Pi	14Ta	23Ge	16Le	23Vi
27	9Cn	0Vi	23Vi	9Sc	12Sg	26Cp	0Pi	20Ar	12Ge	21Cn	13Vi	19Li
29	8Le	27Vi	18Li	3Sg	5Cp	21Aq	26Pi	17Ta	10Cn	19Le	9Li	14Sc
31	6Vi		13Sc		29Cp		23Ar	15Ge		16Vi		8Sg

1965

	Jan	Feb	Mar	Apr	May	Jun	Jul	Aug	Sep	Oct	Nov	Dec
1	20Sg	4Aq	12Aq	28Pi	3Ta	25Ge	4Le	27Vi	17Sc	20Sg	4Aq	6Pi
3	13Cp	28Aq	7Pi	25Ar	2Ge	25Cn	4Vi	25Li	12Sg	14Cp	28Aq	0Ar
5	7Aq	23Pi	2Ar	22Ta	0Cn	24Le	2Li	21Sc	6Cp	8Aq	22Pi	25Ar
7	1Pi	18Ar	29Ar	20Ge	29Cn	22Vi	29Li	15Sg	0Aq	2Pi	17Ar	22Ta
9	26Pi	15Ta	25Ta	18Cn	27Le	19Li	24Sc	9Cp	24Aq	26Pi	14Ta	20Ge
11	22Ar	13Ge	23Ge	16Le	25Vi	14Sc	18Sg	3Aq	18Pi	22Ar	11Ge	19Cn
13	19Ta	12Cn	21Cn	15Vi	22Li	9Sg	12Cp	27Aq	13Ar	18Ta	9Cn	18Le
15	18Ge	11Le	20Le	12Li	18Sc	3Cp	6Aq	21Pi	8Ta	15Ge	8Le	17Vi
17	18Cn	11Vi	19Vi	9Sc	13Sg	27Cp	0Pi	16Ar	4Ge	13Cn	6Vi	15Li
19	18Le	10Li	17Li	4Sg	7Cp	21Aq	24Pi	11Ta	2Cn	11Le	4Li	11Sc
21	18Vi	6Sc	14Sc	29Sg	1Aq	15Pi	19Ar	8Ge	0Le	10Vi	1Sc	7Sg
23	15Li	1Sg	9Sg	23Cp	24Aq	10Ar	15Ta	6Cn	0Vi	8Li	28Sc	2Cp
25	10Sc	25Sg	3Cp	16Aq	19Pi	6Ta	13Ge	6Le	29Vi	6Sc	23Sg	26Cp
27	5Sg	19Cp	27Cp	11Pi	14Ar	4Ge	12Cn	6Vi	28Li	3Sg	18Cp	20Aq
29	28Sg		21Aq	6Ar	12Ta	4Cn	12Le	6Li	25Sc	28Sg	12Aq	14Pi
31	22Cp		15Pi		10Ge		13Vi	4Sc		22Cp		8Ar

1966

	Jan	Feb	Mar	Apr	May	Jun	Jul	Aug	Sep	Oct	Nov	Dec
1	20Ar	8Ge	17Ge	8Le	18Vi	10Sc	17Sg	4Aq	18Pi	21Ar	7Ge	13Cn
3	16Ta	6Cn	14Cn	8Vi	17Li	8Sg	12Cp	28Aq	12Ar	15Ta	3Cn	10Le
5	13Ge	6Le	14Le	8Li	15Sc	4Cp	7Aq	21Pi	6Ta	10Ge	0Le	8Vi
7	13Cn	6Vi	14Vi	7Sc	13Sg	29Cp	1Pi	15Ar	1Ge	6Cn	28Le	7Li
9	13Le	6Li	15Li	5Sg	8Cp	23Aq	25Pi	9Ta	26Ge	3Le	27Vi	5Sc
11	13Vi	5Sc	13Sc	1Cp	3Aq	17Pi	19Ar	5Ge	24Cn	2Vi	26Li	3Sg
13	11Li	1Sg	10Sg	25Cp	27Aq	11Ar	13Ta	1Cn	24Le	2Li	25Sc	1Cp
15	8Sc	26Sg	5Cp	19Aq	21Pi	6Ta	10Ge	0Le	24Vi	2Sc	23Sg	27Cp
17	4Sg	20Cp	29Cp	13Pi	15Ar	1Ge	7Cn	0Vi	24Li	1Sg	19Cp	22Aq
19	29Sg	14Aq	22Aq	7Ar	10Ta	29Ge	7Le	1Li	23Sc	28Sg	14Aq	16Pi
21	23Cp	7Pi	16Pi	2Ta	6Ge	27Cn	6Vi	0Sc	20Sg	24Cp	9Pi	10Ar
23	17Aq	1Ar	10Ar	27Ta	4Cn	26Le	6Li	27Sc	15Cp	18Aq	2Ar	4Ta
25	10Pi	25Ar	5Ta	23Ge	1Le	25Vi	4Sc	23Sg	10Aq	12Pi	26Ar	29Ta
27	4Ar	20Ta	0Ge	21Cn	0Vi	23Li	1Sg	18Cp	4Pi	6Ar	21Ta	25Ge
29	29Ar		26Ge	19Le	28Vi	20Sc	26Sg	13Aq	27Pi	0Ta	16Ge	23Cn
31	24Ta		24Cn		26Li		21Cp	7Pi		25Ta		21Le

1967

	Jan	Feb	Mar	Apr	May	Jun	Jul	Aug	Sep	Oct	Nov	Dec
1	5Vi	28Li	8Sc	29Sg	4Aq	20Pi	21Ar	5Ge	22Cn	27Le	20Li	28Sc
3	4Li	26Sc	6Sg	25Cp	29Aq	13Ar	15Ta	0Cn	19Le	27Vi	20Sc	28Sg
5	2Sc	23Sg	3Cp	20Aq	23Pi	7Ta	9Ge	27Cn	18Vi	27Li	20Sg	27Cp
7	29Sc	19Cp	28Cp	14Pi	17Ar	1Ge	5Cn	25Le	18Li	27Sc	18Cp	23Aq
9	26Sg	14Aq	23Aq	8Ar	10Ta	26Ge	2Le	24Vi	17Sc	25Sg	15Aq	19Pi
11	23Cp	8Pi	17Pi	2Ta	5Ge	22Cn	29Le	23Li	15Sg	23Cp	10Pi	13Ar
13	18Aq	2Ar	11Ar	25Ta	29Ge	19Le	28Vi	21Sc	13Cp	18Aq	4Ar	6Ta
15	12Pi	26Ar	4Ta	20Ge	25Cn	17Vi	26Li	19Sg	9Aq	13Pi	28Ar	0Ge
17	6Ar	20Ta	28Ta	15Cn	22Le	15Li	24Sc	16Cp	4Pi	7Ar	21Ta	24Ge
19	0Ta	14Ge	23Ge	12Le	20Vi	14Sc	22Sg	12Aq	28Pi	1Ta	15Ge	19Cn
21	24Ta	11Cn	19Cn	11Vi	19Li	12Sg	19Cp	7Pi	22Ar	24Ta	10Cn	15Le
23	20Ge	9Le	17Le	10Li	19Sc	11Cp	16Aq	2Ar	16Ta	18Ge	5Le	12Vi
25	17Cn	9Vi	17Vi	11Sc	18Sg	8Aq	11Pi	25Ar	9Ge	13Cn	1Vi	9Li
27	16Le	9Li	17Li	10Sg	16Cp	3Pi	5Ar	19Ta	4Cn	8Le	29Vi	8Sc
29	15Vi		17Sc	8Cp	13Aq	28Pi	29Ar	13Ge	0Le	6Vi	28Li	7Sg
31	14Li		16Sg		8Pi		23Ta	8Cn		5Li		6Cp

278

1968

	Jan	Feb	Mar	Apr	May	Jun	Jul	Aug	Sep	Oct	Nov	Dec
1	20Cp	9Pi	0Ar	14Ta	17Ge	2Le	7Vi	28Li	22Sg	1Aq	21Pi	25Ar
3	18Aq	4Ar	24Ar	8Ge	11Cn	27Le	4Li	26Sc	20Cp	28Aq	16Ar	19Ta
5	14Pi	28Ar	18Ta	2Cn	5Le	24Vi	2Sc	25Sg	18Aq	24Pi	10Ta	13Ge
7	9Ar	22Ta	12Ge	27Cn	1Vi	22Li	1Sg	24Cp	15Pi	19Ar	4Ge	7Cn
9	2Ta	16Ge	6Cn	23Le	29Vi	21Sc	1Cp	23Aq	11Ar	14Ta	28Ge	0Le
11	26Ta	11Cn	1Le	20Vi	28Li	22Sg	0Aq	20Pi	6Ta	8Ge	22Cn	25Le
13	20Ge	7Le	28Le	20Li	28Sc	22Cp	28Aq	15Ar	0Ge	1Cn	16Le	20Vi
15	15Cn	4Vi	27Vi	20Sc	29Sg	20Aq	25Pi	10Ta	23Ge	25Cn	11Vi	17Li
17	12Le	2Li	26Li	20Sg	28Cp	17Pi	20Ar	4Ge	17Cn	20Le	9Li	16Sc
19	8Vi	1Sc	25Sc	18Cp	25Aq	11Ar	14Ta	27Ge	12Le	17Vi	7Sc	16Sg
21	6Li	29Sc	24Sg	15Aq	20Pi	5Ta	7Ge	22Cn	9Vi	15Li	8Sg	16Cp
23	4Sc	27Sg	22Cp	11Pi	14Ar	29Ta	1Cn	17Le	7Li	14Sc	8Cp	16Aq
25	2Sg	25Cp	18Aq	5Ar	8Ta	23Ge	26Cn	14Vi	5Sc	14Sg	7Aq	14Pi
27	1Cp	21Aq	14Pi	29Ar	2Ge	17Cn	21Le	11Li	4Sg	13Cp	5Pi	10Ar
29	29Cp	17Pi	8Ar	23Ta	26Ge	12Le	18Vi	9Sc	3Cp	11Aq	0Ar	4Ta
31	26Aq		3Ta		20Cn		14Li	7Sg		8Pi		28Ta

1969

	Jan	Feb	Mar	Apr	May	Jun	Jul	Aug	Sep	Oct	Nov	Dec
1	10Ge	24Cn	2Le	18Vi	24Li	16Sg	25Cp	18Pi	7Ta	10Ge	24Cn	25Le
3	4Cn	19Le	27Le	15Li	23Sc	16Cp	25Aq	15Ar	2Ge	4Cn	18Le	20Vi
5	28Cn	14Vi	23Vi	13Sc	22Sg	16Aq	23Pi	11Ta	26Ge	28Cn	12Vi	15Li
7	22Le	10Li	20Li	12Sg	21Cp	14Pi	20Ar	6Ge	20Cn	22Le	7Li	12Sc
9	17Vi	7Sc	17Sc	11Cp	20Aq	10Ar	15Ta	0Cn	14Le	16Vi	4Sc	11Sg
11	13Li	5Sg	15Sg	9Aq	17Pi	5Ta	9Ge	23Cn	8Vi	12Li	2Sg	11Cp
13	10Sc	3Cp	14Cp	6Pi	13Ar	0Ge	3Cn	17Le	3Li	9Sc	1Cp	10Aq
15	9Sg	3Aq	12Aq	3Ar	8Ta	24Ge	26Cn	11Vi	29Li	7Sg	0Aq	9Pi
17	9Cp	2Pi	10Pi	29Ar	3Ge	17Cn	20Le	6Li	26Sc	5Cp	28Aq	6Ar
19	9Aq	0Ar	8Ar	24Ta	27Ge	11Le	14Vi	2Sc	24Sg	3Aq	26Pi	2Ta
21	8Pi	26Ar	4Ta	18Ge	21Cn	5Vi	9Li	29Sc	23Cp	2Pi	22Ar	28Ta
23	5Ar	21Ta	28Ta	12Cn	14Le	0Li	6Sc	28Sg	21Aq	29Pi	18Ta	22Ge
25	0Ta	15Ge	22Ge	6Le	9Vi	26Li	4Sg	27Cp	20Pi	26Ar	14Ge	16Cn
27	25Ta	8Cn	16Cn	1Vi	4Li	25Sc	3Cp	27Aq	18Ar	23Ta	8Cn	10Le
29	18Ge		10Le	26Vi	2Sc	25Sg	4Aq	26Pi	15Ta	18Ge	2Le	4Vi
31	12Cn		5Vi		1Sg		3Pi	24Ar	27Ta	12Cn		28Vi

1970

	Jan	Feb	Mar	Apr	May	Jun	Jul	Aug	Sep	Oct	Nov	Dec
1	10Li	28Sc	8Sg	1Aq	10Pi	2Ta	8Ge	24Cn	9Vi	11Li	28Sc	5Cp
3	6Sc	27Sg	6Cp	29Aq	8Ar	28Ta	3Cn	18Le	2Li	6Sc	25Sg	3Aq
5	4Sg	27Cp	5Aq	29Pi	6Ta	24Ge	27Cn	11Vi	26Li	1Sg	22Cp	1Pi
7	4Cp	27Aq	5Pi	27Ar	3Ge	19Cn	21Le	5Li	21Sc	28Sg	20Aq	29Pi
9	4Aq	27Pi	5Ar	25Ta	28Ge	13Le	15Vi	0Sc	18Sg	25Cp	18Pi	27Ar
11	4Pi	25Ar	3Ta	20Ge	23Cn	6Vi	9Li	25Sc	15Cp	24Aq	17Ar	25Ta
13	3Ar	21Ta	0Ge	15Cn	17Le	0Li	3Sc	22Sg	15Aq	23Pi	16Ta	22Ge
15	29Ar	16Ge	25Ge	9Le	10Vi	25Li	0Sg	21Cp	15Pi	23Ar	13Ge	17Cn
17	25Ta	10Cn	19Cn	2Vi	5Li	22Sc	28Sg	21Aq	15Ar	22Ta	9Cn	12Le
19	19Ge	4Le	12Le	27Vi	0Sc	20Sg	28Cp	22Pi	13Ta	19Ge	4Le	6Vi
21	13Cn	28Le	6Vi	22Li	27Sc	19Cp	28Aq	21Ar	11Ge	14Cn	28Le	29Vi
23	7Le	22Vi	1Li	18Sc	25Sg	18Aq	27Pi	18Ta	6Cn	8Le	22Vi	24Li
25	1Vi	16Li	26Li	15Sg	24Cp	17Pi	25Ar	14Ge	0Le	2Vi	16Li	19Sc
27	25Vi	12Sc	22Sc	13Cp	22Aq	15Ar	22Ta	9Cn	24Le	26Vi	11Sc	16Sg
29	19Li		19Sg	11Aq	21Pi	12Ta	18Ge	3Le	17Vi	20Li	7Sg	14Cp
31	15Sc		16Cp		18Ar		12Cn	27Le		15Sc		13Aq

1971

	Jan	Feb	Mar	Apr	May	Jun	Jul	Aug	Sep	Oct	Nov	Dec
1	27Aq	20Ar	0Ta	20Ge	25Cn	9Vi	11Li	25Sc	12Cp	18Aq	11Ar	19Ta
3	26Pi	18Ta	28Ta	16Cn	19Le	3Li	5Sc	20Sg	10Aq	17Pi	11Ta	19Ge
5	24Ar	15Ge	24Ge	11Le	13Vi	27Li	0Sg	17Cp	9Pi	18Ar	11Ge	17Cn
7	21Ta	10Cn	10Cn	4Vi	6Li	21Sc	26Sg	16Aq	9Ar	18Ta	9Cn	13Le
9	18Ge	5Le	14Le	28Vi	0Sc	17Sg	23Cp	15Pi	9Ta	17Ge	5Le	8Vi
11	13Cn	29Le	7Vi	22Li	25Sc	14Cp	21Aq	14Ar	7Ge	14Cn	0Vi	2Li
13	8Le	22Vi	1Li	16Sc	21Sg	11Aq	20Pi	13Ta	4Cn	9Le	24Vi	26Li
15	2Vi	16Li	25Li	11Sg	17Cp	9Pi	18Ar	11Ge	0Le	3Vi	18Li	20Sc
17	26Vi	10Sc	19Sc	7Cp	14Aq	7Ar	16Ta	7Cn	24Le	27Vi	12Sc	15Sg
19	19Li	5Sg	14Sg	4Aq	12Pi	6Ta	14Ge	3Le	18Vi	21Li	6Sg	10Cp
21	14Sc	1Cp	10Cp	2Pi	11Ar	4Ge	11Cn	27Le	12Li	15Sc	1Cp	6Aq
23	10Sg	0Aq	8Aq	1Ar	10Ta	1Cn	6Le	21Vi	6Sc	9Sg	26Cp	3Pi
25	7Cp	29Aq	8Pi	1Ta	9Ge	28Cn	1Vi	15Li	0Sg	4Cp	23Aq	1Ar
27	7Aq	0Ar	8Ar	1Ge	7Cn	23Le	25Vi	9Sc	24Sg	29Cp	21Pi	0Ta
29	6Pi		8Ta	29Ge	3Le	17Vi	19Li	3Sg	20Cp	27Aq	20Ar	29Ta
31	6Ar		7Ge		27Le		13Sc	28Sg		26Pi		27Ge

1972

	Jan	Feb	Mar	Apr	May	Jun	Jul	Aug	Sep	Oct	Nov	Dec
1	11Cn	29Le	20Vi	5Sc	7Sg	23Cp	29Aq	21Ar	14Ge	23Cn	12Vi	16Li
3	8Le	24Vi	14Li	28Sc	1Cp	19Aq	26Pi	19Ta	12Cn	19Le	6Li	10Sc
5	4Vi	18Li	8Sc	22Sg	26Cp	15Pi	24Ar	18Ge	9Le	15Vi	1Sc	3Sg
7	28Vi	12Sc	2Sg	17Cp	22Aq	14Ar	23Ta	16Cn	5Vi	10Li	24Sc	27Sg
9	22Li	6Sg	26Sg	13Aq	20Pi	13Ta	22Ge	13Le	1Li	4Sc	18Sg	21Cp
11	16Sc	1Cp	21Cp	11Pi	19Ar	13Ge	21Cn	10Vi	25Li	28Sc	12Cp	16Aq
13	10Sg	27Cp	18Aq	10Ar	19Ta	12Cn	18Le	]5Li	19Sc	21Sg	6Aq	11Pi
15	6Cp	25Aq	17Pi	11Ta	20Ge	10Le	14Vi	29Li	13Sg	15Cp	2Pi	8Ar
17	2Aq	24Pi	17Ar	11Ge	18Cn	6Vi	9Li	23Sc	7Cp	10Aq	29Pi	7Ta
19	0pi	23Ar	17Ta	9Cn	15Le	1Li	3Sc	17Sg	2Aq	7Pi	28Ar	7Ge
21	28Pi	22Ta	16Ge	6Le	10Vi	25Li	27Sc	12Cp	29Aq	5Ar	29Ta	7Cn
23	26Ar	19Ge	13Cn	1Vi	5Li	29Sc	21Sg	7Aq	27Pi	5Ta	29Ge	6Le
25	25Ta	16Cn	9Le	26Vi	29Li	13Sg	16Cp	4Pi	27Ar	6Ge	28Cn	4Vi
27	23Ge	12Le	4Vi	20Li	22Sc	7Cp	12Aq	3Ar	26Ta	5Cn	25Le	0Li
29	20Cn	7Vi	]29Vi	13Sc	16Sg	3Aq	9Pi	1Ta	25Ge	3Le	21Vi	24Li
31	16Le		23Li		11Cp		7Ar	0Ge		29Le		18Sc

1973

	Jan	Feb	Mar	Apr	May	Jun	Jul	Aug	Sep	Oct	Nov	Dec
1	0Sg	14Cp	22Cp	8Pi	14Ar	7Ge	16Cn	8Vi	27Li	0Sg	13Cp	15Aq
3	24Sg	9Aq	17Aq	6Ar	14Ta	7Cn	15Le	6Li	22Sc	24Sg	7Aq	9Pi
5	18Cp	5Pi	14Pi	5Ta	14Ge	7Le	14Vi	1Sc	16Sg	17Cp	1Pi	5Ar
7	13Aq	1Ar	11Ar	4Ge	13Cn	5Vi	10Li	26Sc	9Cp	11Aq	27Pi	2Ta
9	8Pi	29Ar	10Ta	3Cn	11Le	1Li	5Sc	19Sg	3Aq	6Pi	25Ar	1Ge
11	5Ar	27Ta	8Ge	1Le	8Vi	26Li	29Sc	13Cp	28Aq	3Ar	23Ta	1Cn
13	2Ta	25Ge	6Cn	28Le	4Li	20Sc	23Sg	7Aq	24Pi	0Ta	23Ge	2Le
15	1Ge	24Cn	4Le	24Vi	29Li	14Sg	16Cp	2Pi	21Ar	29Ta	22Cn	0Vi
17	0Cn	22Le	1Vi	20Li	23Sc	8Cp	10Aq	28Pi	19Ta	27Ge	20Le	28Vi
19	0Le	20Vi	28Vi	14Sc	17Sg	1Aq	5Pi	24Ar	17Ge	26Cn	18Vi	24Li
21	28Le	16Li	24Li	8Sg	11Cp	26Aq	1Ar	22Ta	15Cn	24Le	14Li	19Sc
23	25Vi	10Sc	18Sc	2Cp	4Aq	21Pi	27Ar	20Ge	13Le	21Vi	9Sc	13Sg
25	20Li	4Sg	12Sg	26Cp	29Aq	18Ar	25Ta	19Cn	11Vi	17Li	4Sg	7Cp
27	15Sc	28Sg	6Cp	20Aq	25Pi	16Ta	24Ge	18Le	9Li	13Sc	28Sg	0Aq
29	8Sg		0Aq	16Pi	23Ar	16Ge	24Cn	16Vi	5Sc	8Sg	22Cp	24Aq
31	2Cp		25Aq		22Ta		24Le	14Li		2Cp		18Pi

1974

	Jan	Feb	Mar	Apr	May	Jun	Jul	Aug	Sep	Oct	Nov	Dec
1	1Ar	20Ta	0Ge	23Cn	2Vi	23Li	29Sc	14Cp	29Aq	2Ar	19Ta	26Ge
3	27Ar	18Ge	28Ge	21Le	0Li	19Sc	23Sg	8Aq	23Pi	27Ar	16Ge	24Cn
5	25Ta	17Cn	27Cn	20Vi	27Li	14Sg	17Cp	2Pi	18Ar	23Ta	14Cn	23Le
7	24Ge	18Le	26Le	18Li	23Sc	9Cp	11Aq	26Pi	13Ta	20Ge	12Le	22Vi
9	25Cn	17Vi	25Vi	15Sc	18Sg	2Aq	5Pi	20Ar	9Ge	17Cn	11Vi	19Li
11	25Le	16Li	23Li	10Sg	12Cp	26Aq	29Pi	16Ta	7Cn	16Le	9Li	16Sc
13	24Vi	12Sc	20Sc	5Cp	6Aq	20Pi	24Ar	13Ge	6Le	15Vi	7Sc	12Sg
15	20Li	7Sg	15Sg	28Cp	0Pi	15Ar	20Ta	12Cn	6Vi	14Li	4Sg	7Cp
17	16Sc	0Cp	9Cp	22Aq	25Pi	12Ta	19Ge	12Le	5Li	12Sc	29Sg	2Aq
19	10Sg	24Cp	2Aq	17Pi	20Ar	10Ge	18Cn	12Vi	4Sc	9Sg	24Cp	25Aq
21	4Cp	18Aq	26Aq	12Ar	18Ta	10Cn	19Le	12Li	1Sg	4Cp	18Aq	19Pi
23	27Cp	12Pi	21Pi	9Ta	16Ge	10Le	19Vi	9Sc	26Sg	28Cp	11Pi	13Ar
25	21Aq	7Ar	17Ar	7Ge	15Cn	9Vi	17Li	5Sg	20Cp	22Aq	6Ar	9Ta
27	15Pi	3Ta	13Ta	5Cn	14Le	7Li	13Sc	29Sg	13Aq	16Pi	1Ta	6Ge
29	10Ar		11Ge	4Le	13Vi	3Sc	8Sg	23Cp	7Pi	10Ar	28Ta	4Cn
31	6Ta		8Cn		10Li		2Cp	17Aq		6Ta		4Le

1975

	Jan	Feb	Mar	Apr	May	Jun	Jul	Aug	Sep	Oct	Nov	Dec
1	19Le	12Li	21Li	11Sg	14Cp	29Aq	0Ar	15Ta	2Cn	9Le	2Li	11Sc
3	18Vi	10Sc	19Sc	6Cp	9Aq	23Pi	24Ar	10Ge	0Le	8Vi	2Sc	9Sg
5	16Li	6Sg	15Sg	1Aq	3Pi	17Ar	19Ta	7Cn	0Vi	9Li	1Sg	7Cp
7	13Sc	1Cp	10Cp	24Aq	26Pi	11Ta	16Ge	6Le	0Li	9Sc	29Sg	3Aq
9	9Sg	25Cp	4Aq	18Pi	21Ar	7Ge	13Cn	6Vi	0Sc	7Sg	25Cp	28Aq
11	4Cp	19Aq	28Aq	12Ar	16Ta	4Cn	12Le	6Li	29Sc	4Cp	20Aq	22Pi
13	28Cp	12Pi	21Pi	7Ta	12Ge	3Le	12Vi	5Sc	25Sg	29Cp	14Pi	16Ar
15	22Aq	6Ar	15Ar	2Ge	8Cn	1Vi	11Li	2Sg	20Cp	24Aq	8Ar	10Ta
17	16Pi	0Ta	10Ta	28Ge	6Le	0Li	8Sc	28Sg	15Aq	17Pi	2Ta	5Ge
19	9Ar	25Ta	5Ge	25Cn	4Vi	28Li	5Sg	23Cp	9Pi	11Ar	26Ta	1Cn
21	4Ta	22Ge	1Cn	24Le	3Li	25Sc	1Cp	18Aq	2Ar	5Ta	22Ge	28Cn
23	0Ge	20Cn	29Cn	23Vi	2Sc	22Sg	26Cp	12Pi	26Ar	0Ge	18Cn	26Le
25	28Ge	20Le	29Le	22Li	0Sg	18Cp	21Aq	5Ar	20Ta	25Ge	15Le	24Vi
27	27Cn	21Vi	29Vi	21Sc	26Sg	13Aq	15Pi	29Ar	15Ge	21Cn	13Vi	22Li
29	27Le		29Li	19Sg	22Cp	7Pi	9Ar	23Ta	11Cn	18Le	12Li	20Sc
31	28Vi		27Sc		17Aq		3Ta	19Ge		17Vi		18Sg

1976

	Jan	Feb	Mar	Apr	May	Jun	Jul	Aug	Sep	Oct	Nov	Dec
1	2Cp	19Aq	19Pi	25Ar	27Ta	14Cn	21Le	13Li	6Sg	14Cp	3Pi	6Ar
3	28Cp	14Pi	4Ar	18Ta	22Ge	10Le	18Vi	11Sc	4Cp	10Aq	27Pi	0Ta
5	24Aq	8Ar	28Ar	12Ge	17Cn	7Vi	16Li	9Sg	0Aq	6Pi	21Ar	23Ta
7	18Pi	1Ta	22Ta	7Cn	13Le	5Li	15Sc	7Cp	26Aq	0Ar	15Ta	17Ge
9	12Ar	25Ta	16Ge	4Le	11Vi	4Sc	13Sg	4Aq	21Pi	24Ar	8Ge	12Cn
11	5Ta	20Ge	11Cn	2Vi	10Li	4Sg	11Cp	0Pi	15Ar	18Ta	2Cn	7Le
13	0Ge	17Cn	9Le	1Li	10Sc	3Cp	9Aq	25Pi	9Ta	11Ge	27Cn	3Vi
15	26Ge	15Le	8Vi	2Sc	10Sg	0Aq	4Pi	19Ar	3Ge	5Cn	23Le	0Li
17	23Cn	15Vi	9Li	2Sg	9Cp	26Aq	29Pi	13Ta	27Ge	1Le	20Vi	28Li
19	21Le	15Li	9Sc	0Cp	6Aq	21Pi	23Ar	7Ge	22Cn	28Le	19Li	28Sc
21	20Vi	14Sc	7Sg	27Cp	1Pi	15Ar	17Ta	1Cn	19Le	26Vi	19Sc	28Sg
23	19Li	11Sg	5Cp	22Aq	25Pi	9Ta	11Ge	28Cn	18Vi	26Li	20Sg	27Cp
25	17Sc	8Cp	0Aq	16Pi	19Ar	3Ge	6Cn	25Le	18Li	26Sc	19Cp	24Aq
27	14Sg	3Aq	25Aq	10Ar	12Ta	28Ge	3Le	24Vi	18Sc	26Sg	16Aq	20Pi
29	11Cp	28Aq	19Pi	4Ta	6Ge	24Cn	0Vi	23Li	17Sg	24Cp	12Pi	14Ar
31	7Aq		13Ar		1Cn		29Vi	22Sc		20Aq		8Ta

1977

	Jan	Feb	Mar	Apr	May	Jun	Jul	Aug	Sep	Oct	Nov	Dec
1	20Ta	4Cn	12Cn	29Le	5Li	28Sc	7Cp	29Aq	17Ar	19Ta	3Cn	6Le
3	14Ge	29Cn	7Le	27Vi	4Sc	28Sg	6Aq	26Pi	11Ta	13Ge	27Cn	0Vi
5	8Cn	26Le	5Vi	26Li	5Sg	28Cp	4Pi	21Ar	5Ge	7Cn	21Le	25Vi
7	4Le	23Vi	3Li	26Sc	4Cp	26Aq	1Ar	15Ta	29Ge	1Le	17Vi	23Li
9	0Vi	21Li	2Sc	25Sg	3Aq	22Pi	25Ar	9Ge	23Cn	26Le	15Li	22Sc
11	27Vi	19Sc	0Sg	23Cp	0Pi	17Ar	19Ta	3Cn	18Le	23Vi	14Sc	22Sg
13	24Li	18Sg	29Sg	20Aq	25Pi	10Ta	13Ge	27Cn	15Vi	21Li	14Sg	23Cp
15	23Sc	16Cp	26Cp	16Pi	20Ar	4Ge	7Cn	23Le	12Li	20Sc	14Cp	22Aq
17	22Sg	13Aq	23Aq	10Ar	13Ta	28Ge	1Le	19Vi	10Sc	19Sg	12Aq	19Pi
19	21Cp	10Pi	19Pi	4Ta	7Ge	22Cn	26Le	16Li	9Sg	18Cp	9Pi	15Ar
21	19Aq	6Ar	14Ar	28Ta	1Cn	17Le	22Vi	14Sc	7Cp	16Aq	5Ar	9Ta
23	15Pi	0Ta	8Ta	22Ge	25Cn	12Vi	19Li	12Sg	5Aq	12Pi	0Ta	3Ge
25	10Ar	24Ta	2Ge	16Cn	20Le	9Li	17Sc	11Cp	3Pi	8Ar	24Ta	27Ge
27	4Ta	17Ge	25Ge	11Le	16Vi	7Sc	16Sg	9Aq	29Pi	3Ta	18Ge	21Cn
29	28Ta		20Cn	7Vi	13Li	6Sg	15Cp	7Pi	25Ar	27Ta	12Cn	15Le
31	22Ge		15Le		13Sc		15Aq	4Ar		21Ge		9Vi

1978

	Jan	Feb	Mar	Apr	May	Jun	Jul	Aug	Sep	Oct	Nov	Dec
1	22Vi	11Sc	22Sc	15Cp	24Aq	15Ar	20Ta	5Cn	19Le	22Vi	10Sc	17Sg
3	18Li	10Sg	20Sg	14Aq	22Pi	10Ta	14Ge	28Cn	13Vi	18Li	8Sg	16Cp
5	16Sc	9Cp	19Cp	11Pi	18Ar	5Ge	8Cn	22Le	8Li	14Sc	6Cp	15Aq
7	15Sg	9Aq	18Aq	9Ar	13Ta	29Ge	1Le	16Vi	4Sc	12Sg	5Aq	14Pi
9	15Cp	8Pi	16Pi	5Ta	8Ge	23Cn	25Le	11Li	1Sg	10Cp	3Pi	11Ar
11	16Aq	6Ar	14Ar	0Ge	2Cn	16Le	19Vi	7Sc	29Sg	8Aq	1Ar	7Ta
13	14Pi	2Ta	9Ta	24Ge	26Cn	10Vi	14Li	4Sg	28Cp	6Pi	28Ar	3Ge
15	11Ar	26Ta	4Ge	18Cn	20Le	5Li	11Sc	3Cp	27Aq	5Ar	24Ta	28Ge
17	6Ta	20Ge	28Ge	12Le	14Vi	2Sc	9Sg	3Aq	26Pi	2Ta	19Ge	22Cn
19	0Ge	14Cn	22Cn	6Vi	10Li	1Sg	9Cp	3Pi	24Ar	28Ta	14Cn	15Le
21	24Ge	8Le	16Le	2Li	8Sc	1Cp	10Aq	2Ar	21Ta	23Ge	7Le	9Vi
23	17Cn	3Vi	11Vi	0Sc	7Sg	1Aq	10Pi	29Ar	16Ge	18Cn	1Vi	3Li
25	12Le	28Vi	7Li	28Sc	7Cp	1Pi	8Ar	25Ta	10Cn	11Le	25Vi	29Li
27	6Vi	25Li	5Sc	27Sg	7Aq	28Pi	4Ta	20Ge	3Le	5Vi	21Li	26Sc
29	2Li		3Sg	26Cp	5Pi	25Ar	29Ta	13Cn	27Le	0Li	18Sc	25Sg
31	28Li		1Cp		2Ar		23Ge	7Le		26Li		25Cp

1979

	Jan	Feb	Mar	Apr	May	Jun	Jul	Aug	Sep	Oct	Nov	Dec
1	10Aq	3Ar	11Ar	1Ge	4Cn	18Le	20Vi	5Sc	23Sg	0Aq	23Pi	2Ta
3	10Pi	1Ta	9Ta	26Ge	29Cn	12Vi	14Li	1Sg	21Cp	29Aq	23Ar	0Ge
5	8Ar	27Ta	5Ge	21Cn	22Le	6Li	9Sc	28Sg	21Aq	29Pi	22Ta	27Ge
7	4Ta	21Ge	0Cn	14Le	16Vi	1Sc	6Sg	27Cp	21Pi	29Ar	19Ge	23Cn
9	0Ge	15Cn	24Cn	8Vi	10Li	28Sc	4Cp	28Aq	21Ar	28Ta	15Cn	18Le
11	24Ge	9Le	18Le	2Li	6Sc	26Sg	4Aq	28Pi	19Ta	25Ge	10Le	12Vi
13	18Cn	3Vi	12Vi	27Li	3Sg	25Cp	4Pi	26Ar	16Ge	20Cn	4Vi	5Li
15	12Le	27Vi	6Li	23Sc	0Cp	24Aq	2Ar	24Ta	11Cn	14Le	27Vi	29Li
17	6Vi	21Li	1Sc	20Sg	29Cp	22Pi	0Ta	19Ge	5Le	7Vi	22Li	25Sc
19	0Li	16Sc	26Sc	18Cp	27Aq	20Ar	27Ta	14Cn	29Le	1Li	17Sc	22Sg
21	24Li	13Sg	23Sg	16Aq	25Pi	17Ta	22Ge	8Le	22Vi	25Li	13Sg	19Cp
23	20Sc	12Cp	21Cp	15Pi	23Ar	13Ge	17Cn	2Vi	16Li	20Sc	10Cp	18Aq
25	18Sg	11Aq	20Aq	13Ar	20Ta	8Cn	11Le	25Vi	11Sc	16Sg	7Aq	16Pi
27	18Cp	12Pi	20Pi	11Ta	17Ge	3Le	5Vi	19Li	6Sg	13Cp	5Pi	14Ar
29	18Aq		19Ar	8Ge	12Cn	26Le	28Vi	14Sc	2Cp	10Aq	3Ar	12Ta
31	18Pi		17Ta		6Le		22Li	9Sg		9Pi		9Ge

1980

	Jan	Feb	Mar	Apr	May	Jun	Jul	Aug	Sep	Oct	Nov	Dec
1	23Ge	10Le	1Vi	15Li	18Sc	5Cp	12Aq	5Ar	28Ta	6Cn	23Le	26Vi
3	19Cn	4Vi	24Vi	9Sc	13Sg	2Aq	10Pi	4Ta	26Ge	2Le	17Vi	20Li
5	14Le	28Vi	18Li	3Sg	9Cp	29Aq	9Ar	2Ge	22Cn	26Le	11Li	13Sc
7	8Vi	21Li	12Sc	29Sg	5Aq	27Pi	7Ta	29Ge	17Le	20Vi	5Sc	8Sg
9	1Li	15Sc	6Sg	25Cp	3Pi	26Ar	5Ge	25Cn	11Vi	14Li	29Sc	3Cp
11	25Li	11Sg	2Cp	23Aq	1Ar	25Ta	2Cn	20Le	5Li	8Sc	23Sg	28Cp
13	20Sc	7Cp	0Aq	22Pi	1Ta	23Ge	29Cn	15Vi	29Li	2Sg	18Cp	24Aq
15	16Sg	6Aq	29Aq	22Ar	1Ge	21Cn	24Le	9Li	23Sc	26Sg	14Aq	22Pi
17	14Cp	6Pi	29Pi	22Ta	29Ge	16Le	19Vi	2Sc	17Sg	21Cp	11Pi	20Ar
19	13Aq	6Ar	29Ar	21Ge	26Cn	11Vi	12Li	26Sc	13Cp	18Aq	10Ar	19Ta
21	12Pi	5Ta	28Ta	17Cn	21Le	4Li	6Sc	21Sg	10Aq	17Pi	10Ta	19Ge
23	11Ar	3Ge	26Ge	12Le	15Vi	28Li	1Sg	18Cp	8Pi	17Ar	10Ge	17Cn
25	9Ta	29Ge	21Cn	6Vi	8Li	23Sc	26Sg	16Aq	9Ar	17Ta	9Cn	14Le
27	6Ge	24Cn	16Le	0Li	2Sc	18Sg	23Cp	15Pi	9Ta	17Ge	6Le	10Vi
29	2Cn	19Le	9Vi	24Li	27Sc	15Cp	22Aq	15Ar	8Ge	15Cn	2Vi	4Li
31	27Cn		3Li		22Sg		21Pi	14Ta		11Le		28Li

1981

	Jan	Feb	Mar	Apr	May	Jun	Jul	Aug	Sep	Oct	Nov	Dec
1	10Sc	24Sg	2Cp	19Ag	25Pi	19Ta	28Ge	19Le	6Li	9Sc	23Sg	26Cp
3	4Sg	20Cp	27Cp	17Pi	25Ar	19Ge	27Cn	15Vi	1Sc	3Sg	17Cp	20Aq
5	29Sg	17Aq	25Aq	17Ar	26Ta	19Cn	24Le	11Li	25Sc	27Sg	11Aq	16Pi
7	24Cp	15Pi	23Pi	17Ta	26Ge	16Le	20Vi	5Sc	19Sg	21Cp	7Pi	14Ar
9	21Aq	13Ar	23Ar	17Ge	24Cn	12Vi	15Li	29Sc	13Cp	16Aq	5Ar	13Ta
11	19Pi	12Ta	22Ta	15Cn	21Le	7Li	9Sc	23Sg	8Aq	13Pi	5Ta	13Ge
13	17Ar	10Ge	21Ge	11Le	16Vi	1Sc	3Sg	17Cp	5Pi	12Ar	5Ge	13Cn
15	15Ta	8Cn	18Cn	6Vi	10Li	24Sc	27Sg	13Aq	3Ar	12Ta	5Cn	13Le
17	14Ge	4Le	14Le	1Li	4Sc	18Sg	22Cp	10Pi	2Ta	11Ge	4Le	10Vi
19	12Cn	0Vi	9Vi	25Li	27Sc	13Cp	17Aq	8Ar	1Ge	10Cn	1Vi	5Li
21	9Le	25Vi	4Li	19Sc	21Sg	8Aq	14Pi	6Ta	0Cn	8Le	26Vi	0Sc
23	5Vi	20Li	28Li	12Sg	16Cp	3Pi	11Ar	5Ge	27Cn	4Vi	21Li	24Sc
25	0Li	13Sc	22Sc	6Cp	11Aq	0Ar	9Ta	3Cn	24Le	29Vi	15Sc	17Sg
27	24Li	7Sg	15Sg	1Aq	7Pi	29Ar	8Ge	1Le	20Vi	24Li	8Sg	11Cp
29	17Sc		10Cp	27Aq	4Ar	28Ta	7Cn	28Le	15Li	18Sc	2Cp	5Aq
31	12Sg		5Aq		4Ta		5Le	24Vi		11Sg		0Pi

1982

	Jan	Feb	Mar	Apr	May	Jun	Jul	Aug	Sep	Oct	Nov	Dec
1	13Pi	4Ta	14Ta	8Cn	16Le	6Li	10Sc	25Sg	9Aq	12Pi	1Ta	8Ge
3	9Ar	2Ge	13Ge	5Le	13Vi	1Sc	4Sg	18Cp	4Pi	8Ar	29Ta	8Cn
5	7Ta	1Cn	11Cn	3Vi	9Li	25Sc	28Sg	12Aq	29Pi	6Ta	28Ge	7Le
7	6Ge	0Le	9Le	29Vi	4Sc	19Sg	22Cp	7Pi	26Ar	4Ge	27Cn	6Vi
9	6Cn	28Le	7Vi	25Li	28Sc	13Cp	15Aq	3Ar	23Ta	2Cn	25Le	3Li
11	6Le	26Vi	4Li	20Sc	22Sg	6Aq	10Pi	29Ar	21Ge	0Le	22Vi	29Li
13	4Vi	22Li	29Li	14Sg	16Cp	1Pi	6Ar	26Ta	19Cn	28Le	19Li	24Sc
15	1Li	16Sc	24Sc	8Cp	10Aq	26Pi	2Ta	25Ge	18Le	26Vi	15Sc	18Sg
17	26Li	10Sg	18Sg	1Aq	4Pi	23Ar	1Ge	24Cn	17Vi	23Li	9Sg	12Cp
19	20Sc	4Cp	11Cp	26Aq	1Ar	22Ta	0Cn	24Le	14Li	19Sc	3Cp	5Aq
21	14Sg	28Cp	6Aq	22Pi	29Ar	22Ge	0Le	22Vi	11Sc	13Sg	27Cp	29Aq
23	8Cp	23Aq	1Pi	20Ar	28Ta	22Cn	0Vi	20Li	5Sg	7Cp	21Aq	23Pi
25	2Aq	19Pi	28Pi	20Ta	28Ge	21Le	28Vi	15Sc	29Sg	1Aq	15Pi	19Ar
27	27Aq	16Ar	26Ar	19Ge	28Cn	19Vi	24Li	9Sg	23Cp	25Aq	11Ar	16Ta
29	23Pi		25Ta	18Cn	26Le	15Li	19Sc	3Cp	17Aq	20Pi	9Ta	16Ge
31	20Ar		24Ge		23Vi		13Sg	27Cp		17Ar		16Cn

293

1983

	Jan	Feb	Mar	Apr	May	Jun	Jul	Aug	Sep	Oct	Nov	Dec
1	1Le	24Vi	2Li	21Sc	24Sg	8Aq	10Pi	26Ar	14Ge	22Cn	15Vi	24Li
3	1Vi	21Li	0Sc	16Sg	18Cp	2Pi	4Ar	21Ta	12Cn	21Le	14Li	21Sc
5	29Vi	17Sc	26Sc	10Cp	12Aq	26Pi	29Ar	19Ge	11Le	20Vi	12Sc	18Sg
7	26Li	12Sg	20Sg	4Aq	6Pi	21Ar	26Ta	18Cn	12Vi	20Li	9Sg	13Cp
9	21Sc	6Cp	14Cp	28Aq	0Ar	18Ta	25Ge	18Le	12Li	18Sc	5Cp	7Aq
11	15Sg	29Cp	8Aq	22Pi	26Ar	16Ge	25Cn	19Vi	10Sc	15Sg	29Cp	1Pi
13	9Cp	23Aq	2Pi	18Ar	24Ta	16Cn	25Le	18Li	6Sg	9Cp	23Aq	25Pi
15	2Aq	17Pi	26Pi	15Ta	22Ge	15Le	24Vi	15Sc	1Cp	3Aq	17Pi	19Ar
17	26Aq	12Ar	22Ar	12Ge	21Cn	14Vi	22Li	10Sg	25Cp	27Aq	12Ar	15Ta
19	20Pi	8Ta	18Ta	10Cn	19Le	12Li	18Sc	5Cp	19Aq	21Pi	7Ta	12Ge
21	15Ar	5Ge	15Ge	8Le	17Vi	8Sc	13Sg	28Cp	13Pi	16Ar	4Ge	10Cn
23	11Ta	3Cn	13Cn	6Vi	15Li	4Sg	7Cp	22Aq	7Ar	11Ta	1Cn	9Le
25	9Ge	2Le	12Le	5Li	11Sc	28Sg	1Aq	16Pi	2Ta	8Ge	29Cn	9Vi
27	9Cn	2Vi	11Vi	2Sc	7Sg	23Cp	25Aq	10Ar	28Ta	5Cn	28Le	7Li
29	9Le		10Li	29Sc	2Cp	16Aq	19Pi	5Ta	24Ge	3Le	26Vi	4Sc
31	9Vi		7Sc		26Cp		13Ar	1Ge		1Vi		1Sg

1984

	Jan	Feb	Mar	Apr	May	Jun	Jul	Aug	Sep	Oct	Nov	Dec
1	14Sg	0Aq	21Aq	5Ar	9Ta	26Ge	3Le	27Vi	20Sc	27Sg	13Aq	16Pi
3	9Cp	24Aq	15Pi	0Ta	4Ge	24Cn	2Vi	26Li	17Sg	22Cp	8Pi	10Ar
5	3Aq	18Pi	8Ar	24Ta	0Cn	22Le	1Li	24Sc	13Cp	17Aq	1Ar	3Ta
7	27Aq	11Ar	2Ta	20Ge	27Cn	20Vi	29Li	20Sg	8Aq	11Pi	25Ar	28Ta
9	21Pi	6Ta	27Ta	16Cn	25Le	18Li	27Sc	16Cp	2Pi	5Ar	19Ta	23Ge
11	15Ar	1Ge	23Ge	14Le	24Vi	17Sc	23Sg	11Aq	26Pi	28Ar	14Ge	19Cn
13	10Ta	28Ge	20Cn	14Vi	23Li	14Sg	19Cp	5Pi	19Ar	22Ta	9Cn	16Le
15	6Ge	26Cn	20Le	14Li	21Sc	11Cp	14Aq	29Pi	13Ta	17Ge	6Le	14Vi
17	4Cn	27Le	20Vi	13Sc	19Sg	6Aq	8Pi	22Ar	8Ge	12Cn	4Vi	13Li
19	3Le	27Vi	20Li	11Sg	15Cp	0Pi	2Ar	16Ta	3Cn	9Le	2Li	11Sc
21	4Vi	27Li	19Sc	7Cp	10Aq	24Pi	26Ar	11Ge	0Le	8Vi	2Sc	10Sg
23	3Li	24Sc	16Sg	2Aq	4Pi	18Ar	20Ta	8Cn	29Le	8Li	1Sg	7Cp
25	1Sc	20Sg	12Cp	26Aq	28Pi	13Ta	16Ge	6Le	0Li	8Sc	29Sg	4Aq
27	28Sc	15Cp	6Aq	20Pi	22Ar	8Ge	14Cn	6Vi	0Sc	7Sg	26Cp	29Aq
29	23Sg	9Aq	0Pi	14Ar	17Ta	5Cn	13Le	6Li	29Sc	5Cp	22Aq	24Pi
31	18Cp		23Pi		13Ge		12Vi	6Sc		1Aq		17Ar

1985

	Jan	Feb	Mar	Apr	May	Jun	Jul	Aug	Sep	Oct	Nov	Dec
1	29Ar	13Ge	21Ge	9Le	16Vi	10Sc	19Sg	9Aq	27Pi	29Ar	13Ge	17Cn
3	23Ta	9Cn	17Cn	8Vi	16Li	10Sg	17Cp	6Pi	21Ar	23Ta	7Cn	12Le
5	18Ge	7Le	15Le	8Li	16Sc	9Cp	14Aq	1Ar	15Ta	16Ge	2Le	8Vi
7	15Cn	6Vi	15Vi	8Sc	16Sg	6Aq	10Pi	25Ar	8Ge	11Cn	28Le	5Li
9	13Le	6Li	15Li	8Sg	15Cp	2Pi	5Ar	18Ta	3Cn	6Le	26Vi	4Sc
11	11Vi	4Sc	14Sc	6Cp	11Aq	27Pi	29Ar	12Ge	28Cn	3Vi	25Li	4Sg
13	9Li	2Sg	13Sg	2Aq	6Pi	21Ar	22Ta	7Cn	25Le	2Li	26Sc	4Cp
15	8Sc	29Sg	9Cp	27Aq	0Ar	14Ta	17Ge	3Le	24Vi	3Sc	26Sg	3Aq
17	5Sg	25Cp	5Aq	21Pi	24Ar	8Ge	12Cn	1Vi	24Li	3Sg	25Cp	0Pi
19	3Cp	21Aq	0Pi	15Ar	18Ta	3Cn	8Le	0Li	23Sc	2Cp	22Aq	26Pi
21	29Cp	16Pi	24Pi	9Ta	12Ge	29Cn	6Vi	28Li	22Sg	29Cp	17Pi	20Ar
23	25Aq	10Ar	18Ar	2Ge	6Cn	25Le	4Li	27Sc	19Cp	25Aq	11Ar	13Ta
25	19Pi	3Ta	12Ta	27Ge	2Le	23Vi	2Sc	25Sg	15Aq	20Pi	5Ta	7Ge
27	13Ar	27Ta	5Ge	22Cn	28Le	21Li	0Sg	22Cp	11Pi	14Ar	28Ta	1Cn
29	7Ta		0Cn	18Le	26Vi	20Sc	28Sg	18Aq	5Ar	8Ta	22Ge	26Cn
31	1Ge		26Cn		25Li		26Cp	14Pi		1Ge		22Le

1986

	Jan	Feb	Mar	Apr	May	Jun	Jul	Aug	Sep	Oct	Nov	Dec
1	5Vi	26Li	7Sc	0Cp	8Aq	27Pi	1Ta	15Ge	29Cn	2Vi	21Li	28Sc
3	1Li	24Sc	5Sg	28Cp	5Pi	22Ar	24Ta	8Cn	24Le	29Vi	20Sc	29Sg
5	29Li	22Sg	3Cp	25Aq	0Ar	15Ta	18Ge	3Le	20Vi	27Li	20Sg	29Cp
7	28Sc	21Cp	1Aq	20Pi	24Ar	9Ge	12Cn	28Le	17Li	25Sc	19Cp	27Aq
9	27Sg	19Aq	28Aq	15Ar	18Ta	3Cn	6Le	24Vi	15Sc	24Sg	17Aq	24Pi
11	26Cp	16Pi	24Pi	10Ta	12Ge	27Cn	1Vi	21Li	13Sg	23Cp	14Pi	20Ar
13	25Aq	11Ar	19Ar	4Ge	6Cn	21Le	27Vi	18Sc	12Cp	20Aq	10Ar	14Ta
15	21Pi	6Ta	14Ta	27Ge	0Le	17Vi	24Li	17Sg	10Aq	17Pi	5Ta	8Ge
17	16Ar	29Ta	7Ge	21Cn	25Le	14Li	22Sc	16Cp	8Pi	13Ar	29Ta	2Cn
19	10Ta	23Ge	1Cn	16Le	21Vi	12Sc	21Sg	15Aq	5Ar	9Ta	23Ge	26Cn
21	3Ge	18Cn	25Cn	13Vi	19Li	12Sg	21Cp	13Pi	0Ta	3Ge	17Cn	20Le
23	27Ge	13Le	21Le	11Li	19Sc	13Cp	21Aq	10Ar	25Ta	27Ge	11Le	14Vi
25	22Cn	10Vi	19Vi	11Sc	19Sg	12Aq	18Pi	5Ta	19Ge	20Cn	5Vi	10Li
27	18Le	8Li	17Li	11Sg	19Cp	10Pi	14Ar	29Ta	13Cn	15Le	1Li	7Sc
29	15Vi		17Sc	10Cp	18Aq	6Ar	9Ta	23Ge	7Le	10Vi	29Li	6Sg
31	12Li		16Sg		14Pi		3Ge	17Cn		7Li		7Cp

1987

	Jan	Feb	Mar	Apr	May	Jun	Jul	Aug	Sep	Oct	Nov	Dec
1	22Cp	14Pi	22Pi	10Ta	14Ge	28Cn	0Vi	16Li	6Sg	14Cp	8Pi	16Ar
3	22Aq	12Ar	20Ar	6Ge	8Cn	22Le	24Vi	12Sc	4Cp	13Aq	5Ar	12Ta
5	20Pi	7Ta	15Ta	0Cn	1Le	16Vi	20Li	10Sg	3Aq	12Pi	3Ta	8Ge
7	16Ar	2Ge	10Ge	24Cn	25Le	11Li	16Sc	9Cp	3Pi	10Ar	29Ta	3Cn
9	11Ta	26Ge	4Cn	18Le	20Vi	8Sc	15Sg	9Aq	2Ar	8Ta	25Ge	27Cn
11	5Ge	19Cn	28Cn	12Vi	16Li	7Sg	16Cp	9Pi	0Ta	4Ge	19Cn	21Le
13	29Ge	13Le	22Le	8Li	14Sc	7Cp	16Aq	8Ar	26Ta	29Ge	13Le	15Vi
15	23Cn	8Vi	17Vi	5Sc	13Sg	7Aq	15Pi	5Ta	21Ge	23Cn	7Vi	9Li
17	17Le	3Li	13Li	4Sg	13Cp	6Pi	13Ar	1Ge	15Cn	17Le	1Li	5Sc
19	11Vi	29Li	10Sc	2Cp	12Aq	3Ar	9Ta	25Ge	9Le	11Vi	27Li	2Sg
21	6Li	27Sc	7Sg	1Aq	10Pi	20Ar	4Ge	19Cn	3Vi	6Li	24Sc	1Cp
23	3Sc	25Sg	6Cp	29Aq	6Ar	24Ta	28Ge	12Le	27Vi	2Sc	23Sg	1Aq
25	0Sg	24Cp	4Aq	26Pi	2Ta	19Ge	22Cn	6Vi	23Li	29Sc	22Cp	1Pi
27	0Cp	23Aq	3Pi	23Ar	27Ta	13Cn	15Le	1Li	19Sc	27Sg	20Aq	29Pi
29	0Aq		1Ar	19Ta	22Ge	6Le	9Vi	26Li	16Sg	25Cp	18Pi	26Ar
31	0Pi		27Ar		16Cn		4Li	22Sc		23Aq		22Ta

1988

	Jan	Feb	Mar	Apr	May	Jun	Jul	Aug	Sep	Oct	Nov	Dec
1	5Ge	21Cn	11Le	25Vi	29Li	17Sg	25Cp	19Pi	11Ta	17Ge	4Le	5Vi
3	29Ge	14Le	5Vi	20Li	25Sc	15Cp	24Aq	18Ar	8Ge	13Cn	28Le	29Vi
5	24Cn	8Vi	29Vi	15Sc	22Sg	14Aq	23Pi	15Ta	4Cn	7Le	21Vi	23Li
7	17Le	2Li	23Li	11Sg	19Cp	12Pi	21Ar	12Ge	28Cn	1Vi	15Li	18Sc
9	11Vi	26Li	18Sc	8Cp	17Aq	11Ar	18Ta	7Cn	22Le	25Vi	9Sc	14Sg
11	5Li	21Sc	14Sg	6Aq	16Pi	8Ta	15Ge	1Le	16Vi	18Li	5Sg	11Cp
13	0Sc	19Sg	12Cp	5Pi	14Ar	5Ge	10Cn	25Le	9Li	13Sc	1Cp	9Aq
15	26Sc	17Cp	11Aq	5Ar	12Ta	1Cn	4Le	19Vi	3Sc	8Sg	28Cp	7Pi
17	24Sg	18Aq	11Pi	3Ta	9Ge	26Cn	28Le	12Li	28Sc	4Cp	26Aq	5Ar
19	24Cp	18Pi	11Ar	1Ge	5Cn	20Le	22Vi	7Sc	24Sg	1Aq	24Pi	3Ta
21	25Aq	17Ar	9Ta	27Ge	0Le	14Vi	16Li	2Sg	21Cp	0Pi	23Ar	1Ge
23	24Pi	15Ta	6Ge	22Cn	24Le	8Li	10Sc	28Sg	20Aq	29Pi	22Ta	28Ge
25	22Ar	11Ge	2Cn	16Le	18Vi	2Sc	6Sg	27Cp	20Pi	29Ar	20Ge	24Cn
27	19Ta	5Cn	26Cn	10Vi	12Li	28Sc	4Cp	27Aq	21Ar	28Ta	16Cn	19Le
29	14Ge	29Cn	20Le	4Li	7Sc	26Sg	4Aq	27Pi	20Ta	25Ge	11Le	13Vi
31	8Cn		13Vi		3Sg		4Pi	27Ar		21Cn		7Li

1989

	Jan	Feb	Mar	Apr	May	Jun	Jul	Aug	Sep	Oct	Nov	Dec
1	19Li	3Sg	12Sg	0Aq	8Pi	1Ta	10Ge	0Le	17Vi	19Li	4Sg	8Cp
3	13Sc	0Cp	8Cp	29Aq	7Ar	1Ge	8Cn	26Le	11Li	13Sc	28Sg	3Aq
5	9Sg	28Cp	6Aq	28Pi	7Ta	29Ge	5Le	20Vi	4Sc	7Sg	23Cp	29Aq
7	6Cp	27Aq	5Pi	29Ar	7Ge	27Cn	0Vi	14Li	28Sc	1Cp	19Aq	26Pi
9	4Aq	27Pi	5Ar	29Ta	5Cn	22Le	24Vi	8Sc	23Sg	27Cp	17Pi	25Ar
11	3Pi	26Ar	5Ta	27Ge	1Le	16Vi	18Li	2Sg	18Cp	24Aq	16Ar	25Ta
13	2Ar	24Ta	4Ge	23Cn	26Le	10Li	12Sc	27Sg	16Aq	23Pi	17Ta	25Ge
15	0Ta	21Ge	1Cn	18Le	20Vi	4Sc	7Sg	24Cp	15Pi	23Ar	17Ge	23Cn
17	27Ta	17Cn	26Cn	12Vi	14Li	28Sc	2Cp	22Aq	15Ar	24Ta	15Cn	20Le
19	24Ge	12Le	21Le	5Li	8Sc	24Sg	29Cp	21Pi	15Ta	23Ge	12Le	15Vi
21	20Cn	6Vi	15Vi	29Li	2Sg	20Cp	27Aq	20Ar	14Ge	20Cn	7Vi	10Li
23	15Le	29Vi	8Li	23Sc	27Sg	17Aq	26Pi	19Ta	11Cn	16Le	1Li	3Sc
25	9Vi	23Li	2Sc	18Sg	23Cp	15Pi	24Ar	17Ge	7Le	10Vi	25Li	27Sc
27	3Li	17Sc	26Sc	13Cp	20Aq	13Ar	22Ta	14Cn	1Vi	4Li	19Sc	22Sg
29	27Li		21Sg	10Aq	18Pi	12Ta	20Ge	9Le	25Vi	28Li	13Sg	17Cp
31	21Sc		17Cp		17Ar		17Cn	4Vi		22Sc		13Aq

1990

	Jan	Feb	Mar	Apr	May	Jun	Jul	Aug	Sep	Oct	Nov	Dec
1	26Aq	18Ar	28Ar	22Ge	29Cn	17Vi	21Li	4Sg	19Cp	22Aq	11Ar	19Ta
3	23Pi	16Ta	27Ta	20Cn	26Le	12Li	14Sc	28Sg	14Aq	19Pi	11Ta	20Ge
5	21Ar	15Ge	25Ge	16Le	21Vi	6Sc	8Sg	23Cp	11Pi	18Ar	11Ge	20Cn
7	20Ta	13Cn	23Cn	11Vi	15Li	0Sg	2Cp	19Aq	9Ar	17Ta	11Cn	18Le
9	19Ge	10Le	19Le	6Li	9Sc	23Sg	27Cp	15Pi	7Ta	17Ge	9Le	15Vi
11	17Cn	6Vi	14Vi	0Sc	3Sg	18Cp	22Aq	13Ar	6Ge	15Cn	6Vi	10Li
13	15Le	1Li	9Li	24Sc	26Sg	12Aq	18Pi	11Ta	4Cn	12Le	1Li	5Sc
15	11Vi	25Li	3Sc	17Sg	21Cp	8Pi	16Ar	9Ge	2Le	9Vi	26Li	29Sc
17	5Li	19Sc	27Sc	11Cp	15Aq	5Ar	14Ta	8Cn	29Le	4Li	20Sc	22Sg
19	29Li	13Sg	21Sg	6Aq	12Pi	4Ta	13Ge	6Le	25Vi	29Li	14Sg	16Cp
21	23Sc	8Cp	15Cp	3Pi	10Ar	4Ge	12Cn	3Vi	20Li	23Sc	7Cp	10Aq
23	17Sg	3Aq	11Aq	1Ar	10Ta	4Cn	11Le	29Vi	15Sc	17Sg	1Aq	5Pi
25	12Cp	1Pi	9Pi	1Ta	10Ge	3Le	8Vi	24Li	8Sg	10Cp	26Aq	1Ar
27	9Aq	29Pi	8Ar	2Ge	10Cn	0Vi	4Li	19Sc	2Cp	4Aq	22Pi	28Ar
29	6Pi		8Ta	2Cn	8Le	26Vi	29Li	12Sg	26Cp	0Pi	19Ar	27Ta
31	4Ar		8Ge		5Vi		23Sc	6Cp		27Pi		28Ge

1991

	Jan	Feb	Mar	Apr	May	Jun	Jul	Aug	Sep	Oct	Nov	Dec
1	13Cn	4Vi	12Vi	1Sc	4Sg	18Cp	20Aq	7Ar	28Ta	7Cn	0Vi	7Li
3	12Le	2Li	9Li	25Sc	28Sg	12Aq	15Pi	4Ta	26Ge	5Le	27Vi	3Sc
5	10Vi	27Li	5Sc	19Sg	21Cp	6Pi	11Ar	1Ge	25Cn	3Vi	24Li	29Sc
7	7Li	22Sc	0Sg	13Cp	15Aq	1Ar	8Ta	0Cn	24Le	1Li	20Sc	23Sg
9	2Sc	16Sg	23Sg	7Aq	10Pi	29Ar	6Ge	0Le	23Vi	28Li	15Sg	17Cp
11	26Sc	9Cp	17Cp	2Pi	7Ar	28Ta	6Cn	0Vi	20Li	24Sc	9Cp	11Aq
13	19Sg	3Aq	12Aq	28Pi	5Ta	28Ge	7Le	28Vi	16Sc	19Sg	2Aq	4Pi
15	13Cp	28Aq	7Pi	26Ar	4Ge	28Cn	6Vi	25Li	11Sg	13Cp	26Aq	29Pi
17	7Aq	24Pi	4Ar	25Ta	4Cn	27Le	4Li	21Sc	5Cp	6Aq	21Pi	25Ar
19	2Pi	21Ar	1Ta	25Ge	3Le	25Vi	0Sc	15Sg	29Cp	1Pi	17Ar	23Ta
21	28Pi	19Ta	0Ge	23Cn	1Vi	20Li	24Sc	9Cp	23Aq	26Pi	15Ta	22Ge
23	24Ar	17Ge	28Ge	21Le	28Vi	15Sc	18Sg	2Aq	18Pi	23Ar	14Ge	22Cn
25	22Ta	16Cn	26Cn	18Vi	23Li	9Sg	12Cp	26Aq	14Ar	21Ta	13Cn	22Le
27	21Ge	14Le	24Le	14Li	18Sc	3Cp	6Aq	22Pi	11Ta	19Ge	12Le	21Vi
29	21Cn		21Vi	9Sc	12Sg	27Cp	0Pi	17Ar	9Ge	18Cn	10Vi	18Li
31	20Le		18Li		6Cp		25Pi	14Ta		16Le		13Sc

1992

	Jan	Feb	Mar	Apr	May	Jun	Jul	Aug	Sep	Oct	Nov	Dec
1	26Sc	11Cp	1Aq	16Pi	19Ar	8Ge	16Cn	10Vi	2Sc	7Sg	23Cp	25Aq
3	20Sg	4Aq	25Aq	11Ar	16Ta	7Cn	16Le	9Li	29Sc	3Cp	17Aq	19Pi
5	14Cp	28Aq	19Pi	6Ta	13Ge	6Le	15Vi	7Sc	24Sg	27Cp	11Pi	13Ar
7	7Aq	22Pi	14Ar	3Ge	11Cn	5Vi	13Li	3Sg	19Cp	21Aq	5Ar	8Ta
9	1Pi	17Ar	10Ta	0Cn	9Le	3Li	10Sc	27Sg	12Aq	15Pi	0Ta	4Ge
11	25Pi	13Ta	6Ge	28Cn	8Vi	0Sc	6Sg	22Cp	6Pi	9Ar	26Ta	2Cn
13	20Ar	10Ge	4Cn	27Le	6Li	26Sc	0Cp	15Aq	0Ar	4Ta	23Ge	0Le
15	17Ta	8Cn	2Le	26Vi	3Sc	21Sg	25Cp	9Pi	24Ar	29Ta	20Cn	29Le
17	15Ge	8Le	2Vi	24Li	0Sg	16Cp	18Aq	3Ar	20Ta	26Ge	18Le	27Vi
19	15Cn	8Vi	1Li	21Sc	25Sg	10Aq	12Pi	27Ar	16Ge	23Cn	16Vi	25Li
21	15Le	8Li	0Sc	17Sg	20Cp	3Pi	6Ar	23Ta	13Cn	21Le	15Li	22Sc
23	15Vi	6Sc	27Sc	12Cp	13Aq	27Pi	1Ta	19Ge	11Le	21Vi	13Sc	19Sg
25	14Li	1Sg	22Sg	6Aq	7Pi	22Ar	27Ta	18Cn	11Vi	20Li	10Sg	14Cp
27	10Sc	26Sg	16Cp	29Aq	2Ar	19Ta	25Ge	18Le	11Li	18Sc	6Cp	9Aq
29	5Sg	19Cp	9Aq	24Pi	27Ar	16Ge	24Cn	18Vi	10Sc	15Sg	1Aq	3Pi
31	29Sg		3Pi		24Ta		24Le	18Li		11Cp		26Pi

1993

	Jan	Feb	Mar	Apr	May	Jun	Jul	Aug	Sep	Oct	Nov	Dec
1	8Ar	23Ta	2Ge	21Cn	29Le	23Li	2Sg	21Cp	7Pi	10Ar	24Ta	28Ge
3	3Ta	20Ge	28Ge	20Le	29Vi	22Sc	29Sg	16Aq	1Ar	3Ta	19Ge	24Cn
5	29Ta	18Cn	26Cn	19Vi	28Li	20Sg	25Cp	10Pi	24Ar	27Ta	14Cn	21Le
7	26Ge	18Le	26Le	20Li	27Sc	16Cp	20Aq	4Ar	18Ta	22Ge	11Le	19Vi
9	25Cn	18Vi	26Vi	19Sc	25Sg	12Aq	14Pi	28Ar	13Ge	17Cn	8Vi	17Li
11	24Le	18Li	27Li	17Sg	21Cp	6Pi	8Ar	22Ta	8Cn	15Le	8Li	16Sc
13	24Vi	16Sc	25Sc	13Cp	16Aq	0Ar	2Ta	17Ge	6Le	14Vi	8Sc	15Sg
15	22Li	12Sg	22Sg	8Aq	10Pi	24Ar	26Ta	14Cn	6Vi	14Li	7Sg	13Cp
17	19Sc	8Cp	17Cp	2Pi	4Ar	18Ta	22Ge	12Le	6Li	15Sc	6Cp	10Aq
19	15Sg	2Aq	11Aq	25Pi	28Ar	14Ge	20Cn	12Vi	6Sc	14Sg	2Aq	5Pi
21	11Cp	26Aq	5Pi	19Ar	23Ta	11Cn	18Le	12Li	5Sg	11Cp	27Aq	29Pi
23	5Aq	20Pi	29Pi	14Ta	18Ge	9Le	18Vi	11Sc	2Cp	6Aq	21Pi	23Ar
25	29Aq	13Ar	22Ar	9Ge	15Cn	7Vi	17Li	9Sg	27Cp	1Pi	15Ar	17Ta
27	23Pi	7Ta	17Ta	5Cn	12Le	6Li	15Sc	5Cp	22Aq	25Pi	9Ta	12Ge
29	17Ar		12Ge	1Le	10Vi	4Sc	12Sg	0Aq	16Pi	18Ar	3Ge	7Cn
31	11Ta		8Cn		9Li		8Cp	25Aq		12Ta		4Le

1994

	Jan	Feb	Mar	Apr	May	Jun	Jul	Aug	Sep	Oct	Nov	Dec
1	18Le	11Li	20Li	13Sg	20Cp	8Pi	11Ar	24Ta	8Cn	12Le	2Li	10Sc
3	16Vi	9Sc	20Sc	11Cp	17Aq	2Ar	4Ta	18Ge	4Le	10Vi	2Sc	10Sg
5	14Li	7Sg	17Sg	7Aq	11Pi	26Ar	28Ta	13Cn	2Vi	9Li	2Sg	10Cp
7	12Sc	4Cp	14Cp	2Pi	5Ar	20Ta	22Ge	9Le	0Li	9Sc	2Cp	9Aq
9	10Sg	0Aq	10Aq	26Pi	29Ar	14Ge	17Cn	7Vi	29Li	8Sg	0Aq	6Pi
11	8Cp	26Aq	5Pi	20Ar	23Ta	8Cn	13Le	5Li	28Sc	7Cp	27Aq	1Ar
13	5Aq	21Pi	0Ar	14Ta	17Ge	4Le	10Vi	3Sc	26Sg	4Aq	22Pi	25Ar
15	1Pi	15Ar	23Ar	8Ge	11Cn	0Vi	8Li	1Sg	24Cp	0Pi	16Ar	19Ta
17	25Pi	9Ta	17Ta	2Cn	7Le	27Vi	6Sc	29Sg	20Aq	25Pi	10Ta	12Ge
19	19Ar	2Ge	11Ge	27Cn	3Vi	26Li	5Sg	27Cp	16Pi	19Ar	4Ge	6Cn
21	13Ta	27Ge	5Cn	24Le	1Li	25Sc	3Cp	24Aq	11Ar	13Ta	27Ge	1Le
23	7Ge	23Cn	1Le	22Vi	1Sc	24Sg	1Aq	20Pi	5Ta	7Ge	22Cn	26Le
25	2Cn	21Le	29Le	22Li	1Sg	23Cp	28Aq	14Ar	28Ta	0Cn	16Le	23Vi
27	29Cn	21Vi	29Vi	23Sc	1Cp	20Aq	24Pi	8Ta	22Ge	25Cn	13Vi	20Li
29	27Le		29Li	22Sg	29Cp	16Pi	18Ar	2Ge	16Cn	20Le	10Li	19Sc
31	26Vi		29Sc		25Aq		12Ta	26Ge		18Vi		18Sg

305

1995

	Jan	Feb	Mar	Apr	May	Jun	Jul	Aug	Sep	Oct	Nov	Dec
1	3Cp	25Aq	3Pi	21Ar	24Ta	8Cn	11Le	29Vi	20Sc	29Sg	22Aq	29Pi
3	3Aq	22Pi	0Ar	15Ta	17Ge	2Le	6Vi	25Li	18Sg	27Cp	19Pi	24Ar
5	1Pi	17Ar	25Ar	9Ge	11Cn	26Le	2Li	23Sc	16Cp	25Aq	15Ar	19Ta
7	27Pi	11Ta	19Ta	3Cn	5Le	22Vi	29Li	22Sg	15Aq	22Pi	10Ta	13Ge
9	22Ar	5Ge	13Ge	27Cn	0Vi	19Li	27Sc	21Cp	13Pi	19Ar	5Ge	7Cn
11	15Ta	29Ge	7Cn	22Le	27Vi	18Sc	27Sg	21Aq	10Ar	14Ta	29Ge	1Le
13	9Ge	23Cn	1Le	19Vi	25Li	19Sg	27Cp	19Pi	6Ta	8Ge	22Cn	25Le
15	3Cn	19Le	27Le	17Li	25Sc	19Cp	27Aq	16Ar	1Ge	2Cn	16Le	19Vi
17	28Cn	16Vi	25Vi	17Sc	25Sg	18Aq	24Pi	11Ta	24Ge	26Cn	11Vi	15Li
19	23Le	13Li	23Li	16Sg	25Cp	16Pi	20Ar	5Ge	18Cn	21Le	7Li	13Sc
21	20Vi	11Sc	22Sc	15Cp	23Aq	11Ar	14Ta	28Ge	13Le	16Vi	5Sc	12Sg
23	17Li	9Sg	20Sg	13Aq	19Pi	6Ta	8Ge	22Cn	8Vi	13Li	5Sg	13Cp
25	14Sc	8Cp	18Cp	9Pi	14Ar	29Ta	2Cn	17Le	5Li	11Sc	5Cp	13Aq
27	13Sg	6Aq	16Aq	5Ar	9Ta	23Ge	26Cn	12Vi	2Sc	11Sg	4Aq	12Pi
29	12Cp		13Pi	0Ta	2Ge	17Cn	21Le	9Li	0Sg	10Cp	2Pi	9Ar
31	11Aq		8Ar		26Ge		16Vi	6Sc		8Aq		4Ta

1996

	Jan	Feb	Mar	Apr	May	Jun	Jul	Aug	Sep	Oct	Nov	Dec
1	16Ta	1Cn	21Cn	6Vi	9Li	28Sc	7Cp	1Pi	22Ar	27Ta	13Cn	15Le
3	10Ge	25Cn	15Le	1Li	6Sc	28Sg	7Aq	0Ar	19Ta	23Ge	7Le	8Vi
5	4Cn	19Le	10Vi	27Li	4Sg	28Cp	7Pi	28Ar	15Ge	17Cn	1Vi	2Li
7	28Cn	13Vi	5Li	25Sc	3Cp	27Aq	5Ar	23Ta	9Cn	11Le	25Vi	28Li
9	22Le	8Li	1Sc	23Sg	2Aq	25Pi	1Ta	18Ge	3Le	5Vi	20Li	24Sc
11	16Vi	4Sc	28Sc	21Cp	0Pi	21Ar	26Ta	12Cn	26Le	29Vi	16Sc	23Sg
13	11Li	1Sg	26Sg	20Aq	28Pi	17Ta	21Ge	6Le	20Vi	24Li	14Sg	22Cp
15	8Sc	0Cp	25Cp	18Pi	24Ar	12Ge	15Cn	29Le	15Li	20Sc	12Cp	21Aq
17	6Sg	0Aq	24Aq	15Ar	20Ta	6Cn	9Le	23Vi	11Sc	18Sg	11Aq	20Pi
19	6Cp	29Aq	22Pi	11Ta	15Ge	0Le	2Vi	18Li	7Sg	15Cp	9Pi	17Ar
21	6Aq	28Pi	20Ar	7Ge	9Cn	24Le	26Vi	14Sc	5Cp	14Aq	7Ar	14Ta
23	6Pi	26Ar	16Ta	1Cn	3Le	17Vi	21Li	10Sg	3Aq	12Pi	4Ta	9Ge
25	4Ar	21Ta	11Ge	25Cn	27Le	12Li	17Sc	9Cp	3Pi	11Ar	0Ge	5Cn
27	0Ta	16Ge	5Cn	19Le	21Vi	9Sc	15Sg	9Aq	2Ar	9Ta	26Ge	29Cn
29	25Ta	9Cn	29Cn	13Vi	17Li	7Sg	15Cp	9Pi	0Ta	5Ge	21Cn	23Le
31	19Ge		23Le		14Sc		16Aq	8Ar		1Cn		16Vi

307

1997

	Jan	Feb	Mar	Apr	May	Jun	Jul	Aug	Sep	Oct	Nov	Dec
1	28Vi	14Sc	23Sc	13Cp	22Aq	15Ar	23Ta	12Cn	27Le	0Li	15Sc	19Sg
3	23Li	10Sg	19Sg	11Aq	21Pi	13Ta	20Ge	6Le	21Vi	24Li	10Sg	16Cp
5	18Sc	9Cp	17Cp	11Pi	19Ar	10Ge	15Cn	0Vi	15Li	18Sc	6Cp	13Aq
7	16Sg	9Aq	17Aq	10Ar	18Ta	6Cn	10Le	24Vi	8Sc	13Sg	3Aq	11Pi
9	16Cp	9Pi	17Pi	9Ta	15Ge	2Le	4Vi	18Li	3Sg	9Cp	0Pi	9Ar
11	16Aq	9Ar	17Ar	7Ge	11Cn	26Le	27Vi	12Sc	29Sg	6Aq	29Pi	8Ta
13	16Pi	7Ta	16Ta	3Cn	6Le	19Vi	21Li	7Sg	27Cp	5Pi	28Ar	6Ge
15	14Ar	3Ge	12Ge	28Cn	0Vi	13Li	16Sc	4Cp	26Aq	5Ar	28Ta	4Cn
17	11Ta	28Ge	7Cn	22Le	23Vi	8Sc	12Sg	3Aq	27Pi	5Ta	26Ge	0Le
19	6Ge	23Cn	1Le	15Vi	17Li	4Sg	10Cp	3Pi	27Ar	4Ge	22Cn	25Le
21	1Cn	16Le	25Le	9Li	13Sc	2Cp	10Aq	3Ar	26Ta	1Cn	17Le	19Vi
23	26Cn	10Vi	19Vi	4Sc	9Sg	1Aq	9Pi	2Ta	23Ge	27Cn	11Vi	13Li
25	19Le	4Li	13Li	0Sg	7Cp	29Aq	8Ar	0Ge	18Cn	21Le	5Li	7Sc
27	13Vi	28Li	7Sc	26Sg	5Aq	28Pi	6Ta	26Ge	12Le	15Vi	29Li	2Sg
29	7Li		3Sg	24Cp	3Pi	26Ar	3Ge	21Cn	6Vi	8Li	23Sc	28Sg
31	1Sc		29Sg		1Ar		29Ge	15Le		2Sc		25Cp

1998

	Jan	Feb	Mar	Apr	May	Jun	Jul	Aug	Sep	Oct	Nov	Dec
1	9Aq	2Ar	12Ar	5Ge	11Cn	28Le	0Li	14Sc	28Sg	2Aq	23Pi	1Ta
3	8Pi	1Ta	11Ta	2Cn	7Le	22Vi	24Li	8Sg	24Cp	0Pi	22Ar	1Ge
5	6Ar	29Ta	9Ge	28Cn	2Vi	16Li	18Sc	3Cp	22Aq	29Pi	23Ta	1Cn
7	4Ta	26Ge	6Cn	23Le	25Vi	9Sc	12Sg	0Aq	21Pi	0Ta	23Ge	0Le
9	2Ge	22Cn	1Le	17Vi	19Li	4Sg	8Cp	28Aq	21Ar	0Ge	21Cn	26Le
11	29Ge	17Le	26Le	10Li	13Sc	29Sg	5Aq	26Pi	20Ta	28Ge	18Le	21Vi
13	25Cn	11Vi	20Vi	4Sc	7Sg	25Cp	2Pi	25Ar	18Ge	25Cn	12Vi	15Li
15	21Le	5Li	13Li	28Sc	2Cp	22Aq	0Ar	24Ta	15Cn	21Le	6Li	9Sc
17	15Vi	28Li	7Sc	23Sg	28Cp	19Pi	29Ar	22Ge	11Le	15Vi	0Sc	3Sg
19	8Li	22Sc	1Sg	18Cp	25Aq	18Ar	27Ta	19Cn	6Vi	9Li	24Sc	27Sg
21	2Sc	17Sg	26Sg	15Aq	23Pi	17Ta	25Ge	15Le	1Li	3Sc	18Sg	22Cp
23	27Sc	14Cp	22Cp	13Pi	22Ar	15Ge	22Cn	10Vi	24Li	27Sc	12Cp	18Aq
25	22Sg	12Aq	20Aq	13Ar	22Ta	14Cn	19Le	4Li	18Sc	21Sg	8Aq	14Pi
27	20Cp	12Pi	20Pi	13Ta	21Ge	10Le	14Vi	28Li	12Sg	15Cp	4Pi	12Ar
29	18Aq		20Ar	13Ge	19Cn	6Vi	8Li	22Sc	7Cp	11Aq	2Ar	10Ta
31	18Pi		20Ta		15Le		2Sc	16Sg		8Pi		10Ge

1999

	Jan	Feb	Mar	Apr	May	Jun	Jul	Aug	Sep	Oct	Nov	Dec
1	24Ge	15Le	24Le	11Li	14Sc	28Sg	2Aq	20Pi	12Ta	21Ge	14Le	20Vi
3	23Cn	12Vi	20Vi	5Sc	8Sg	23Cp	27Aq	17Ar	11Ge	20Cn	10Vi	15Li
5	21Le	7Li	15Li	29Sc	1Cp	17Aq	23Pi	15Ta	9Cn	17Le	6Li	10Sc
7	17Vi	1Sc	9Sc	23Sg	26Cp	13Pi	20Ar	14Ge	7Le	13Vi	1Sc	4Sg
9	11Li	25Sc	3Sg	17Cp	21Aq	10Ar	19Ta	13Cn	4Vi	9Li	25Sc	27Sg
11	5Sc	19Sg	27Sg	12Aq	17Pi	10Ta	19Ge	11Le	0Li	4Sc	19Sg	21Cp
13	29Sc	13Cp	21Cp	9Pi	16Ar	10Ge	18Cn	9Vi	26Li	28Sc	12Cp	15Aq
15	23Sg	9Aq	17Aq	8Ar	16Ta	10Cn	17Le	5Li	20Sc	22Sg	6Aq	10Pi
17	18Cp	7Pi	15Pi	8Ta	17Ge	9Le	14Vi	0Sc	14Sg	16Cp	1Pi	6Ar
19	14Aq	5Ar	14Ar	8Ge	16Cn	6Vi	10Li	24Sc	8Cp	10Aq	27Pi	4Ta
21	11Pi	3Ta	14Ta	7Cn	14Le	1Li	4Sc	18Sg	2Aq	6Pi	26Ar	4Ge
23	9Ar	2Ge	13Ge	4Le	10Vi	26Li	28Sc	12Cp	28Aq	3Ar	26Ta	4Cn
25	7Ta	0Cn	11Cn	1Vi	5Li	20Sc	22Sg	7Aq	25Pi	2Ta	26Ge	4Le
27	5Ge	27Cn	8Le	26Vi	29Li	13Sg	16Cp	3Pi	24Ar	2Ge	26Cn	3Vi
29	4Cn		3Vi	20Li	23Sc	7Cp	11Aq	0Ar	23Ta	2Cn	24Le	29Vi
31	2Le		29Vi		17Sg		7Pi	28Ar		0Le		25Li

2000

	Jan	Feb	Mar	Apr	May	Jun	Jul	Aug	Sep	Oct	Nov	Dec
1	7Sc	21Sg	11Cp	25Aq	29Pi	19Ta	28Ge	21Le	13Li	17Sc	2Cp	4Aq
3	1Sg	15Cp	5Aq	21Pi	27Ar	19Ge	28Cn	20Vi	9Sc	13Sg	26Cp	28Aq
5	24Sg	9Aq	0Pi	18Ar	26Ta	19Cn	28Le	18Li	5Sg	7Cp	20Aq	22Pi
7	18Cp	4Pi	26Pi	16Ta	25Ge	18Le	26Vi	14Sc	29Sg	0Aq	14Pi	18Ar
9	12Aq	29Pi	23Ar	15Ge	24Cn	16Vi	22Li	8Sg	22Cp	24Aq	10Ar	15Ta
11	7Pi	26Ar	20Ta	14Cn	22Le	13Li	17Sc	2Cp	16Aq	19Pi	7Ta	14Ge
13	2Ar	23Ta	18Ge	12Le	19Vi	8Sc	11Sg	26Cp	11Pi	15Ar	5Ge	13Cn
15	29Ar	22Ge	17Cn	9Vi	16Li	2Sg	5Cp	20Aq	6Ar	12Ta	4Cn	13Le
17	27Ta	21Cn	15Le	6Li	11Sc	26Sg	29Cp	14Pi	2Ta	10Ge	3Le	12Vi
19	27Ge	20Le	13Vi	2Sc	6Sg	20Cp	23Aq	9Ar	29Ta	8Cn	1Vi	9Li
21	27Cn	18Vi	10Li	27Sc	29Sg	14Aq	17Pi	5Ta	27Ge	6Le	29Vi	5Sc
23	26Le	15Li	6Sc	21Sg	23Cp	8Pi	12Ar	2Ge	25Cn	4Vi	25Li	1Sg
25	24Vi	11Sc	1Sg	15Cp	17Aq	3Ar	9Ta	1Cn	24Le	2Li	21Sc	25Sg
27	21Li	5Sg	25Sg	9Aq	11Pi	29Ar	7Ge	0Le	23Vi	29Li	16Sg	19Cp
29	15Sc	29Sg	19Cp	3Pi	7Ar	28Ta	6Cn	0Vi	21Li	25Sc	11Cp	13Aq
31	9Sg		13Aq		5Ta		6Le	29Vi		20Sg		6Pi

APPENDIX 2

The Questionnaire

The ideas which I have put into this book are taken directly from my observations of real people and the unfolding of their lives rather than a scholarly re-hash of old astrological ideas. In order to help myself and to add freshness and immediacy to the book, I compiled a questionnaire made up of distinctly *lunar* questions which I then foisted on to as many victims as I could find. I gave copies wholesale to friends who in turn, passed them on to *their* friends. I did not ask for names and addresses, I only requested the gender and marital status of each subject, along with the usual astrological data of date, time and place of birth.

The information gleaned as a result of this exercise was totally fascinating; for instance, all five Moon in Taurus subjects made a point of saying that they couldn't stand the sight of blood, especially their own! It proved to be almost impossible to collect information from lunar Sagittarius, Virgo or Capricorn subjects. The Sagittarians were always too busy and the Capricorns and Virgos would have preferred it to be gone over first by their solicitors! One person who stared and stared at the form and couldn't bring herself to fill it in was *me*!! Moon in the tenth in Pisces — obviously can't face reality, even to myself!

Astrological Survey

Here is the questionnaire which I handed out. I have reproduced it here as a matter of interest and a possible means of research for future astrologers.

In order to give you some idea of the kind of information which

I am researching, here is a list of things with which the Moon is associated.

1. Being born or giving birth.
2. Attitude of your parents to you, your attitude to your own children.
3. Parent figures (especially mother figures).
4. Emotional response and reactive behaviour.
5. Inner needs, inner fears.
6. Attitude to and experience of domestic life.
7. Personal habits.
8. Gut reaction.
9. Ancestors.
10. Memories.
11. Health matters and attitude to health.
12. Digestive system, stomach, breasts, fluids, nerves.

——————The Questionnaire——————

If you have knowledge of astrology and you know where your Sun, Moon and Ascendant are, could you please enter it here.....
....

If not could you please put the following:
Date of birth: ....
Place of birth: ....
Time of birth (if known):...

Male/female: ....
Marital status: ....

Did your mother have an easy or a hard time giving birth to you?
....

Do you enjoy being a parent (if you are one)? Any comments about how you see your role as a parent would be useful. Were your children born easily or was there difficulty?..........................
....

Any comments about your domestic life would be helpful. For

instance practical comments such as 'I hate housework/love being at home' or, emotional comments such as, 'I see my home as a haven from the world/a place to dump my things and get out of as soon as possible' ....
....
....

Your feelings about and attitude to your parents when you were younger.
....
....
....

Your feelings and attitudes about them now.
....
....
....

Is family background and family history important to you?
....
....
....

Are your real needs expressed outwardly, i.e. are you secretly ambitious? Are you really seeking an easy life? Any comment which shows the real inner wants and needs (please be very honest) will help me immensely. A remark such as, 'I never really wanted children' or 'I really want to be an opera singer', could be very useful as long as it is totally honest and true.
....
....
....
....

If you could have your childhood over again, would you?
....
....

Were you expected to succeed at school or in hobbies, was parental pressure put on you?
....
....

....

Are you aware of being very different on the inside to what you show on the outside? If so, how?

....

....

....

....

If someone were to push in front of you in a queue, how would you react? Would you always react in the same manner?

....

....

....

....

If someone new joins your group do you feel that you want to welcome them or are you suspicious of them until you have sussed them out?

....

....

....

....

If someone is in dire trouble, do you have a strong desire to help? Do you feel embarrassed by their problems? Do you want to put distance between you and them?

....

....

....

....

Have you a strong sense of smell, taste, touch etc. Do you like to see, feel, smell, hear lovely things and which sense would be the most important? Which sense is the easily upset, i.e. are you funny about the taste of food, the sight of blood, harsh or discordant noises? Any information here would be useful.

....

....

....

....

Do you seek to fit into any situation you find yourself in. Or do you tend to be yourself whatever the situation? Do you try to manipulate situations to suit yourself?

....

....

....

Do you mainly use others or are you mainly used by others or a bit of both?

....

....

....

Recall one event which made you really angry.

....

....

....

....

Recall one event which made you really happy.

....

....

....

....

Any other emotional reactions, peculiarities you have could be helpful here. How do you honestly feel about the following (i.e. either need, love, hate, couldn't care less about):

1. Your home. ....
2. The sea. ....
3. Money...
4. Having a partner in your life. ....
5. Sex. ....
6. Your parents. ....
7. Your children...
8. The countryside, ecology..
9. Personal advancement, ambitions etc. ....
10. Being seen as a success by others. ....
11. Other, more successful people..
12. What is your favourite season of the year? ....

In a close relationship, do you play the part of parent or child?

....

....

....

Any comments about love relationships could be useful, if there is anything special which makes you react in a loving way, an angry way.

....

....

....

....

This book is not going to contain too much about sex but anything you can tell me would help me to understand each Moon sign that much more. For instance, if there is a particular type of person you are attracted to. How important is sex in your life generally; in any relationships specifically i.e. 'I would still think my partner is smashing even without the sex (or otherwise)' etc.

....

....

....

....

Health section:

Are you basically fit? ....
If you have any particular illness, some kind of permanent condition such as diabetes, rheumatism, please state.

....

....

....

Any operations?

....

....

....

RISING SIGNS

Discover the truth
about your personality

The sign of the zodiac rising on the eastern horizon when you are born — your Rising sign — reveals details about your outer personality and how it masks what is underneath: your looks, actions and outward behaviour may all be determined by your Rising sign. And, being based on the actual *time* of birth, it is a far more personal indicator of character than the more general Sun sign.

Here Sasha Fenton shows how to find your Rising sign and explains how it applies to you. In addition, she examines decanates, the modifying 'thirds' of the zodiac signs, and their subsidiary effects on the horoscope.

SUN SIGNS	1 85538 021 8	£4.99 ☐
RISING SIGNS	0 85030 751 1	£4.99 ☐
UNDERSTANDING ASTROLOGY	1 85538 065 X	£4.99 ☐
THE COMPLETE SUN SIGN GUIDE	0 85030 777 5	£6.99 ☐
POWER ASTROLOGY	1 85538 160 5	£4.99 ☐
SUN SIGN SECRETS	1 85538 076 5	£3.99 ☐
THE CHINESE ASTROLOGY WORKBOOK	0 85030 641 8	£7.99 ☐

All these books are available from your local bookseller or can be ordered direct from the publishers.

To order direct just tick the titles you want and fill in the form below:

Name: _____

Address: _____

_____

_____Postcode:_____

Send to Thorsons Mail Order, Dept 31B, HarperCollins*Publishers*, Westerhill Road, Bishopbriggs, Glasgow G64 2QT.
Please enclose a cheque or postal order or your authority to debit your Visa/Access account —

Credit card no: _____

Expiry date: _____

Signature: _____

— to the value of the cover price plus:
UK & BFPO: Add £1.00 for the first book and 25p for each additional book ordered.
Overseas orders including Eire: Please add £2.95 service charge. Books will be sent by surface mail but quotes for airmail despatches will be given on request.

24 HOUR TELEPHONE ORDERING SERVICE FOR ACCESS/ VISA CARDHOLDERS — TEL: 041-772 2281.